WALTER BENJAMIN

# WALTER BENJAMIN

An Introduction to His Work and Thought

UWE STEINER

*Translated by* Michael Winkler

THE UNIVERSITY OF CHICAGO PRESS

CHICAGO AND LONDON

The University of Chicago Press, Chicago 60637
The University of Chicago Press, Ltd., London
© 2010 by The University of Chicago
All rights reserved. Published 2010.
Paperback edition 2012
Printed in the United States of America

Original German language edition: Uwe Steiner, *Walter Benjamin* © 2004 J. B.
Metzlersche Verlagsbuchhandlung und Carl Ernst Poeschel Verglag GmbH in
Stuttgart, Germany.

21  20  19  18  17  16  15  14  13  12       1  2  3  4  5

ISBN-13: 978-0-226-77221-9 (cloth)
ISBN-10: 0-226-77221-7 (cloth)
ISBN-13: 978-0-226-77222-6 (paper)
ISBN-10: 0-226-77222-5 (paper)

Library of Congress-in-Publication Data

Steiner, Uwe.
    Walter Benjamin : an introduction to his work and thought / Uwe Steiner;
translated by Michael Winkler.
        p.  cm.
    Original German language edition published by J. B. Metzlersche Verlagsbuchhan-
dlung und Carl Ernst Poeschel Verlag GmbH, Stuttgart, Germany, 2004.
    Includes biographical references and index.
    ISBN-13: 978-0-226-77221-9 (cloth : alk. paper)
    ISBN-10: 0-226-77221-7 (cloth : alk. paper)   1. Benjamin, Walter, 1892–1940—
Criticism and interpretation.   I. Title.
    PT603.E455Z89474   2010
    838'.91209—dc22

                                                                    2009049779

♾ This paper meets the requirements of ANSI/NISO Z39.48-1992 (Permanence of
Paper).

# CONTENTS

The present volume is an introduction to the writings of Walter Benjamin. It traces the intellectual momentum that finds expression in the internal tensions of his thought and is revealed in the controversial discussions that have accompanied his work to this day. This book is not, however, a report on the current status of Benjamin scholarship. The primary aim of my text is to let Benjamin speak for himself and to place his various writings in the context of his entire oeuvre and of his time. To accomplish this, I have largely refrained from an extensive discussion of scholarly research. The critical studies I consulted and other helpful literature are listed in the bibliography.

I would like to take this opportunity to express my gratitude to individual colleagues who, in their own way, have contributed to making this book possible.

I owe thanks, first of all, to Jane O. Newman and John Smith, who invited me to teach and pursue research in the Department of German at the University of California, Irvine. As the Max Kade Distinguished Visiting Professor, I enjoyed the hospitality of the Department of German Studies at Indiana University in Bloomington, for which I am especially grateful to William W. Rasch. In the same capacity I was a guest of the Department of Germanics at the University of Washington (Seattle), thanks especially to Richard Gray's and Sabine Wilke's support. My guest professorships in the United States would not have been possible without the good offices and patience of the two directors of the *Forschungszentrum Europäische Aufklärung* in Potsdam, Günther Lottes and Eberhardt Lämmert. They have repeatedly relieved me of the obligations demanded by my fellowship at this research center. I am grateful to Michael W. Jennings of Princeton

University, who has been a great help at all times since my first sojourn in the New World.

Finally, I owe a special debt of gratitude to Gary Wihl, dean of the School of Humanities at Rice University, whose award of a stipend enabled me to complete this book, and who contributed a generous subsidy to facilitate its translation.

Uwe Steiner

For all quotations, I have adopted, faithfully and with gratitude, the English-language versions established by Benjamin's (and others') original translators. Only in a very few instances have I made slight changes, both for technical reasons and to make sure that certain nuances in Steiner's analysis do not conflict with the text that is quoted to support them. I have resisted the temptation, however, to make Benjamin's at times opaque and idiosyncratic style more easily accessible to readers whose native language does not favor an equal degree of abstraction and density.

Obviously, different translators have approached their task differently. Hence, there is no uniformity in the way that some of his key concepts have been rendered—a fact that is not recognizable in this book. In deciding from which of the existing versions to borrow, I have tried to avoid diversity and be as consistent as possible instead. Therefore, I have throughout used "primal history" for Benjamin's term "Urgeschichte," a utopian concept denoting a "mythic" image of history and central to his idea of "Ursprung" (origin). By contrast, "Vorgeschichte" (prehistory) is concerned with persons, events, or objects as precursors of things to come. Likewise, "die Moderne" as the time in which, for example, Baudelaire lived and which he tried to give the *Gestalt* of an experience, is "modernity" (in analogy to "antiquity"). When "die Moderne" identifies an artistic style, for example, that of Kafka, it is "modernism."

"Das Epische," in the context of its "restitution" or "reinstatement," refers not to the ancient genre (*das Epos*) of Homer or Virgil. Rather, Benjamin uses this abstract noun to advocate an application to prose fiction of structuring principles that correspond to Brecht's technique of the "epic theater." Hence, I prefer "epic narration" over "the epic," knowing full well that this locution also requires commentary. For the Nietzschean neologism "der Übermensch," when it is part of a direct quotation from Walter Kaufmann's reading of Nietzsche, I have kept "the overman"; elsewhere I have opted for "the superhuman." And finally, Benjamin's use of "profan" reflects the original meaning of "profane" more closely that does "secular."

Steiner's book, originally written for German, primarily academic, readers, presupposes greater familiarity with historical and cultural contexts than its non-German audience may bring to it. In instances where it was easily possible, I have, with the author's consent, added very brief comments that may help to uncomplicate what are for the most part rather demanding arguments. But it was not possible to expand such commentary into what would have amounted to the addition of separate annotations. A case in point is Rang's memorandum of 1924 titled *Deutsche Bauhütte* (German Masons's Guild). It is an anti-idealistic plea for a philosophical politics that calls for groups of volunteers to provide practical help in the rebuilding of war-ravaged towns, which act of conscience would contribute to alleviating ideological antagonisms.

I thank my wife, Mary Grace Winkler, for her frequent reminders that "English does not accommodate itself to the Russian nested-doll-construction of some of your German sentences."

Michael Winkler

# BENJAMIN'S WORKS CITED IN THIS STUDY

## GERMAN-LANGUAGE EDITIONS

*Gesammelte Schriften.* 7 Bände und Supplementa, unter Mitwirkung von Theodor W. Adorno und Gershom Scholem herausgegeben von Rolf Tiedemann. Frankfurt am Main: Suhrkamp, 1972–99.

*Werke und Nachlaß. Kritische Gesamtausgabe.* Im Auftrag der Hamburger Stiftung zur Förderung von Wissenschaft und Kultur herausgegeben von Christoph Gödde und Henri Lonitz. Band 3: *Der Begriff der Kunstkritik in der deutschen Romantik*, herausgegeben von Uwe Steiner. Frankfurt am Main: Suhrkamp, 2008; Band 10: *Deutsche Menschen*, herausgegeben von Momme Brodersen. Frankfurt am Main: Suhrkamp, 2008.

*Gesammelte Briefe.* 6 Bände, herausgegeben vom Theodor W. Adorno Archiv. Frankfurt am Main: Suhrkamp, 1995–2000.

*Walter Benjamin. Gershom Scholem: Briefwechsel, 1933–1940.* Herausgegeben von Gershom Scholem. Frankfurt am Main: Suhrkamp, 1980.

*Theodor W. Adorno. Walter Benjamin: Briefwechsel, 1928–1940.* Herausgegeben von Henri Lonitz. Frankfurt am Main: Suhrkamp, 1994.

*Gretel Adorno. Walter Benjamin: Briefwechsel, 1930–1940.* Herausgegeben von Christoph Gödde und Henri Lonitz. Frankfurt am Main: Suhrkamp, 2005.

*Das Adressbuch des Exils, 1933–1940.* Herausgegeben von Christine Fischer-Defoy. Leipzig: Koehler & Amelang, 2006.

## ENGLISH-LANGUAGE EDITIONS

*Selected Writings.* Edited by Michael W. Jennings, general editor. 4 vols. Cambridge, MA: Harvard University Press, Belknap Press, 1996–2003.

*The Arcades Project.* Translated by Howard Eiland and Kevin McLaughlin. Cambridge, MA: Harvard University Press, Belknap Press, 1999.

*The Origin of German Tragic Drama*. Translated by John Osborne. London: New Left Books, 1977.

*Moscow Diary*. Edited by Gary Smith, translated by Richard Sieburth. Cambridge, MA: Harvard University Press, 1986.

*The Correspondence of Walter Benjamin, 1910–1940*. Edited by Gershom Scholem and Theodor W. Adorno, translated by Manfred R. Jacobson and Evelyn Jacobson. Chicago, IL: Chicago University Press, 1994.

*The Correspondence of Walter Benjamin and Gershom Scholem, 1932–1940*. Edited by Gershom Scholem, translated by Gary Smith and André Lefevre. New York: Schocken Books, 1989.

*Theodor W. Adorno and Walter Benjamin: The Complete Correspondence, 1928–1940*. Edited by Henri Lonitz, translated by Nicholas Walker. Cambridge, UK: Polity Press and Cambridge, MA: Harvard University Press, Belknap Press, 1999.

*Gretel Adorno and Walter Benjamin: Correspondence, 1930–1940*. Edited by Henri Lonitz and Christoph Gödde, translated by Wieland Hoban. Cambridge, UK: Polity Press, 2008.

## CHAPTER ONE

# Introduction

## 1. A Contemporary of Modernity

"A generation that had gone to school in horse-drawn streetcars now stood in the open air amid a landscape in which nothing was the same except the clouds, and, at its center, exposed to a force field of destructive torrents and explosions, the tiny, fragile human body."[1] Walter Benjamin, describing in 1933 the experience of his own generation, dated his childhood to the period around 1900. Although he was in fact born a few years earlier, in 1892, the turn of the century became for him the privileged span of time in which things familiar and long-established collided with new and strange phenomena. This experience is illustrated nowhere more vividly than in the development of technology, evoked here in the shape of a dramatic arc. And it is only as a technological event that the First World War, to which the quotation alludes, became the fiery signal for his generation.

When the writer and literary historian Samuel Lublinski (1868–1910) drew up the balance sheet of Modernity in his book *Die Bilanz der Moderne* (1904), the year 1890, in which Bismarck submitted his resignation, served as the decisive juncture: "The fall of Bismarck also marked the end of the major achievement that defined his statecraft during his final years in office: the emergency law against Social Democracy of 1878. This law signified a complete turning point in Germany's political life; it was without a doubt the most significant event since the founding of the Reich." Lublinski argued that the rise of Social Democracy had given the masses a clear political profile, and that, for the first time in world history, a mass of millions of citizens had turned into a political entity whose organizational shrewdness and unified drive for power could stand up to the Prussian conservatives. But it was technology no less than the masses that had shaped the true face of modernity: "It is our charging locomotives, our incessantly hammering machines, our science and technology" that assign the modern poets their material, and they must prove themselves worthy of it.[2]

In one of his first published texts, the short essay "Das Dornröschen" (Sleeping Beauty) of 1911, Benjamin announced that he considers himself a contemporary of this type of Modernity, which he sees as "the age of socialism, of the women's movement, of traffic, of individualism."[3] Barely twenty years later, *Berlin Childhood around 1900* (which we, knowing of its author's demurral, should be rather hesitant to read as an autobiography) captures, in its own way, an image of this time. An image not only of the time but even more of the place, that is, of locales indissolubly bound up with memory. In other words, Benjamin's carefully chosen title denotes a "time-space" (*Zeit-Raum*); and his childhood memories focus on a life lived not *in* but "with Berlin."[4] It is a life that continued there through the time when *Berlin Childhood* was being written, a life lived with the city of Berlin that, at the beginning of the 1930s, is no longer the same place it had once been. The child's gaze, conjuring up the text's memory images from the perspective of the second half of the nineteenth century, is directed at the city, at "matter-of-fact and noisy Berlin, the city of labor and the metropolis of business."[5] In these images, however, the child's gaze meets the countering look of the adult, who recognizes in them the prehistory of his own present.

In the sequence of Benjamin's works, *Berlin Childhood* belongs to a series of significant studies and essays, some of them extensive, that are associated with the *Arcades Project*. These works occupied his attention almost exclusively until his death in 1940, their importance to him being equal to that of the *opus maximum* he was not able to complete. What unifies these studies thematically—studies ranging from "The Work of Art in the Age of Its Technological Reproducibility" through the "exposé" of the *Arcades Project* to the essays on Baudelaire—is Benjamin's attempt, grounded in a philosophy of history, to render the nineteenth century as the a priori for all critical insights into the present era, and thus to make this era intellectually perceptible as the prehistory of his own time.

The Paris on which the "exposé" programmatically bestows the honorary title of "Capital City of the Nineteenth Century" is also the Paris of Charles Baudelaire (1821–1867), whom Benjamin, in the title of a projected book, calls a "Lyric Poet in the Era of High Capitalism." Baudelaire, who decisively shaped the concept of modernity, personified for Benjamin two essential aspects: he is the poet whose poetry strove unsuccessfully to endow the consciously experienced, though quickly forgotten, facts (*Erlebnis*) of *modernité* with "the weight of insights that are based on long experience,"[6] which have become part of memory (*Erfahrung*). He is also the contemporary of the workers' movement that was taking shape during the Second Empire. More specifically, he witnesses those class struggles in France whose history and political theory Karl Marx wrote. Toward the end of his first essay on Baudelaire, Benjamin states that Blanqui's doctrine of action had been "the sister of Baudelaire's dream."[7] Benjamin's capital city of the nineteenth century, however, is also the Paris of the industrial revolution then spreading through all of Europe, a revolution symbolized by the railroad. Locomotives were the harbingers of a rapidly expanding transit system. They were also the first beneficiaries of an industrially produced construction material—iron—which, when combined with glass, revolutionized architecture. Early examples of this phenomenon are the halls of railroad stations that were being built in the heart of Europe's cities, and, no less importantly, the Parisian arcades.

Paris, finally, is also the site of the world's fairs, of those "pilgrimage sites that display the fetish called commodities."[8] For the first time in 1855, at one of these expositions, a special exhibit had been devoted to photography. And for the visual arts, it is photography that inaugurates the age of their technological reproducibility. Going back to the middle of the nineteenth century, Benjamin traces the development of photography and, as a parallel process, the revolutionary transformation of both art and human perception—a process that culminates in the art of film. The latest productions of the studios in Berlin-Babelsberg, Hollywood, and Moscow are, in the mid-1930s, the subject of those theses in which he seeks to decode, by way of a prognosis, the then current trends in the development of art and to clarify their political implications.

It is not difficult to show the cross-connections that tie the memory images of *Berlin Childhood* to the various sections of the *Arcades Project* and to other writings that revolve around it.

During my childhood I was a prisoner of both the old and new western suburbs of Berlin. In those days, my clan lived in these two neighborhoods with an attitude compounded of doggedness and self-esteem, a frame of mind that turned their world into a ghetto they considered their fiefdom. I remained confined within this prosperous district without any knowledge of a different world outside. Poor people—as far as rich children my age were concerned—existed only as beggars.[9]

In the imagination of a child brought up in a wealthy middle-class family, poverty is only a shameful humiliation, unconnected to its economic and social causes. In this way of seeing, the person humiliated has no other recourse but to revolt. In retrospect, the lure of an "escape into sabotage and anarchism," which for a long time cast a spell on Benjamin's nascent political awareness, is a limitation he held responsible for all the difficulty faced by an intellectual from this milieu trying to "see things as they really are."[10] It is hardly fortuitous that he sees Baudelaire's political insights, in principle, as not extending beyond the rebellious pathos of a revolt such as characterizes the posture of the *bohémien*. The radical questioning of the intellectual's role in society, which for the Benjamin of the 1920s turns out to be a one-way street into politics, is prefigured *ex negativo* in the apolitical attitudes with which the fin-de-siècle bourgeoisie took over the heritage of a century that was coming to its end. Political insight, however, was for him most closely connected to an understanding of the technological status of things, a fact registered subliminally but precisely in his book of memories.

According to a passage in *Berlin Chronicle*, the posthumously published first version of *Berlin Childhood*, the latter book was written at a time "when the railroads were beginning to become obsolete." One consequence of this, he says, is the fact that the train stations, generally speaking, were "no longer the true 'gateways' through which the city unrolls its outskirts, as it does nowadays along the approach roads built for the *Automobilist*, the driver of a car."[11]

In 1921, a good ten years before Benjamin jotted down this observation, the *Avus (Auto-Versuchs- und Übungsstraße)*, the so-called Auto Test and Practice Road in Berlin, had been officially opened after a long period of construction that had been interrupted by the war. It is a road of nearly ten kilometers, perfectly straight and without intersections, whose two separate lanes were reserved exclusively for automobiles. It led from the southwestern suburbs directly into the western center of the city. This first autobahn in the world was open to all motorists for a small fee, day and night. It was also less than a year before the publication of Benjamin's *One-Way Street* (1928) that one-way streets and the appropriate traffic signs (which Sasha Stone used in the photo montage he designed for the book's dust cover) had been officially introduced in Germany. The first filling stations—"Tankstelle" is the title of the book's first piece—appeared in 1924.[12]

It is not known whether Benjamin shared Brecht's appreciation for the products of the Steyr Company. But as a front-seat passenger in the car of a friend, the writer Wilhelm Speyer (1887–1952), he gathered relevant experiences during various vacation trips. In a letter he reports, for example, that after several starts they had succeeded in crossing the Gotthard Pass, though not without incurring some damage to the car.[13] In September 1932, during another trip to Italy with Speyer, he used the unpleasant delay caused by a flat tire to start writing the first draft of *Berlin Childhood*.[14] In the summer of 1927—the same year in which, on May 21, Charles Lindbergh had safely landed his plane, the *Spirit of St. Louis*, at Le Bourget Airport near Paris, thereby bringing the first airborne nonstop crossing of the Atlantic to a triumphal conclusion—Benjamin announced on a postcard mailed from Corsica that he is about to "drive" (*fahren*) in an airplane from there to Antibes on the Côte d'Azur.[15]

Technological progress is a fact of life that Benjamin faced with an open mind and as an observer who is given to ambitious theorizing. He perceived that the new means of transportation also bring about a no less fundamental change of perception that in turn accompanies the fundamental transformation of the technological media. The railroad station, he continues his note in *Berlin Chronicle*, issues, as it were,

> the instructions for a surprise attack, but it is an outdated maneuver, one
> that strikes at nothing but things of the past. And this is very much true
> of photography, even including the snapshot. Only the cinema opens up
> optical access roads into the center of the urban environment, the same
> way these new roads guide the motorist into the new City.[16]

Around 1900, however, it was still the *Kaiserpanorama* (Imperial Panorama) in Berlin, a late successor of the panorama Daguerre had set up in Paris in 1822, that marks the state of affairs with respect to media technology.[17] But Daguerre's name is associated more closely with photography, an invention that Benjamin, child of a bourgeois family, experienced as a veritable sacrificial victim when he was taken to a photographer's studio.[18] This child was still able to watch the horse-drawn streetcar from his parents' apartment, and it was a "rattling hackney" that took him to Berlin's railroad stations, to those departure points and final destinations for summer journeys that were inevitably taken by train.[19] The one technological innovation of the nineteenth century, however, that was especially close to Benjamin's heart was the telephone, an invention Alexander Graham Bell had patented in 1876. The telephone, he remembers, made its entry into the apartments of Berlin's prosperous bourgeoisie at precisely the same time that he himself did, which is the reason why, in *Berlin Childhood*, he welcomes it as his "twin brother."[20]

The image of Benjamin the esoteric scholar is incomplete, to say the least. It is the image of a man who, in the Bibliothèque nationale in Paris, buries himself under books on the cultural history of the nineteenth century, reading incessantly and accumulating innumerable excerpts and notes, the results of his studies, as far as we know them, nowadays providing the material and starting point for learned endeavors that seem at times no less esoteric than Benjamin's. The image is incomplete not only because the bookish scholar had started as early as the beginning of 1927 now and then to exchange his workplace in the library for a place behind the microphone of a radio station. It is characteristic in Benjamin's case that a good measure of close attention and perspicacity is required to discover in the outlines of his thematically diverse oeuvre those traces that his life—during politically turbulent years and during every other kind of upheaval—has left in it.

Benjamin claimed self-assuredly that he "writes a better style of German than most writers" of his generation thanks to observing one little rule: "Never use the word 'I' except in letters."[21] As a result, he included autobiographical information in his writings as infrequently as he referred directly to historical events. His own time provides him with the material not for historical, but for philosophical, inquiries. Likewise, the memory images of *Berlin Childhood*, which give a kind of spectral shape to the child's experience during the era around the turn of the century, reveal the inescapable experience of obsolescence to the adult. It is not the past with its pieces of historical evidence that, in this book and in others, constitute Benjamin's true interest. Rather, the real issue for him is the experience of time itself and, therefore, the philosophical question: what are the conditions that make experience possible in an era in which experience has become problematic?

We encounter the concept of experience in both Benjamin's earliest and final writings. Even as a young student, he devoted an essay to this concept, trying to wrest it from the grip of the adults. His protest titled "Experience" (1913) is directed against the debasement of "experience" into a mask for resignation, and against its abuse as an instrument used to disillusion "inexperienced" youth.[22] A few years later, a different concept of experience becomes central to his endeavor to outline the *Program of the Future Philosophy*. It is a concept that, following Kant and through a critical reading of neo-Kantianism, has reformulated experience from the perspective of the philosophy of language, and has upscaled it metaphysically. In certain ways, the inquiries of the Baudelaire studies into how experience is possible under the conditions of modernity return to the philosophical-systematic questions raised in the early writings. In turn, their implications concerning a philosophy of history are further probed in the theses titled "On the Concept of History" (1940).[23] Compared with the essay of 1913, "Experience and Poverty," published in 1933, assumes significantly greater importance due to its provocative linking of "experience" and "poverty." Owing to the "tremendous development of technology," he writes, "a completely new kind of wretchedness has descended on mankind."[24] The poverty of experience perceived since the end of the war should not, however, be misunderstood to indicate that people were yearning for new experiences. On the contrary, they were yearning to fight free of experiences because a "total absence of illusion about the age and at the same time an unlimited commitment to it"[25] define the only appropriate attitude, and indeed the indispensable condition, for understanding this present age.

In a retrospective note probably written in 1929, Benjamin states that in the early essay "he had mobilized every rebellious force of youth against the word 'experience.'" By contrast, this same word had now become, as he puts it, a foundational element in many of his pieces. But even so, he has remained true to himself, he insists, because "my attack, penetrating as it did to the center of the issue, cut through this word without annihilating it."[26] The validity of this self-interpretation could with some justification be extended to include his entire oeuvre. There has been a sustained discussion about this issue, which for a long time dominated Benjamin's reception. It revolved around the notion that his works can be divided into two phases: an early period of metaphysical-theological interests, and a later period with a Marxist orientation. This division is justified, while at the same time unjustified. At any rate, one can easily discern that a nearly identical dichotomy also characterizes the spirit and the reception of the works of Ernst Bloch (1885–1977) and Georg Lukács (1885–1971). Their writings offer an instructive parallel, even though it is one that has been discussed less controversially.

Bloch had made Benjamin's personal acquaintance in Switzerland in 1919 and remained on friendly terms with him, even though their friendship was never free of tensions, until they both went into exile. The influence of Lukács's early writings—the essay collection *Soul and Forms* (1911), *The Theory of the Novel* (1920), and especially *History and Class Consciousness* (1923)—on Benjamin can hardly be overestimated. This is no less true for the writings of the French Surrealists, most of all for the development of the movement's two protagonists, André Breton (1896–1966) and Louis Aragon (1897–1982). "The Last Snapshot of the European Intelligentsia"

is the ostensible subtitle of Benjamin's essay on Surrealism, in which, toward the end of the 1920s, he surveyed what remained of the bourgeois
intellectual's domain, an area that in the end he saw as inescapably dominated by politics.

Benjamin did not live long enough to act as an advocate for himself and
for his works by writing introductions or afterthoughts to revised or repub-
lished editions of his books. But even so he has left numerous documents, in
which, on the one hand, he speaks about a reorientation in his thinking, but
on the other emphasizes the continuity of his fundamental conceptions. For
example, letters from the middle of the 1930s, that is, the decisive, second
phase of his work on the *Arcades Project*, mention that "a mass of ideas
and images" originating in the very distant past when he "thought in purely
metaphysical, and indeed theological terms" had to undergo a "process of
complete and radical change."[27] These letters also refer to "a melting-pot
process" that has moved the "whole mass of ideas originally animated by
metaphysics" toward a new "aggregate condition," where they would be
safe from the objections "provoked by metaphysics."[28]

In spite of any number of specific differences, one can claim that Bloch
and Lukács engaged in the same retrospective self-analysis through which,
during the middle of the 1920s, Benjamin tried to account for his intellectual origins and for his current position:

> I belong to the generation that is now between thirty and forty years
> old. The intelligentsia of this generation will presumably be the last for
> a long time to have enjoyed a completely apolitical education. The war
> caught its most left-leaning elements in the camp of a more or less radi-
> cal pacifism. The history of Germany in the postwar period is in part
> the history of the revolutionary education of this originally left-bourgeois
> wing of the intelligentsia. It may confidently be asserted that the revolu-
> tion of 1918, which was defeated by the petty-bourgeois, parvenu spirit
> of German Social Democracy, did more to radicalize this generation
> than did the war itself. In Germany, it is increasingly the case—and this
> is the feature of particular importance in this entire process—that the
> status of the independent writer is being called into question, and one
> gradually realizes that the writer (like the intellectual in the wide sense),
> willy-nilly, consciously or unconsciously, works in the service of a class
> and receives his mandate from a class. The fact that the economic basis
> of the intellectual's existence is becoming ever more constricted has
> hastened this realization in recent times.[29]

## 2. Life and Works

The path that leads from a well-protected childhood around 1900 to the insight quoted above was not predetermined by the particular circumstances of this childhood. It can nevertheless be considered paradigmatic. Walter Benjamin was born on July 15, 1892, the oldest of three children. In view of the scanty information he gives about his parents, his sister, Dora (1901–1946), and his brother, Georg (1895–1942), Benjamin was justified in refusing to call *Berlin Childhood* an autobiography. But it is noteworthy even so that his brother, a socially active physician, joined the German Communist Party early in his career. (His wife, Hilde Benjamin [1902–1989], future attorney general [*Justizministerin*] of East Germany, has described the course of his life until his murder in the Mauthausen concentration camp in her book, *Georg Benjamin. Eine Biographie,* published in 1977.) The children grew up in a prosperous, assimilated Jewish family, cared for by a nanny and a French governess. In his various curricula vitae, Benjamin refers to the professional affiliation of his father, Emil Benjamin (1856–1926), simply as *Kaufmann,* businessman.[30] Only *Berlin Chronicle* provides a few more details about the diversity of his activities.[31]

It was not his studies at the classically oriented *Gymnasium,* but his personal encounters with a teacher, Gustav Wyneken (1875–1964), whom he met during the two years he spent as a boarder at a private school in Haubinda (Thuringia), that became the incisive experience, spiritually and intellectually, for the schoolboy and for the student of philosophy. Wyneken was a pedagogue and school reformer who represented the idealistic-radical wing of the Youth Movement, and it was the program of this group that, until the outbreak of the war, elicited Benjamin's intensive engagement with issues relating to academic policy, even at the expense of his university studies. But his demonstrative breach with this revered teacher was perhaps an even more incisive decision. It was brought about by Wyneken's support of the war, which Benjamin castigated as a betrayal of the ideals of youth, using it as the occasion for a letter written in March 1915, in which he renounces his mentor "completely and unconditionally."[32]

Benjamin's high expectations of the university, inspired as they were by the ideals of the Youth Movement, met with disappointment. Predictably, neither the institution nor any one particular academic teacher were able to satisfy them. Quite early in his life as a student, to be sure, he had become convinced that "the university ... simply is not the place to engage in studies."[33] But neo-Kantianism, at that time the dominant philosophical school at German universities, did leave clearly discernible traces in his early writings. During the course of his studies, Benjamin had come into contact with its principal representatives: the Marburg School and its epistemological orientation as personified by Hermann Cohen (1842–1918), who taught in Berlin at the end of his career; and the Southwest German School with its emphasis on axiology, the theory of values. Benjamin heard lectures by that school's most important proponent, Heinrich Rickert (1863–1936), in Freiburg. Classified as unfit for military service, Benjamin concluded his studies in neutral Switzerland. Married by now and the father of a son, he was graduated summa cum laude in Berne in 1919 with a dissertation titled "The Concept of Criticism in German Romanticism." In this study, as he writes in one of his curricula vitae, his "interest had come to focus on the philosophical content of imaginative literature and of artistic forms."[34]

His prospects for an academic career came to an abrupt end, however, when the faculty at the university in Frankfurt am Main advised him to withdraw his *Habilitation* thesis, "Origin of German Tragic Drama," which he had submitted in 1925. Erich Rothacker (1888–1965), a philosopher and the coeditor of the *Deutsche Vierteljahrsschrift für Literaturwissenschaft und Geistesgeschichte*, who had been asked to write an evaluation of the *Elective Affinities* essay,[35] is said to have remarked "that intellect (*Geist*) cannot be habilitated," a "wickedly insolent statement"[36] aimed at his collegues' gross misjudgments. Their circumstances have since been fully reconstructed and the story has entered the annals of a German university's recent history as an academic tragedy.

When Ernst Rowohlt's recently established publishing house put out his *Origin of German Tragic Drama* as a book in 1928, its author could not have demonstrated his renunciation of all academic ambitions more clearly. To make his point, Benjamin had his book published together with *One-Way Street*, a collection of aphorisms he had written in order to prove himself, in form and content, an equal of the intellectual and artistic avant-garde. Looking back at the book on Baroque drama, Benjamin would at times mention that this project had marked the end of the academic studies among his published output.[37] But there is no doubt that, in addition to the two major works he wrote as a professional Germanist, "Goethe's *Elective Affinities*," written at the beginning of the 1920s and published in 1924–25, is to be counted among Benjamin's "academic" group of writings, and that its significance and critical challenge are in no way secondary to his book on seventeenth-century drama.

Henceforth, Benjamin would devote himself intensively to journalistic work, which, for the most part, appeared in the literary section of the news-

paper *Frankfurter Zeitung* and in *Literarische Welt*, edited by Willy Haas
(1891–1973) and published by Rowohlt. His self-perception as an intellectual during the "golden era" of the Weimar Republic is summarized in a letter he wrote at the beginning of 1930. There he states that he had succeeded,
admittedly only to a modest degree, in making a name for himself in Germany. He said that he had not as yet reached his goal of being recognized
as the foremost critic of German literature, but that he was getting close to
it. The difficulty he confronted had to do with the fact that literary criticism was not considered a respectable genre in Germany. For this reason,
he thought, one would basically have to reinvent criticism as a genre if one
sought to be respected as a critic.[38]

It was not by chance that his self-description, whose claims would probably have surprised many of his contemporaries, was written in French. For
Benjamin had already established a modest reputation not only as a critic,
but also as a translator of Baudelaire as well as of Proust, whose grand sequence of novels he was translating in collaboration with a close friend, the
writer Franz Hessel (1880–1941). Much as the letter quoted above shows
that Benjamin's theoretical concept of criticism was still tied to his work
as a Germanist, there is equally strong evidence that his practice as a critic
had discarded its exclusively aesthetic criteria some time ago. Benjamin's
participation in the intellectual debates, and the increasing attention with
which he followed the development of literature in France—an interest that
was increasing during the following years—is most clearly connected with
the different phases in the conception of the *Arcades*, a project he had first
mentioned in a letter of 1927. Beyond that, the expansion of his literary purview to France contributed its share to the political radicalization that finds
expression in the topics and in the temper that characterize his journalistic
contributions but also other writings.

Benjamin has attributed his "conversion to political thinking"[39] to his
meeting Asja Lacis (1891–1979), the "Russian revolutionary from Riga,"
whose acquaintance he had made on Capri as early as 1924, while he was
living in seclusion there during the writing of his book on Baroque drama.[40]
The essays and reviews he wrote during the next years testify to the decision he had reached to turn more intensively toward politics.

At the same time, the continuing disintegration of Benjamin's marriage—a breakdown that had started in the early 1920s—brought about decisive changes also in his private life. His frequent and extended trips, his
repeated sojourns in Paris, and his stay in Moscow at the turn of 1926–27—a
sojourn he has described in an essay and in his *Moscow Diary*—are clear
evidence of this disorder. When, at the beginning of 1930, his marriage to

Dora Benjamin (1890–1964) ended in divorce, Benjamin found himself "at the threshold of forty, without property and position, apartment and assets."[41] This sobering description of his situation held true for the remaining years before his exile. When he casually remarked in a letter that for the first time in his life he felt "like an adult,"[42] his material difficulties, according to his own paradoxical admission, played as much a part in this state of affairs as did the fact that he was finally able to live in an apartment he could call his own. But this does not mean at all that the circumstances of his life had stabilized. On the contrary: during these years Benjamin was repeatedly contemplating suicide.

Speaking about the fate of his writings in a letter he wrote to Scholem on July 26, 1932, shortly after his fortieth birthday, he took stock of his life and came to a bitter conclusion: "And though many—or a good number—of my works have been small-scale victories, they are offset by large-scale defeats. I do not want to mention the projects that had remained unfinished, or even untouched, but rather to enumerate here at least the four books that identify the true site of ruination and catastrophe whose distant boundary I am still unable to detect when I let my eye wander over the next years of my life. They include the *Parisian Arcades*, the *Collected Essays on Literature*, the *Letters*, and a truly exceptional book about hashish."[43] During his exile in France, where in March 1933 Benjamin had found refuge from National Socialist persecution, work on the *Parisian Arcades* was to occupy him more intensively than any of his other projects. And even though the volume of essays, for which he had signed a contract with Rowohlt in April 1930, did not materialize, most of the studies he had intended to include in this book had either been completed already or were written during the following years.

And as for the "Letters": without identifying himself as the editor, Benjamin had published in the *Frankfurter Zeitung*, at irregular intervals from April 1931 until May 1932, a sequence of unknown letters by notable people from the era between 1783 and 1883, adding to each a brief commentary as an introduction. Four years after the newspaper had printed the last of these twenty-six letters, Benjamin, using a pseudonym and contributing a short preface, succeeded in having this collection published under the inconspicuous title of *Deutsche Menschen* (German Men and Women). The book's Swiss publisher, Vita Nova Verlag in Lucerne, also guaranteed its distribution in Germany.

And finally "the truly exceptional book about hashish": in addition to the essay "Hashish in Marseille,"[44] published in 1932, a number of notes and medical minutes have been found among Benjamin's papers. They record experiments with different drugs that he had been undertaking since

1927, some together with Ernst Bloch and in the presence of two physician friends, Ernst Joël and Fritz Fränkel.

The material circumstances of Benjamin's life in exile were extremely constrained. Most of the time he felt highly uncertain about his immediate and more distant future. Though at first he had turned to Paris, where the Bibliothèque nationale had become the indispensable resource for his work, he needed to leave his principal residence at certain times due to the rather high living expenses in the French capital. A few times—during the off-season—he went to San Remo, where his former wife operated a small private hotel, and until the outbreak of war, he repeatedly accepted Brecht's offer to spend the summer months with him in his Danish exile in Skovs-bostrand near Svendborg.

Aside from meager honoraria paid him for an ever diminishing number of brief or more substantial publications, it is the Institute for Social Research, with which he had established contacts even before his exile, that became his most important, though not his only, source of income. From now on, Benjamin's most significant studies, many of them commissioned by the Institute, appeared in its *Zeitschrift für Sozialforschung,* which was first published in 1932. These contributions found both an energetic supporter and a resolute critic in Theodor W. Adorno.

One should keep in mind the circumstances under which the following studies were conceived and brought to fruition: the theses on "The Work of Art in the Age of Its Technological Reproducibility," the two versions of the Baudelaire essay, the study dealing with Social Democratic art and cultural historian Eduard Fuchs, and finally the edition of the essay "Die Rückschritte der Poesie" (The Regressions of Poetry) by Carl Gustav Jochmann (1789–1830), which had first been published posthumously in 1837. One should add to these works the important essays on Kafka and on the storyteller Nikolai Leskov, which he wrote independently of the Institute. Moreover, one must include his continual, tenacious work on the *Arcades.* Then one cannot help but think that Benjamin's unwavering commitment to his production as a writer had become his guarantee for survival, and not only in a strictly material sense. His oeuvre certainly assumed a new justification. Written in defiance of the most hostile external conditions, and held up against a political situation that—in view of the Spanish Civil War, the show trials in Moscow, and the ever increasing threat of war—was becoming more and more impenetrable and hopeless, this intellectual enterprise was undergoing a change: it was no longer the means to make a living but had turned into the purpose of his life.

The quintessence of this work, at least since the "exposé" of 1935, was the *Arcades Project,* a project supported by a stipend from the Institute, now located in New York City, whose regular collaborator Benjamin became in 1937. Even his last completed work, the theses "On the Concept of History," is part of the closer context of the *Arcades Project.* They were written in Paris, probably at the beginning of 1940, after Benjamin had returned there for a short time following his internment at the outbreak of war.

When it became obvious that France was facing a military disaster, Benjamin fled to the unoccupied part of the country, evading the German troops and his impending extradition to a Germany that had revoked his citizenship on March 25, 1939. With Max Horkheimer acting as an intermediary, he had obtained an entrance visa for the USA in August 1940; but he lacked an exit visa from France. As a result, his attempt to escape from Europe by crossing the Pyrenees into Spain and then proceeding to Portugal failed at the Spanish border. Probably on the erroneous assumption that the harassment he experienced at the hands of the Spanish border police was meant to signal his deportation and his subsequent surrender to the German authorities in France, Benjamin put an end to his life in the border town of Port Bou on September 26, 1940.

## 3. Companions, Influences

Perhaps even more than the stations along the course of Benjamin's life, it is the very heterogeneous circle of people with whom he kept company that reflects the internal tensions and great diversity of his oeuvre. The disparate response to his work as a whole and the competing interpretations of specific writings have frequently been attributed to the equally controversial influences they are said to have incorporated. But was it merely mystery mongering—as Adorno reports—that made Benjamin keep his friends apart from one another? In an essay of 1972 that provoked its own controversial reactions, Habermas found it very easy to dispel this claim, suggesting that it was only as a surrealistic scene that one could imagine "Scholem, Adorno, and Brecht sitting around a table for a peaceful symposium, with Breton and Aragon crouching nearby, while Wyneken stands by the door, all gathered for a debate on Bloch's *Spirit of Utopia* (1918) or even Klages's *Mind as Adversary of the Soul* (1929)."[45] The impression that a tension-filled disparateness characterizes his work is left in equal measure by the multiplicity of its themes and by the various theoretical approaches he employs. And this impression does not change even when one limits the influence of a specific individual to only one of the different "cycles of productivity" that Benjamin himself would on occasion single out. It is helpful to remember in this context that his oeuvre is distinguished not only by the heterogeneity of these cycles of production but frequently enough by the fact that, at least during the early stage of a particular project, they overlap.

There can be no doubt that Gustav Wyneken was of special importance for Benjamin's earliest writings, a fact that is given expression *ex negativo* by the irreconcilable hostility with which Benjamin renounced him and by the hurtful severity with which he ended his connections with many friends and companions of these years. Yet Benjamin remained loyal to his intellectual beginnings. One example of this attachment is the cycle of seventy-three sonnets he wrote to mourn and memorialize his friend the poet Fritz Heinle (1894–1914), who, on August 8, 1914, had joined in a suicide pact with Rika Seligson (1891–1914) in protest against the war. In a very stimulating and persuasive essay, the cultural historian Peter Gay has traced the spiritual and intellectual complexion of the years immediately preceding the war by analyzing the veneration accorded the figure of the poet.[46] Gay shows this attitude to be no less relevant for the formative period of the Weimar Republic. The names that represent such a close to cultic adulation—Stefan George, Rainer Maria Rilke, Heinrich von Kleist, the Swiss epic poet Carl Spitteler (1846–1924), and, above all, Friedrich Hölderlin—were idolized also in Wickersdorf, where Wyneken had founded his own *Freie Schulgemeinde* (Free School Community) in 1906. They also demarcate the intellectual horizon within which the young Benjamin was moving at this time and from which he was beginning to separate himself in his earliest writings.

Gershom Scholem (1897–1982), the militant Benjamin interpreter, Kabbalah scholar, and resolute Zionist, whose acquaintance Benjamin had made in July 1915, never really became aware of this and other aspects of his friend's background. He remained, in fact, rather impervious to them. Instead, Benjamin found in Scholem a vigorous and eloquent advocate who favored a metaphysical-theological interpretation of his writings and saw them as closely linked to a genuinely Jewish tradition and its spiritual as well as intellectual world (*Geisteswelt*). Scholem's work as an editor, commentator, and interpreter of Benjamin's oeuvre is excellent, and so is his knowledge of the way in which its different parts are connected with each other and with their author's biographical circumstances. His book of recollections, *Walter Benjamin: The Story of a Friendship* (1981), is a moving memorial to this friendship, and it has remained an invaluable source for scholars to this day.[47] But Scholem had left Germany as early as 1923 in order to emigrate to Palestine. When Benjamin says about (and to) him: "I have come to know living Judaism in absolutely no form other than you" and adds that the question of his relationship to Judaism is always also the question of how he stands "in relation to the forces (Scholem) has touched in him,"[48] he leaves the impression that he is referring to a *geistig* realm to which he feels close without considering himself a part of it, and which he approached with an open-minded interest while being fully aware that it lies outside his competence.

It is symptomatic that Scholem reacted to Ernst Bloch and his *Spirit of Utopia* (1918) with undisguised antipathy when they met him during their sojourn together in Bern, whereas Benjamin, by his own admission, owed crucial, and not the least political, stimulation to both the book and its author. This divergence masks the beginning of the controversy about Benjamin's turn to political theory, a dispute that Scholem, at times with hurtful stridency, fought out with him toward the end of the 1920s in a sequence of epistolary exchanges. But in spite of their disagreements, Benjamin did not hesitate—in a last will and testament he had executed in 1932—to entrust Scholem with his unpublished literary estate. This was his way of sanctioning that private archive in Jerusalem whose importance, especially for the years of his exile, can hardly be overrated. In defiance of every burden that strained their friendship, and through an unspoken understanding, this collection became the place where the letters as well as the contributions to so many different journals and, most importantly, the unpublished writings of Scholem's friend, were reliably gathered and where the seeds were planted for Benjamin's posthumous renown.

In a letter dated February 19, 1925, while he was close to completing his *Habilitation* thesis, Benjamin emphasized that this work contained various things about which it would be extremely important for him to have Scholem's response. He was alluding specifically to those parts that relate directly to his own early writings on philosophical issues, above all to his philosophy of language. In the same letter he wrote that, strictly speaking, the recent death of Florens Christian Rang (1864–1924) had robbed his book on Baroque drama of "the reader for whom it was intended."[49] And there is good reason aside from this remark to associate Rang—an administrative lawyer and later Protestant pastor and then a private scholar, whose acquaintance Benjamin had made in Berlin in 1922—with the academic/ "philological" phase of his production. Rang's thinking, which was decisively influenced by Nietzsche, was rather individualistic. But it was rooted in a remarkably comprehensive cultural and intellectual background, his specific scholarly interests focusing on Greek tragedy, Goethe's *Divan*-poems, and Shakespeare's sonnets. For Benjamin he had become an important partner and an authoritative source of information in their exchanges about the central theses in his book on Baroque drama.

A letter found among the papers in Rang's estate shows that he had read Benjamin's dissertation with the kind of critical understanding that he had hoped would extend also to his *Habilitation* thesis. But Rang had died—in October 1924—before this study was completed. Benjamin paid tribute to him as a man to whom he was indebted

> for whatever essential element of German culture I have internalized. Not only the main subjects of our tenacious reflections in this area were almost all identical. But also I have seen the life that inhabits these great subjects humanely manifested in him alone, bursting forth from him with all the more volcanic force when it lay paralyzed beneath the crust of the rest of Germany.[50]

When, to his surprise, Benjamin received an offer from the Heidelberg publisher Richard Weißbach to draw up plans for a new journal and serve as its editor, the first issue was to include, aside from his own essay on the "Task of the Translator," a few pieces from Heinle's literary estate as well as contributions by Scholem and Rang. Remarks in letters show, however, that the prospective editor looked at Rang's work far from uncritically. On the contrary, at times he read it with extreme reservations. Not a single issue of the journal, which Benjamin had titled *Angelus Novus* after a drawing by Paul Klee, nor even its (already typeset) "Announcement" were published. This meant, of course, that the essay "Goethe's *Elective Affinities*" had also lost the venue where it was first projected to appear. But on Rang's initiative and with him acting as an intermediary, Benjamin had meanwhile contacted Hugo von Hofmannsthal (1874–1929), who considered himself fortunate to print the essay in his *Neue Deutsche Beiträge* (New German Contributions). Rang did not see the printed version of the Goethe essay nor the book on the origin of German *Trauerspiel* (literally, mourning play). But in the end, Benjamin was indebted to him also for helping to have an excerpt from this book published in *Beiträge*, thus making Hofmannsthal "its first, most perceptive, and—in the term's most beautiful sense—its 'dearest reader.'"[51]

In 1924, Rang published a political-philosophical memorandum (*Denkschrift*) titled "Deutsche Bauhütte," to which Benjamin contributed a "Zuschrift" (Reply),[52] that is, one of several dedicatory appreciations in the form of a letter that were appended to this treatise. And so Benjamin once again found himself confronted with politics. It is most probably this context to which he was referring barely a year later when, in the fall of 1924, he wrote from Capri about the "actual and political elements" of his thinking, which henceforth, under the impression of Communist political praxis, he intends "no longer to mask in the good, old German way" but "to develop, experimentally, to an extreme degree."[53] This extreme position was exemplified for him by a person, the Latvian Bolshevik and theater director Asja Lacis, and by a book, Georg Lukács's essay collection *History and Class Consciousness* (1923). The Marxist orientation of Benjamin's last works, however, is first and foremost linked with Bertolt Brecht (1898–1956), whom he had met through Asja Lacis in November 1924. Benjamin has always and enthusiastically acknowledged the importance of Brecht—they had become close friends in May 1929[54]—for his various projects and for his intellectual development. His commentaries on a number of works by Brecht testify to this, as do plans for collaborative ventures, which, however, either remained just that, plans, or ultimately failed, as did, for example, the project of a journal, *Krisis und Kritik,* that they abandoned in January 1931.

To be sure, Scholem considered Brecht's influence on Benjamin's production of the 1930s to be "pernicious and in some respects even catastrophic."[55] But Scholem was not the only person to whom he had to defend his continuing engagement with the playwright's work, an interest he maintained even during their time in exile. His association with Brecht and his circle, especially his acquaintance with the Marxist theoretician Karl Korsch (1886–1961), was no doubt a decisive factor in imbuing Benjamin's studies from the end of the 1920s with a clearly noticeable Marxist accent. Even so, Brecht's influence on the tendencies and themes that distinguished the late writings from the early ones should not be overestimated. This is true for various reasons, but mainly because Brecht had reservations about many, if not most, of Benjamin's works, or indeed rejected them outright, while Benjamin, in turn, found himself frequently confronted with "the difficulty inherent in any form of collaboration with Brecht."[56]

Even while he was working on *Origin of German Tragic Drama,* Benjamin established contacts in Frankfurt with a circle of people who would provide an important background for his works during the time of his exile. First among them was Siegfried Kracauer (1889–1966), an editor at *Frankfurter Zeitung* who had accomplished the remarkable feat of reviewing *Origin* and *One-Way Street* in one essay and who deserves considerable credit for the success of Benjamin's journalistic reorientation after the failure of his academic plans.[57] Beyond that, the production cycle around *One-Way Street* clearly owes many an insight to Kracauer's own works. Indirectly linking these writings to his own, Benjamin said about them that they pin-point "the decline of the petit-bourgeois class in a very remarkable, 'loving' description of its heritage."[58]

No less important than Kracauer during this phase of Benjamin's work was Franz Hessel, who became central to his creative interests during their sojourn together in Paris, where they began translating Proust's *Recherche*. Their collaborative work on this translation, though begun with a good pros-pect for success, was never completed because their publisher abandoned the project. But under the knowledgeable guidance of Hessel the passionate *flâneur*, Benjamin was introduced into the secret inner life of the city. It was at this time also, in the summer of 1927, that his plan for an essay on the Parisian arcades, the earliest phase of the *Arcades Project*, was taking shape. After their return to Berlin, Hessel became the editor of Rowohlt Verlag, in which capacity he accepted Benjamin's two books for publication in 1928.

Benjamin's most important partner in discussions and a very stimulat-ing critic during the decisive second phase of this project was Theodor Wie-sengrund Adorno (1903–1969). His junior by eleven years, Adorno, whom he had met, as he had Kracauer, in 1923, was offering (as a *Privatdozent* at the University in Frankfurt) as late as 1932 a seminar on *Origin of German Tragic Drama*. It was also on Adorno's recommendation that Benjamin had arranged (with Max Horkheimer [1895–1973], also in 1932) to contribute his first article to *Zeitschrift für Sozialforschung*, the journal of the Frank-furt Institute for Social Research, of which Horkheimer had become the director in October 1930. As it would turn out, this contact would be instru-mental in securing the material support for his survival in exile. Throughout the 1930s, moreover, in his epistolary debates with Adorno about his works, he confronted a variant of historical materialism at a theoretically most exacting level. For Adorno, the influence Brecht was gaining on the *Arcades Project* meant not only a grave threat to its metaphysical dimension but even more to its historical-materialist aspects: two conflicting claims that needed to be mediated in however tension-filled a way.

Adorno, like Scholem, had the highest expectations of Benjamin's works and followed them with passionate interest. This engagement was ex-pressed nowhere with stronger emphasis than in the letter in which he en-thusiastically welcomed Benjamin's decision to start the *opus maximum* at last, calling it the happiest news he had received from him in many years. Adorno assured him that he understood this project to be "our destined con-tibution to *prima philosophia*," also asserting that he had every confidence in Benjamin's ability to accomplish its completion. Nevertheless, he found it necessary to warn him of a false respect "for any objections stemming

## CHAPTER TWO

# Early Writings, 1914–18

## 1. Apotheosis of the Mind (*Geist*):
## Beginnings inside the Youth Movement

It is often an all too easy ploy, and it is always tempting, to find evidence that a thinker's earliest writings foreshadow all of his later ideas. The passage that introduces Benjamin's first published essay, "The Life of Students"[1] of 1915, appears to fully vindicate this approach. Based on two lectures he gave in May and June 1914, as the newly elected president of Berlin's Free Students (*Freie Studentenschaft*) group, this text, along with the "Dialogue about Contemporary Religiosity" (1912), represents what is perhaps the most concentrated expression of the direction his thoughts were taking at that time. In a broad sweep, the young student of philosophy at the universities of Freiburg and Berlin placed his attempt to describe the spiritual (*geistig*) situation of student life, an existence circumscribed by the university and the state and by intellectual pursuits and professional demands, within the horizon of a metaphysical concept of history centered in an understanding of the present.

This present, said Benjamin, will elude a view of history that approaches it with the idea of progress, trusting in the infinity of time. In contrast, his own thinking proceeded from a utopian final state of history whose elements, no matter how imperfectly accomplished, manifest themselves in every present, are indeed immanent in it. It is "the historical task" to "disclose this immanent state of perfection and make it absolute, to make it visible and dominant in the present."[2] This task makes it necessary, however, to capture this immanent state not in terms of its historical details, but rather to grasp its metaphysical structure. As with the messianic realm or the idea of the French Revolution, it is necessary to perceive the historical significance of the university and its students, which means to describe "the form of their present existence . . . as a metaphor, as an image of the highest, the metaphysical state of history."[3] To be sure, this claim can be adequately fulfilled only within the framework of a philosophical system. "So long as the preconditions needed for this are absent, there is no other choice but to liberate the future from its deformations in the present by an act of cognition." According to Benjamin's programmatic summary of his long first paragraph, this "must be the exclusive task of criticism."[4]

It is easy to draw a line connecting these ideas with the critique of progress as formulated in the late theses "On the Concept of History" and, even more directly, with the essay "On the Program of the Coming Philosophy" of 1918,[5] in which Benjamin took up the discussion of philosophy, which the earlier text had merely hinted at. But focusing on the concept of "critique"—in his early writings he used this term again in the title of the long essay "Critique of Violence"[6]—marks not only his attempt to connect with philosophy. Rather, his conception of himself as a literary critic can, even in his final works, be traced back to the adaptation of Kantian criticism (Kritizismus) by the early Romantics and to the transformation of this concept in their theory of art, the principal topic of his dissertation. Yet it is advisable not to try to understand his early writings by relating them all too hastily to his later work but to see them within the specific context of their origin.

As a member of the Free Students—for a time in a leadership position—Benjamin was closely associated with the Youth Movement whose vehement and diffuse criticism of civilization had found a much admired precursor in Nietzsche, especially in *Thus Spoke Zarathustra*. When he was preparing his lecture, he therefore consulted both Nietzsche's "Thoughts on the Future of Our Educational Institutions" (1872) and Fichte's memorandum on founding the University of Berlin, "Deduzierter Plan einer in Berlin zu errichtenden höheren Lehranstalt."[7] He also followed closely on the path that his mentor Gustav Wyneken had established in his numerous writings on school reform. But there is a world of difference between his lecture of early 1914 and versions published in 1915 (in *Der Neue Merkur*) and 1916 (in Hiller's *Ziel*).

The outbreak of war and, even more, the protest against it that motivated the suicide of two of his close friends did not fundamentally change Benjamin's intellectual self-perception but rather radicalized it. This self-perception did not renounce what it owed to that section of the Youth Movement that had been shaped by Wyneken, even though Benjamin was no less intent on retaining his autonomy. But from early on, since his first experiences as a student and through his organizational work on behalf of the Free Students, Benjamin had firmed up his conviction that the dictates of the moment demand the creation of "a community of young people that is only internally and intrinsically grounded, and not at all politically."[8] At the same time, he was fully prepared to accept his incipient detachment from Wyneken in the bargain. After the outbreak of war and under the impact of his friends' suicide, this attitude is expressed in a letter of October 25, 1914, in which Benjamin states that the university as presently constituted "is capable even of poisoning our turn to the spirit" and that he has come to realize "that our radicalism [had been] too much a gesture, and that a harder, purer, more invisible radicalism should become axiomatic for us."[9]

Benjamin's letter to Wyneken dated March 9, 1915, in which he "totally and unconditionally"[10] dissociated himself from this previously admired pedagogue, must be read as a consequence of this insight. The fact that Wyneken had come out in support of the war gave Benjamin the ostensible impetus for this break. But the real issue for him was not the war itself. Rather, through his commitment to war, Benjamin considered his revered teacher guilty of betraying the "idea" and youth. Wyneken, he wrote, had been "the first person to introduce me to the life of the spirit."[11] The idea of youth, to which Benjamin declared his loyalty in this letter and in numerous other writings from this time, clearly does not refer to a stage of life but to an attitude toward life. Youth, in Benjamin's fluctuating terminology, means the experience (as "Erlebnis" or "Erfahrung") of an absolute commitment to what he calls the idea or pure spirit (*Geist*). His later effort to regain a comprehensive concept of experience through metacritical recourse to Kant's critiques is unmistakably rooted in these early attempts to attain both an intellectual and an existential orientation. The idea of youth, "this constantly reverberating feeling for the abstractness of pure spirit,"[12] had to be defended against Wyneken. Its legacy—that is, to live with the idea—Benjamin is now intent on "wresting" from his teacher, as he wrote with a gesture of radical decisiveness in the final sentence of his letter.

What imbues Benjamin's early writings with a strained and at times straining pathos is to a considerable extent that gesture of absoluteness that perceives any form of concreteness as a betrayal, if not of the idea, then of its unconditionality and purity. It is not merely in the nature of things but clearly the author's intention that this pathos occasionally verges on the religious. Not surprisingly, "contemporary religiosity" is the hardly fortuitous theme of a dialogue written in 1912. It discusses the conditions required to make a new religion possible. Obvious expectations, however, that

Benjamin might show himself to be a partisan, for example, of the Jewish Renewal prominently associated with Martin Buber (1878–1965), the Jewish philosopher of religion, or even of Zionism, met with disappointment.

An exchange of letters with the young Zionist Ludwig Strauß (1892–1953) gave him an opportunity even before the war to account for the reasons of his commitment to Wyneken while he kept himself at a distance from Zionism.[13] He wrote that he had had his decisive intellectual (*geistig*) experience before Judaism had become important or problematical to him. He continues that it is against this background that he had found his Jewishness, had "discovered as Jewish what he considered the highest ground that ideas and human beings" could attain. This experience, he stated in a different letter, had given him the insight that the Jews represent an elite among the people of spirit (*die Geistigen*). For Judaism was to him "in no respect an end in itself but a most noble upholder and representative of the spiritual." Exemplary evidence of a "cultural Zionism"[14] or of an esoteric "Zionism of the spirit,"[15] to which he would profess his loyalty, he found in Hegel (whom he read through Wyneken's eyes) as well as in Buber's then popular *Three Addresses on Judaism* (1911), but also in Goethe and of course in Nietzsche's *Zarathustra*.

A political Zionism, to which Strauß was trying to convert him, had no place in this mental household. Politics, according to a formulation indicative of Benjamin's later political philosophy, is "a consequence of a spiritual turn of mind that is no longer being carried out through the spirit [*am Geiste*]."[16] In view of the absolute primacy of the spiritual, politics assumed a secondary, relative significance. When he located his political position "somewhere on the left," he did not base it on a conviction that could properly be called political. A more specific justification for this nonchalant option in favor of a "leftist liberalism" or a "social-democratic wing"[17] is the expectation that Wyneken's plans for school reforms would be supported here more likely than anywhere else. This kind of "socialism by instinct,"[18] though widespread throughout the Youth Movement, was politically ignorant and later turned out to be dangerously ambivalent. It was based on the vague experience of community that the campfire romanticism of the *Wandervogel* conveyed in much the same way as the Wickersdorf school community did. In Benjamin's early writings, the ideology of community is given its specific contours as a corollary of an ethically grounded individualistic reservation.

As early as in his correspondence with Ludwig Strauß, Benjamin characterized what his idealistic (*geistig*) attitude as motivated by Wyneken has in common with Judaism. He did so in terms of a "strictly dualistic view of life."[19] This outlook also defines the position that, in the (posthumously published) "Dialogue on Contemporary Religiosity," quite unequivocally represents his own conviction. The partner in this dialogue, by contrast, reveals himself to be an adherent of monism, a pantheistic view of the world that, invoking the doctrines of Gustav Theodor Fechner (1802–87), wielded considerable influence on the intellectual life of Wilhelmine Germany. This decidedly modern view of the world, replacing religion and metaphysics with science and technological progress and finding a kind of *ersatz* religion by believing in the perfectibility of the world, is countered in the dialogue by the "honesty of dualism."[20] By religion Benjamin means the "sum of duties as . . . divine commands,"[21] a definition that allows him, as it did Kant (who is his authoritative source), to stay altogether within the boundaries of "philosophical morality." Moral community, to which also in others of his early writings he consistently accorded religious attributes, is absolutely predicated on the individual experience of moral autonomy, on the "dualism of duty and person,"[22] as he occasionally calls this experience in the "Dialogue." Religion, he wrote, in the final analysis arises in one's inward self, which, out of need, creates a final objective for itself, and, to emphasize this point, is not at all limited to confidence in evolution or to the developing of a pantheistic sense of life.

At first sight it is surprising and surely indicative of a certain flair for the provocative when Benjamin calls coffeehouse literati (to whom he also refers in "The Life of Students") the bearers of a religious spirit that points beyond the present age. The reference to "literati," to a modern phenomenon, places the concept of culture in the context of the "Dialogue on Contemporary Religiosity." The literati become martyrs of the new *religion* that, in an emphatic sense, has also to be understood as *culture*. Their martyrdom is the consequence of two aspects: they "want to transform values (*die Werte*) into life, into convention,"[23] and they take the forms of culture seriously, dedicating their lives all the more rigorously to, for example, art, of which they are dilettantes at best. By becoming social outsiders through their absolute love of art, their contradicting of society serves to demonstrate society's religious neediness. Thus they reveal, he says, how far removed, in the final analysis, the present age is from a culture in which this dualism had been overcome. This religion and its promise, the new human being (*der neue Mensch*) to which the present age will give birth, have already had their prophets: Tolstoy, Nietzsche, Strindberg.

The philosopher and sociologist Georg Simmel (1858–1918) as never before had made culture, its concepts and its phenomena, the object of philosophical reflection. In 1911, he published his important essay "The Concept and Tragedy of Culture," wherein he describes culture as the arena of a conflict that takes place between the soul and the constructs of the objective spirit that that soul itself had originally created. Tragedy takes its course where the objective products of the soul close themselves off more and more to form an independent cosmos, in the process creating a fully differentiated sphere of values with a logic and development all its own. Even culture is no exception to the general tendency of Modernity to isolate the various sectors of society from each other as a consequence of the advancing division of labor. In following Marx, Simmel speaks of the "fetishizing" of cultural products, which leads to an alienation of the soul from its own creations. What we call culture, the path of the subject via the objective products to itself, its formative process, "runs into a cul-de-sac or a vacuity of our innermost and most genuine life."[24]

The neo-Kantian philosopher Heinrich Rickert, with whom Benjamin had studied in Freiburg, had ventured to make an epistemological distinction between the cultural sciences as based on the validity of value judgments, and the natural sciences. It is a neo-Kantian concept of culture that left its traces in Max Weber's (1864–1920) famous phrase about the "disenchantment of the world" through modern science and through an uncompromising rationalism in the conduct of life. It is no less evident in Nietzsche's program of a "revaluation of all values." Yet as little as the cultural sciences can dispense with value judgments, it is also not within their power and competency, Weber argued, to justify their partisanship in favor of specific values. Such preferences, to the contrary, would always turn out to be decisions against other, equally legitimate values. Thus, the cultural sciences cannot but accept the fact that the contest of value systems is in principle insoluble. At the culmination of Modernity, Weber diagnosed a regression into polytheism: "The numerous gods of yore, divested of their magic and hence assuming the shape of impersonal forces, arise from their graves, strive for power over our lives, and resume their eternal struggle among themselves." These words from his lecture "Science as a Vocation" of November 7, 1917 (published 1919), are specifically addressed to members of the young generation. He called them the ones who experience the greatest difficulty when they have to meet the challenges of everyday life that the "iron cage" of rationalistic-technocratic Modernity offers. All chasing after "experience" is evidence of weakness. For it is weakness "to be unable to look the fate of the age into its solemn face."[25]

Already the title of Georg Lukács's essay collection *Soul and Forms* (1911) indicates that this volume is a reprise of the "tragedy of culture" that Simmel had diagnosed so vividly. Lukács like Ernst Bloch was a student of Simmel, whose lectures Benjamin also attended as a student of philosophy at the Friedrich-Wilhelms-Universität in Berlin, where he studied in the winter semester of 1912–13 and again from 1913–14 until the summer semester of 1915. (In 1912 and 1913 he spent two semesters in Freiburg). One would not err in reading these essays on different authors and on questions of both ethics and aesthetics as so many explorations that seek to break through the alienation and isolation of modern culture in the name of a new "totality." Lukács writes that the fragmentation of modern life has been overcome when the intended closed form, be it that of the artwork or of a community, has been accomplished. Even his *Theory of the Novel* (written under the impact of the war and first published in 1916) moves within this intellectual (*geistig*) gravitational field. Inasmuch as this new book projects its author's high-flying expectations onto Tolstoy and even more onto Dostoevsky, it makes use of an intellectual fashion. Yet while this vogue had become stuck in the rut of indistinct derogations of its age, Lukács's critique turns an intellectual fad into a utopian vision that is forcefully coherent. Thus, it is no coincidence that Tolstoy emerged as one of the prophets of the new culture in Benjamin's "Dialogue," and that Benjamin, in 1917, will devote one of his earliest pieces of literary criticism to Dostoevsky's novel *The Idiot*.

The young Benjamin was as unwilling as Lukács, close to ten years his senior, to accept Weber's stoic submission to modern culture along with his diagnosis of it. In "The Life of Students" he mapped out the image of a community that submits itself unconditionally to Idea (*die Idee*) and is pervaded by it. In the form of an ultimatum, he contrasts this image with a view of university studies as preparation for a professional job: "Where the idea that governs student life is office and profession, there can be no true learning."[26] With the same logical consistency, Benjamin's community of learners and teachers, which has been established in the spirit of genuine science (and for Benjamin that means of course philosophy), demands the inclusion of women. For just as student life is no mere transitional stage on the road to a profession, so should it not be misunderstood as an intermediate stage of erotic liberality during a period preceding a bourgeois marriage. Benjamin makes it an irrefutable demand that the *Idee* of a way of life founded on the friendship of creative minds must take charge of every individual. Whoever accepts this idea, he writes in the final sentence of the essay, thus directing his focus back on the historical-philosophical reflection at the end of the first paragraph, will succeed in "liberating the future from its deformed existence in the womb of the present."[27]

It took a relatively long time before this speech saw print, early in 1916 in the first of Kurt Hiller's (1885–1972) *Ziel* (*Target*) yearbooks. This delay was the reason that this talk was published there together with an essay by Wyneken, from whom Benjamin had withdrawn his allegiance barely a year before. In Wyneken's opinion, the war had begun with the antici-pated victory of unifying the people as a whole, even including the party of the proletarians. Thus, he wrote, the state of wartime emergency prede-termines the coming peace, for which guidance emanating from "the idea, from that which absolutely shall be,"[28] would have to become obligatory. It is the task of *"Creative Education,"* to quote the title of Wyneken's essay, to bring up a generation with an absolute will, a generation that is prepared to meet the validity of absolute values with a willingness to commit itself to unconditional service. To the fundamental issue of the new age, which he perceived to be the choice between "culture or socialism," Wyneken re-sponded by professing his faith in the necessity of a new culture. Alluding to Wickersdorf, he evoked the school as the venue where the idea of a youth culture based on the living community of youth and its leaders has become a precedent-setting reality for society. The supremacy of *Geist,* in its mani-festation as mind, spirit, and intellect as it had been made real here, the theocracy of *Geist,* knows no hierarchy other than that of *geistig* achieve-ment and vocation.

It is hardly possible to deny that such ideas show an occasionally amaz-ing proximity to Benjamin's essay in the same volume, Wyneken's tribute to war notwithstanding. One may assume, therefore, that Benjamin felt all the more urgently the necessity of subjecting the basic reasons for keeping his distance from Wyneken to a critical revision. This reassessment, no less than his renunciation of Wyneken and, a short time later, his abrupt break with most of his companions from the time of the Youth Movement, took place along the intellectual paths he outlined rather than fully laid out in his early writings. In 1916, Benjamin was still far from the insight he was to note in *Berlin Chronicle* that "no one can improve his school or his pa-rental home without first smashing the state that needs bad ones."[29] For the time being it was Nietzsche who prominently delimited the horizon of his thinking. Nietzsche, in "The Uses and Disadvantages of History for Life" (1874), the second of his *Untimely Meditations,* had addressed a dramatic appeal to that very youth whose mission it is, he said, to bring about a new culture, one that had overcome the paralyzing historicism and the level-ing materialism of the present age. "You should not seek an escape into some metaphysics but should sacrifice yourselves actively to the *emerging culture (der werdenden Kultur)!*"—an exhortation that was not written by Benjamin but is to be found in a posthumous fragment (no. 19 [154] in a notebook of 1872–73) from the time of Nietzsche's early cultural-critical

writings.[30] Also Benjamin's exhortation in "The Life of Students," "to liberate the future from its deformations in the present by an act of cognition,"[31]
shows him to be a disciple of Nietzsche. To practice "Fernstenliebe" (love
of what is farthest away, as opposed to "Nächstenliebe," love of your neigh-
bor) had been Zarathustra's admonition to his followers, to which he had
added: "Let the future and the farthest be for you the cause of your today: in
your friend you shall love the overman [*Übermensch*] as your cause."[32]

## 2. Life of the Work of Art

According to a curriculum vitae of 1928, Benjamin's interest had in the
course of his university studies gradually come "to focus on the philosophical content of imaginative literature and artistic form" and had ultimately
found expression in the topic of his dissertation.[33] Two essays, both of them
preceding his dissertation, "The Concept of Criticism in German Romanticism" (1919),[34] testify to this direction his interests were taking. The first of
these two studies is the important aesthetic commentary on two poems by
Friedrich Hölderlin, written during the war winter of 1914–15. It remained
unpublished during his lifetime. The second is his critique of Dostoevsky's
novel *The Idiot,* an essay that appeared in *Die Argonauten* in 1921 but had
been written as early as 1917. Benjamin later referred to it as one of his "very
first printed pieces."[35] Both essays also document his attempt to hold on to
the intellectual heritage of the Youth Movement, even after his rigorous
termination of all personal connections. In other words, they appear, both
in their choice of topics and in some biographical allusions, to be still fully
attached to the environment of Benjamin's youth. Yet they corroborate less
his adherence to this ideological milieu than they attest to a different endeavor, that is, he was trying to find in discussions of prominent cultural
issues a more commensurate form for that intellectual disposition to which
he had given a first and, as he soon recognized, inadequate expression during
his commitment to the Youth Movement.

Consequently, his interpretation of *The Idiot* culminates in the thesis
that this novel expresses Dostoevsky's great act of lament "for the failure
of the youth movement."[36] Just as in his political writings that novelist
had hoped for a regeneration of Russia through the powers inherent in the
national heritage, so in his novel he had recognized that the only salvation
for her young people and their country lies in childhood. Youth, according
to Benjamin's interpretation, is a synonym for that immortality that is symbolized by the solitude of a protagonist whose life appears to be moribund
from its beginning as a consequence of his epilepsy.

The autobiographical aspects of this interpretation are no doubt obvious. What is more significant, however, and fraught with consequences, are the methodological reflections on which Benjamin based them. His first and central premise of these deliberations is the rigid rejection of any analysis that seeks to arrive at an understanding of the novel by way of untangling its characters' psychology. By contrast, criticism can justify its right to approach artworks only "by respecting their [distinct] territory and by taking care not to trespass on that forbidden soil."[37] Criticism, the term under whose sign Benjamin had already delivered his speech on the "Life of Students," is now given more specific contours as a concept of literary theory. Benjamin writes that Dostoevsky's novel, like all works of art, is based on an idea. Following Novalis, he accords the *idea* inherent in the artwork an important place in a theory of art criticism whose outlines are taking shape here. In a fragment, Novalis had spoken of the "*necessity* of every work of art"; every one of them "has an a priori ideal," has a "necessity in and of itself for being in the world. This," the fragment continues, makes "a genuine criticism of the painters possible."[38] And Benjamin was convinced that it is the critic's task to articulate this necessity and nothing else.

Benjamin had used the Novalis quotation already in the essay on Hölderlin he had written a few years earlier. There it occupies the center of a methodological reflection that serves as a programmatic introduction to an expansive comparison of two poems or, more precisely, of two versions of an ode by Hölderlin. His essay, he says, should not be misunderstood as a philological commentary of the kind that customarily is intended to explicate works of classical stature. He also is not concerned with an aesthetic investigation that seeks to provide insights into the fundamental rules that define literary genres. Rather, Benjamin wishes to have the essay understood as an "aesthetic commentary on two lyric poems."[39] He does not use the terms "criticism" or "critique" in these preliminary remarks on method. But he paraphrases their task—with reference to the ensuing comparison of the two poems—as making it apparent "that, with respect to lyric poetry, a judgment, even if not provable, can nonetheless be justified."[40]

In this early essay, perhaps even more than in the critique of Dostoevsky's *The Idiot*, subject matter and theoretical reflection are equally remarkable. Some time after the completion of the Hölderlin study, Benjamin wrote (in a letter of February 27, 1917) that his external motivation had been the way Norbert von Hellingrath (1888–1916) had framed the subject in his (academically controversial) dissertation on Hölderlin's Pindar translations. He mentioned also that, before he had learned of the young scholar's death at Verdun in December 1916, he had wanted to give Hellingrath his own Hölderlin essay to read. In Hellingrath's work Benjamin had found the reference to "those revisions and the recasting of older odes" that reveal an increase of pure lyric ability. "One need only to compare 'Blödigkeit' [Timidity] with the first version of 'Dichtermut' [The Poet's Courage] to see how every change there is necessary for imbuing the respective wording with its full being in the world [*Dasein*]."[41] This is the challenge Benjamin accepted in his essay.

Hellingrath is as inseparably linked to Benjamin's essay on Hölderlin as he was instrumental in reorienting the poet's reception at the beginning of the century.[42] He was, first of all, the person who initiated and until his early death supervised the historico-critical edition of Hölderlin's works. But even before its various volumes were published, he had inaugurated, in smaller editions and finally in his dissertation, a fundamental reorientation in the way Hölderlin was read. For this, a revalorization of his late works was symptomatic. Heretofore, the largely unknown poet had been perceived as a minor figure of the Romantic generation. Measured by the standards of German classicism, he was considered a failure. Hellingrath's dissertation, therefore, had to overcome the prevailing value judgments of literary historiography as much as the misgivings of some faculty members who, as regards the poet's mental illness, were of the opinion that the "poetic works of a lunatic" are no material for a scholarly disquisition and that one would have to be concerned for the mind of someone who undertakes it anyway.[43]

Hellingrath's turning away from the standards of classicism in order to introduce a fundamentally new understanding of Hölderlin was accompanied by the close attention he paid to the concrete form into which the language of this poetry had been shaped. He stated that the poet's translations from the Greek have to be taken into consideration when it comes to appreciating both the peculiar originality of these works and the poetological orientation they express. But it was not through abstracting a rule or regulation but through adopting the "inner form of Greek poetry"[44] that Hölderlin's late verse had been given its specific character. Greek rhetoric, Hellingrath emphasized, had made a stylistic distinction between an "austere" and a "smooth" conjoining of linguistic elements. In referring back to this distinction, Hellingrath placed the "austere way of poetizing" alongside the type of rhyming poetry that Goethe had advanced to its highest perfection, and he valued both of them as artistically equal possibilities of lyric expression. The former, he wrote, had found its paradigmatic realization in Hölderlin's late poetic works.[45] Even Adorno's interpretation of the philosophical content of this poetry proceeds, with full acceptance of this distinction, from the serial technique (parataxis) as its characteristic trait. And where Adorno's analysis makes reference to Benjamin, it also, albeit indirectly, acknowledges Hellingrath's fundamental insight and preliminary work to which the former's study had alerted him.[46]

The anticlassical turn in Hellingrath's appreciation of Hölderlin followed a tendency that was prevalent at the turn of the century: (Greek) antiquity was no longer perceived primarily under the sign of its classical but of its archaic era. This revaluation was doubly beholden to Nietzsche, who in *The Birth of Tragedy* had not only prepared the ground for an anticlassicist understanding of antiquity but had also, in prominent parts of his cultural criticism, evoked "the memory of the glorious Hölderlin"[47] as a counter-image to the philistinism of contemporary culture. The parallelisms in the biographies of the *Hyperion* poet and of *Zarathustra*'s author further contributed to attracting to Hellingrath's work a considerable readership, at first above all among the nonacademic public.

It was Hellingrath who, as one of its adherents, played a considerable part in making Hölderlin's works and life accessible to the Stefan George Circle, thereby helping to paradigmatically confirm George's cultic vision of the poet's role. This conception combined Nietzsche's aristocracy of the intellect with a specifically modern understanding of art, one that had been schooled in the refined language of French Symbolism and that made the highest demands on the poet's linguistic sensibility and formal virtuosity. In this manner, that is to say, as a precursor of Modernity, the George Circle accorded Hölderlin his place alongside Baudelaire and Mallarmé. It is not mere chance, therefore, that Benjamin—during that same wartime winter of 1914–15, in which he started writing his study of Hölderlin that Hellingrath had initiated—also began his translations from Baudelaire's *Fleurs du mal*, which were to occupy him for many years.

The emphasis Benjamin places on formal structure and his demonstration that modern writers employ their artistic and linguistic resources in ever more conscious, calculated ways base his comparison of the two Hölderlin poems on criteria that reveal his familiarity with the distinct character of modern lyric poetry. At the theoretical center of his investigation stands the concept of "the poetized" (*das Gedichtete*), a *tertium comparationis* that enables him to include in his discussion an evaluative judgment of poetry, *das Gedichtete* being a concept that shows "the intensity of the coherence of the perceptual and intellectual elements." And to confirm this coherence is, after all, the sole purpose of the comparison.[48] As a sphere to be assumed a priori for every work of poetry, the poetized in the final analysis is identical with "that peculiar domain containing the truth of the poem . . . , which the most serious artists so insistently claim for their creations." In regard to the particular structural configuration (Gestalt) that is the precondition for every single poem, the essay calls this sphere the "inner form," or, following Goethe, the poem's content (Gehalt).[49] It designates the concrete task the poet tries to accomplish through his creative endeavor. In contrast to that, the poetized denotes the form not of the individual work of art, but that of the artwork in general—in Novalis's term, its "necessity."

Within this conceptual force field that is defined by the tension between the potential organization of the elements in the ideal sphere of the poetized and their actual realization in the form of the poem, Benjamin locates the critical space for an aesthetic commentary. It is characteristic of his concept of criticism, as he used it also in later essays, that his thoughts are based on a premise that understands the poetized as "at once the product and the subject of this investigation."[50] In this way he strictly obligates criticism to immanence. Criticism, consequently, amounts less to a judgment *on* rather than to a description *of* the work of art and disregards any preestablished aesthetic and, most of all, extra-aesthetic categories of, for example, a moral, psychological, or biographical nature.

The "peculiar sense of necessity with which the work of art strikes us" was also the starting point for Georg Simmel's reflections on *legitimateness in the work of art* in a posthumously published essay. Going back to ideas first advanced in a lecture course on the philosophy of art during the winter semester of 1913–14, Simmel deduces this "ideal necessity" from a problem that the artwork poses for itself and that consequently can be drawn forth only from the work itself. That is to say that Simmel too thinks of the work of art as an idea, an ideal unity to which the real artwork with its multiple factors is juxtaposed. Any recourse to generally accepted norms, be they rules pertaining to literary genres, ethical demands, or religious conventions, are to be rejected, and an evaluation is to be based only on the individual law of the work in question. Simmel's reflections do not, however, intend to demarcate a theory of art criticism. Rather, the work of art is for him an "ethical analogy." In a strictly formal sense, that is: in its radically individual legitimateness, it serves him as an example to illustrate the need to correct the fundamental error one encounters in nearly every system of ethics, most of all in Kant's critique of practical reason: that of confronting the specific human existence with the general "validity" of the law.[51]

In his Hölderlin essay, Benjamin abstains from incorporating his theory of an immanent art criticism into a philosophical context. His concluding explanation of why the later version of the ode is superior to the poem's first version makes reference to the category of the sublime. But in explicating his reading, Benjamin does not follow the precepts of Kant's aesthetics. Instead, his argumentation paraphrases a thought figure (*Gedankenfigur*) whose origin is to be found in the dualism of his own previous writings. The absoluteness with which he focuses his thoughts on the idea seeks to be faithful to the idea's validity even when it is negated by the given. The work of art thus becomes a medium for the representation of the idea. Determined in its immanent structure by the idea, the work of art represents the idea in the form of its definitive negation, which in turn is being apprehended and described in criticism as the work's necessity. A comparison of Benjamin with Hellingrath shows how closely Benjamin, for example in adopting the concept of "inner form," seeks to connect his theory to the tradition of aesthetic discussions in German classicism and early Romanticism. He will pick up this constellation again in the final chapter (which is in fact the central part) of his dissertation in order to discuss it within the horizon of a contemporary theory of art criticism.

## 3. Defining His Philosophical Position

In the curriculum vitae Benjamin had written toward the end of the 1920s (in which he states—with reference to the topic of his dissertation—that his interest had come to focus on aesthetics), he also mentions that as a university student he had occupied himself in particular with reading and rereading Plato and Kant, and then the philosophy of Husserl and the Marburg School.[52] Coherent or even systematic contributions to philosophical topics are rather infrequent in Benjamin's oeuvre. The most important exception in this respect is the long essay "On the Program of the Coming Philosophy" that he wrote in November 1917, the year he had moved to Switzerland. It is a study that arose from discussions with Gershom Scholem, whom Benjamin had first met in Berlin in July 1915 and with whom he soon developed a close friendship that involved an intensive exchange of ideas. The essay's principal purpose was self-orientation and the desire to clarify his own philosophical position. Benjamin gave no thought to publishing this work. Instead, a copy of it, prepared by Dora Benjamin, was ceremoniously handed over to Scholem when he arrived in Bern in May 1918—he stayed until July 1919—in order to continue his studies there. Scholem has given a detailed report about this time in Bern in his memoirs,[53] writing about their attendance together at seminars and their discussions, and also describing his social life in the company of the young couple and their son, Stefan, born in April 1918.

is situated, at the same time implicitly touching on his specific concerns. Benjamin says that it had been Kant's purpose to erect the theory of knowledge on the foundation of the exact sciences in the interest of restricting the demands made by metaphysical dogmatism. Neo-Kantianism had retained the "plan of development of Kant's thinking" without considering that "the enemy had some time ago been moved to quite a different position." For Kant, the emerging natural sciences constituted an integral part of a worldview "whose historical elevation has had its vanishing point in the realm of freedom and eternal peace."[58] This emancipatory aspect had been lost in the course of the positivistic transformation of the natural sciences. In Helmholtz's, Du Bois-Reymond's, or in Haeckel's image of the world, nature no longer is the material of duty but an instrument for a claim to domination that is based on technological progress and global trade.

The older neo-Kantianism and its most prominent representative Hermann Helmholtz (1821–94) had in fact brought about a rapprochement between philosophy and the natural sciences, which had become all-powerful in consequence of the technological-industrial development. Also, its physiological interpretation of criticism (*Kritizismus*) had at the same time established the basis for the rehabilitation of philosophy as the theory of knowledge, that is, epistemology. To be sure, the physiological approach that Helmholtz had developed in his lecture "Über das Sehen des Menschen" (1855; On the Way Man Sees) and that Friedrich Albert Lange (1828–75) represented in his influential *Geschichte des Materialismus und Kritik seiner Bedeutung in der Gegenwart* (1866; History of Materialism and Criticism of its Present Importance, 1877, 3 vols.) was soon abandoned.[59] Nonetheless, the conception of philosophy as "theory of knowledge," to quote the highly effective catchword that Eduard Zeller had coined with a view toward Kant in 1862, remained obligatory for all variants of neo-Kantianism. A concomitant factor was the inclination to understand the transcendental method as a method of investigation that is equally valid in philosophy and the natural sciences.[60] Hermann Cohen (Lange's disciple and successor to the chair of philosophy at Marburg), while emphatically rejecting the physiological justification for the theory of knowledge, did advocate a view of Kant's conception of experience that, in the final analysis, was identical with the knowledge arrived at in mathematics and the natural sciences.

Benjamin believed that the weakness of neo-Kantianism resulted from its complicity with positivism, of which collusion it itself was not even aware. Hence he considered himself able to recognize this failure especially in the neo-Kantian conception of system. Kant, he says, had put a keystone to his system in *The Critique of Judgment* by granting the imagination and history a place of central importance and, in doing so, has given expression to the *planning* aspect of his conception of system. In neo-Kantianism, most strongly in Cohen, this conception has been reduced to nothing but an interpretative mode. This development from Kant to Cohen reflects a willingness "to make oneself at home in the way things are."[61] It also forms the basis for the interest that a decrepit criticism had taken in language and history. To point out this failing, Benjamin's review uses Hönigswald's study as an equally misguided and offensive example.

The reference in the review to "language" and "history" identifies the two cues that mark the intellectual horizon of the programmatic essay that Benjamin had conceived more than twenty years earlier. In its first sentence he calls it the "central task of the coming philosophy" to "take the deepest intimations it draws from our times and our expectation of a great future, and turn them into knowledge by relating them to the Kantian system."[62] And it is not by chance that this formulation evokes a conception of history that endeavors to provide a metaphysical mediation between present and future, a mediation such as he had outlined in "The Life of Students." But whereas the essay of 1914 –15 had assigned to criticism the task of liberating the future from the present because the systematic foundations for such an undertaking were still lacking, he now is concerned with the problem of laying the systematic groundwork for exactly this cognitive interest. This does not necessarily mean that the coming philosophy itself will have the form of a system. He does say, however, that this philosophy as "truly time-and eternity-conscious"[63] needs to have its claim to knowledge secured, and that he is convinced that, next to Plato, only Kant had more recently endeavored to define obligatory standards for the justification of knowledge.

But there exist two important obstacles to directly linking the coming philosophy to Kant. The first is that the kind of knowledge whose certainty and truth mattered to Kant had been based on a deficient experience of history. Consequently, his *question* of the certainty of knowledge continues to be relevant. The *dignity of the experience,* however, on which that knowledge has been founded, is ephemeral. The second obstacle is that Kant's conception of knowledge had been unable to open up the domain of metaphysics. In part this is true because, as a consequence of its deficient concept of experience, "it contains within itself primitive elements of an unproductive metaphysics which excludes all others."[64] In the interest of a higher, metaphysical experience it would therefore be necessary to overcome both Kant's "conception of knowledge as a relation between some sort of subjects and objects" and the relation of experience and knowledge to "human empirical consciousness."[65]

Benjamin's dispute with Kant may be considered a further example of those more or less creative misunderstandings that characterize the continuation and development of criticism since the era of German Idealism in the historiography of philosophical thought. It is noteworthy, at any rate, that the so-called *Älteste Systemprogramm des deutschen Idealismus* (First Systematic Program of German Idealism)—first edited by Franz Rosenzweig (1886–1929), who thought it probable that Schelling had been its author—was published one year before Benjamin wrote his "Program of the Coming Philosophy." But there is no evidence that Benjamin had ever taken notice of this text.

Instead, Benjamin's outline is quick to emphasize its proximity to Kant and to insist at the very same time that Kant's critical enterprise had originated out of a metaphysical interest. After all, Kant had called the critique of pure reason—especially in the *Prolegomena*, to which Benjamin refers repeatedly and whose title he reclaims for his own project[66]—an indisputable precondition of any future metaphysics. Its rebirth he perceived to be impending all the more inevitably as "the demand for it can never be exhausted, because the interest of human reason in general is much too intimately interwoven with it."[67] The *Critique of Pure Reason* appears to this interest as "a treatise on the method, not a system of the science itself; but it marks out nevertheless the whole plan of that science."[68] But for this very reason, its negative usefulness turns out to be simultaneously a positive one. It is the tangible result of the first *Critique*, to be sure, "that all speculative knowledge of reason is limited to objects of *experience*,"[69] and that we can have knowledge of the things only insofar as they present themselves as objects of sensory perception, that is, as phenomena. But this leaves it perfectly open to us to *think* these same objects as things as such (*Dinge an sich*). The critique of presumed knowledge that goes beyond experience, and thus the restriction of knowledge to experience that is possible, becomes the precondition for extending pure reason in the interest of practical purposes.

While Kant summarized his project by saying that he had to "remove *knowledge*, in order to make room for *belief*,"[70] it is Benjamin's opposite intent—in accordance with the relation between knowledge and experience that Kant had established—to expand them and thereby to obtain space for an epistemologically secured metaphysical conception of experience that also would include "religious experience."[71]

For Benjamin, the path to this higher kind of experience has been laid down as the task of overcoming the historical limitations and systematic restrictions that had blocked such experience for Kant. He sees Kant's orientation toward the sciences and especially toward mathematical physics as a historical consequence of "the religious and historical blindness of the Enlightenment." This firm belief that the worldview of the Enlightenment was "an experience or view of the world . . . of the lowest order"[72] is even the starting point of Benjamin's interpretation of Goethe's *Elective Affinities*. The time in which both Kant and Goethe encountered the preconditions of their works, he wrote in the later essay, was a time in which it was strange to think "that the most essential contents of existence are given their imprint in the world of things and indeed are incapable of fulfilling themselves without this imprint."[73] It is only the question of how this limitation can be overcome productively that eventually leads to Benjamin's critical interest in Goethe.

In his "Program," he gives credit to Kant's contemporaries Moses Mendelssohn and Christian Garve for having done justice to the metaphysical aspect of experience.[74] But it is not through a simple return to precritical positions, against which Kant had defended himself in the *Prolegomena* and in the short essay "What Is Orientation in Thinking?" (*Was heißt: Sich im Denken orientieren?*) of 1786, that the extended conception of experience is to be gained. That objective should be accomplished by continuing what Kant had started. For after all, Kant did nowhere "deny the possibility of a metaphysics."[75]

At first glance, even more difficult to understand is Benjamin's second, systematic objection, that is, his demand to overcome Kant's "conception of knowledge as a relation between some kind of subjects and objects," a conception Benjamin rejected as mythological.[76] Accordingly, he charged the coming theory of knowledge with the task of "finding a sphere of total neutrality in regards to the concepts of both subject and object."[77] It is from this "sphere of pure knowledge" that the looked-for experience that also includes religion must be unfolded so that this experience would then rest upon pure knowledge "as the quintessence of which philosophy alone can and must think God."[78] Benjamin saw signs that confirm the development he desired in phenomenology and neo-Kantianism, which, he states, had clearly understood the necessity of revising Kant's theory of knowledge. This had, however, brought about "a reduction of all experience so exclusively to scientific experience, which had not been Kant's intention."[79]

Only toward the end of his outline does Benjamin indicate the decisive precondition under which the coming philosophy, in turning away from existing approaches, would be able to fulfill the highest metaphysical expectations demanded of it: "The great transformation and correction that must be performed upon the concept of experience, oriented so one-sidedly along mathematical-mechanical lines, can be attained only by relating knowledge to language, as was attempted by Hamann during Kant's lifetime."[80] Consequently, it is in language itself that the sphere of pure knowledge is to be sought. Only a concept of philosophy that has been attained through reflecting on the linguistic nature of knowledge will be able to create a corresponding concept of experience that will also encompass the realm of religion. Thus, the demand made upon the coming philosophy can finally be put in these words: "to create on the basis of the Kantian system a concept of knowledge to which a concept of experience corresponds, the knowledge of which is doctrine (*Lehre*)."[81] A note from the time Benjamin was working on the "Program" puts it even more succinctly: "Philosophy is absolute experience deduced in its systematically symbolic connection as language."[82]

By emphasizing the importance of language for the metaphysical renewal of philosophy as well as by referring to Johann Georg Hamann (1730–88) for support, the "Program" directly continues ideas developed in "On Language as Such and on the Language of Man," a treatise completed barely a year earlier. In his "Metacritique concerning the Purism of Reason," a work that remained unpublished during his lifetime, Hamann had in opposition to Kant insisted not only that language "is the only first and ultimate organon and criterion of reason," but had also objected to Kant's endeavor "to make reason independent of every transmittance, tradition, and faith in it."[83] It appears that Benjamin made productive use of both objections in his idea that the coming philosophy may be transformed to become doctrine or be incorporated in it.

Both Benjamin's concept of doctrine and Hamann's understanding of language and tradition are unthinkable without reference to religion. What is decisive, however, and common to all three concepts is the fact that they divert attention away from metaphysical contents and instead focus on the question of how they are represented and historically mediated. In a letter of October 22, 1917, in which he reflects on the connection of philosophy and doctrine, Benjamin speaks of a "typology of conceiving doctrine," admitting that he is using here a very "vague" expression,[84] but stating at once his conviction "that anyone who does not sense in Kant the struggle to *conceive doctrine itself* and who therefore does not comprehend him with the utmost reverence, looking on even the least letter as a *tradendum*," as something "to be transmitted," knows nothing at all of philosophy.[85] In this manner, however, the process of tradition and exegesis, be it of Kantian philosophy or of philosophy in general, can, finally, no longer be distinguished from doctrine. Once again with obvious reference to the vision of the university as outlined in "The Life of Students," Benjamin approximated the concept of doctrine to that of tradition. Tradition, he wrote in a letter to Scholem in September 1917, "is the medium in which the person who is learning *continually* transforms himself into the person who is teaching," and in "tradition everyone is an educator and a person to be educated and everything is education. These relationships are symbolized and synthesized in the development of doctrine."[86] Both in his theory of language, which forms the basis for the outline of his philosophical program, and in his interpretation of Romanticism, in which he will proceed from his preoccupation with Kant to develop a theory of art criticism, the concepts of mediation and tradition move to the center of Benjamin's thinking.

## 4. The Magic of Language

Benjamin himself in later works repeatedly referred to his reflections on the theory of language. This was his way of emphasizing their relevance not only for his early writings. These reflections have found their most concentrated expression in the notes titled "On Language as Such and on the Language of Man," which he wrote toward the end of 1916 in Munich, where he was a university student before he moved to Bern. Just as the philosophical "Program," this outline was not meant for publication; during his lifetime it circulated in only a few copies.

Even when one concedes that the early theory of language is of exceptional significance in Benjamin's oeuvre, it is not immediately obvious how this theory applies to any specific work. To be sure, thoughts on the philosophy of language can be found again and again in any number of his writings. But if they hint at a systematic connection, Benjamin, in the early outline, hid it from his readers and made no effort to explicate it specifically in the context of a fully elaborated philosophy of language. It must be left open if his outline for a *Habilitation* thesis on the topic of "word and concept," "language and logos,"[87] which he was considering during the early 1920s, may have satisfied this desideratum, or if he had even thought about it. His plan did not progress beyond preliminary studies[88] and was soon abandoned in favor of a *Habilitation* in the discipline of aesthetics.

There remain those writings in which Benjamin implicitly returns to the early work or in which he explicitly expanded it. In view of the themes of "On Language," such a motivation was more than likely behind "The Task of the Translator," a study he wrote in 1921 and used two years later as the preface to his Baudelaire translations. A continued preoccupation with previously formulated ideas is true no less for his interpretation of Baroque theories of language in the *Habilitation* thesis, "Origin of German

Tragic Drama," which he submitted at Frankfurt University in 1925. Benjamin even established an explicit link between the epistemo-critical prolegomena, the "Erkenntniskritische Vorrede," with which he prefaced the book on tragic drama, and his early essay by calling the introduction "a kind of second stage—and I don't know whether it is any better—of my earlier work on language."[89] And finally, the reflections on the theory of language need to be mentioned, which Benjamin wrote in 1933 in two versions, in Berlin and in exile on Ibiza, and for the preparation of which he asked Scholem to mail him the earlier essay because his own copy "now is of course out of reach, since it is among my papers in Berlin."[90] These reflections are titled "Doctrine of the Similar" and "On the Mimetic Faculty."[91]

But the true significance of Benjamin's philosophy of language is discernible not so much as the *theme* of his writings but as their *foundation*. It is in this sense that one can also understand a remark he made (in a letter of March 7, 1931) in answer to a critic of his political commitment during the mid-1920s. He insists that "there is a bridge to the way dialectical materialism looks at things from the perspective of my particular stance on the philosophy of language, however strained and problematical that bridge may be."[92] A further clarification of this standpoint can be found in a letter to Hugo von Hofmannsthal dated January 13, 1924, in which he underscores the philosophical conviction that was guiding him in his literary endeavors. He writes that "every truth has its home, its ancestral palace, in language." The perception that language is symbolic by nature, which imprints the terminology of the various individual disciplines of knowledge "with the most irresponsible arbitrariness," proves to be subordinate to a truth grounded in the fact mentioned above. According to Benjamin, language is not a system of symbols established by convention. It is an "order" (*Ordnung*). Philosophy, by virtue of its insights into this order, is capable of penetrating through the surface of conceptual language to reveal "the forms of linguistic life locked within."[93]

Benjamin has described the way in which this conception of language is linked to his self-understanding as an author in a letter to Martin Buber of July 17, 1916 (the year he wrote the essay "On Language as Such and on the Language of Man"), in which he justified his refusal to accept an offer to contribute to Buber's monthly periodical, *Der Jude* (The Jew). Benjamin had been personally acquainted with Buber since June 1914, when, as president of Berlin's Free Students, Benjamin had invited him to Berlin to join his host in a discussion. After an initially positive response to Buber's writings in his private letters, critically disapproving comments soon predominated.[94] As in his separation from Wyneken the year before, he introduced the topic of

Buber's affirmative attitude toward the war in the first paragraph of his letter of July 17, 1916. But the letter does not mention this particular problem
as the reason for his refusal, stating instead that the war had finally and decisively revealed to him his rejection of "all politically engaged writing."[95]
Insofar as this type of writing is based on a certain conception of the nature
of language, it serves as the background against which Benjamin places his
own point of view.

What characterized for Benjamin the widespread conviction that defines
political writing is the fact that such a tenet considers language in its relation to action only as a means, seeing it as nothing but one medium for
the "more or less suggestive *dissemination* of the motives that determine
a person's actions in his heart of hearts." To this "expansive tendency to
string words together," a procedure in which the action comes about at the
end like the result of an algebraic process, Benjamin opposed an "intensive
aiming of words into the core of an intrinsic falling silent." Only where
this sphere of speechlessness reveals itself can the "magic spark leap between the word and the motivating deed." The basis for this conviction is a
decidedly noninstrumental conception of language. According to this position, the effectiveness of language never derives from an intent that uses it
as a means toward a purpose outside of itself, but solely from having language work an "un-*mediated*" effect. This conception of language—Benjamin
calls it "magic"—seems for him to coincide with "what is actually the
objective and dispassionate manner of writing" and at the same time "to
intimate the relationship between knowledge and action precisely within
linguistic magic."[96]

On close analysis, Benjamin's letter to Buber turns out to be an attempt
to use a philosophy of language to overcome a dilemma into which his interpretation of Kant's ethics in an essay titled "Der Moralunterricht" (Instruc-
tion in Morality) of 1913 had led him. There he had defined the moral will
in Kant's sense as "motivfrei" (free of motivation), using this term—and not
by chance picking it up again in the letter to Buber—to describe his insight
that "not a single empirical manner of exerting influence can guarantee
that we are truly carrying out the moral will as such."[97] To a friend, Carla
Seligson, he explained this idea by stating that no one, in the place where he
is free—in the soul—may or should be influenced by her, or his, will. Every
good deed, he continues, merely symbolizes the freedom of the individual
who effected it: "Deeds, lectures, journals do not change anyone's will,
only a person's behavior, insight, etc. (In the moral realm, however, this is
completely irrelevant)."[98] If moral education then is in principle doomed
to failure, the experience of community does offer the disciple of Wyneken

the guarantee that "morality (*das Sittliche*) is taking shape" as a religious process that defies any closer analysis.[99]

There is good evidence to support the assumption that Benjamin's theory of the magic of language has now taken over the place in his system of thinking previously occupied by the idea of community, which had dominated his earlier reflections. In this sense, the essay on language testifies not least to that process of transformation to which Benjamin subjected his thinking as he was searching for new forms of expression and for more relevant formulations during the years after his break with the Youth Movement. In his letter to Buber, for example, he explicitly refers to his essay on "The Life of Students," which, he states, was entirely in keeping with what he has said above but for which the *Ziel* yearbook had been the wrong outlet. Benjamin concludes his refusal to contribute to *Der Jude* by mentioning the romantic *Athenäum* as a periodical that had come close to his ideal of "objective writing."[100] This declaration of a close affinity he will renew a few years later in the "Announcement" of his own journal, *Angelus Novus.*[101] By contrast, Scholem used Buber's monthly—in a contribution to the issue of March 1917—without reservations, and with Benjamin's approval, as a forum for propagating his idea for a renewal of the Jewish Youth Movement from the spirit of the Hebrew language.[102]

Ernst Schoen (1894–1960), a close friend from their time together in school who as a program director at Southwest German Broadcasting would years later procure commissions for radio features for Benjamin, was the recipient of a letter mailed on February 28, 1918, in which Benjamin, referring to his essay on language, took stock of his own intellectual development. He wrote that he had reached a point that now, for the first time, has allowed him to forge ahead toward an integration of his thought. Discussions with Schoen at a much earlier time are as vivid in his mind as his own "desperate reflections on the foundations of the categorical imperative." Without having arrived at a solution, the way of thinking that had concerned him at that time "has been subsumed into a larger context" that he has tried to develop further. This way of thinking he characterizes by paraphrasing the central idea of the essay "On Language as Such and on the Language of Man" (1916), stating that for him all "questions about the essence of knowledge, justice, and art" are connected with "the question about the origin of all human intellectual utterances in the essence of language."[103]

"On Language as Such" presupposes a comprehensive concept of language as already indicated in its title, which introduces human language as a part of language as such. As in the letter to Buber, language is defined as a medium. Hence, its *"immediacy,"* or *magic,* is declared to be the fundamental problem of linguistic theory.[104] As the medium in which the spiritual essence of all things in animate or inanimate nature communicates itself, language fulfills the demand raised by the philosophical "Program" for a concept of experience that also makes metaphysical experience possible.

The more specific structure of this experience derives from the premise that every "mental being" (*geistiges Wesen*) communicates itself by means of language, to be sure, but that not every "mental being" uses language (*ist sprachlich*) without residue. Hence, language as a medium disintegrates into a multiplicity of languages, which are different from each other merely by degrees, that is, by the intensity with which intellectual and language-using being have been interpenetrated. This idea leads Benjamin to the concept of revelation, which the philosophy of language shares with the philosophy of religion—without, however, letting religion predetermine this concept for philosophy. From the perspective of the philosophy of language, "revelation" denotes the most intensive degree of interpenetration between mind and language, the most intensive "mediateness" (*Medialität*) of language as such. Whereas human language rests on this ultimate essence of the spirit of language, art as a whole rests on a comparatively imperfect language. The "spirit of language in things," to which art testifies "in its consummate beauty,"[105] would have to be placed at the opposite end of Benjamin's scale.

As the philosophy of language in a narrower sense has done since the middle of the eighteenth century, Benjamin considers language not as a means of communication but as the constitutive condition for thinking. With this, he takes up a tradition for which, both in the "Language" essay and in the philosophical "Program," he explicitly refers to Hamann and implicitly—even though it is impossible to prove in detail how extensive his knowledge was—to German Romanticism, Herder and Wilhelm von Humboldt.[106] The concept of revelation that Benjamin introduces into his reflections is subjected to the primacy of language as understood in this way. In a letter to Friedrich Heinrich Jacobi in which he argues against the superstition favoring the mathematical form of Spinoza's and Kant's philosophy, Hamann had emphasized that he himself discusses neither physics nor theology "but language, the *mother* of reason and revelation, its alpha and omega." Also for Benjamin, who uses this quotation,[107] Hamann's not so much theological as epistemological insight is relevant that, after all, "every thing has been made" by language.[108]

At the beginning of his treatise, Benjamin had called his conception of language a "method" that "everywhere raises new questions."[109] Following his explication of the foundations that underpin this conception, he used the Creation story as told in the Book of Genesis as a text that in principle agrees with his own reflections by "presupposing language as an ultimate reality, perceptible only in its manifestation, inexplicable and mystical." But his objective, he says, is "neither biblical interpretation nor subjection of the Bible as revealed truth to objective consideration."[110]

Where an explication of the medial structure of language had led him to the concept of revelation, it is now his purpose, proceeding from the ideal essence of language, to understand its factual complexity. Benjamin distinguishes between a creative divine language and, compared to it, a deficient human language that has been reduced to satisfy the function of knowledge such as he finds in the biblical Creation story. This distinction forms the basis for his description of language as a medium of different density in the first part of the essay. Man's language is creative only in his knowledge of what God has created. Benjamin reconstructs the Adamic procedure of naming things as a "translation of the language of things into that of man."[111] He therefore understands this process as an act of cognition wherein cognition takes place in the medium of an experience that is genuinely linguistic. In this way, that is, in accordance with the coincidence of the philosophy of language and the critique of cognition, the concept of translation, which Benjamin would like to see founded "at the deepest level of linguistic theory,"[112] moves to the center of his reflections.

To support his understanding of the Adamic process of naming things as an act of cognition, Benjamin once again refers to Hamann,[113] this time to *Des Ritters von Rosencreuz letzte Willensmeynung über den göttlichen und menschlichen Ursprung der Sprachen* (Knight von Rosencreuz's Last Will and Testament concerning the Divine and Human Origin of Languages), a short piece that describes its topic in a way that is fundamental to the "Language" essay. Hamann proceeds from a "*communicatio* of divine and human *idiomatum*," which he calls "a fundamental law and the main key to our knowledge and to the visible world of an efficient economy. God is the origin of all great and small effects." Consequently, everything is divine, and the question about the origin of evil in the end amounts to nothing more than a play with words and learned prattle. "But everything divine is also human because man can neither be active nor suffer passively but in analogy to his nature." Insofar as the instruments of language are a gift of nature, the "origin of human language is indeed divine." When a higher being, however, "wants to bring about an effect through our tongue, then such effects . . . must utter themselves analogous to human nature, and in this relationship the origin of language and much less its history can be, and appear as, anything other than human."[114]

From this discrepancy between divine and human language, Benjamin derives not only his concept of translation but also that of the multiplicity of human languages. The language of things, he says, can pass into the language of knowledge (*Erkenntnis*) only through translation—"so many translations, so many languages—once man has fallen from the paradisiacal state that knew only one language." From the viewpoint of a theory of language, the biblical story of the Fall is no subject for reflections pertaining to a theology of morals. It illustrates instead how language further differentiates itself in the course of its development, in its multiplicity "is indeed forced to differentiate itself."[115] Even when Benjamin describes postlapsarian human language as a parodistic distortion of the divine language, the theological scandal of the Fall is not decisive for its understanding. Rather, it is as necessary as ever before to understand that language is structured as a medium and despite its increasing differentiatedness and complexity has therefore remained fundamentally unchanged.

To be sure, the instrumental use made of human languages has, after the "Fall of the spirit of language," become the predominant characteristic of human languages. But even so, this does not exhaust their essence. While the languages have become, "in one part at any rate, a *mere* sign, in another part the immediacy in them lives on"—even if, as Benjamin emphasizes, "no longer undamaged."[116]

In a direct continuation of Benjamin's early theory of language, the "Doctrine of the Similar"[117] illuminates its fundamental idea by conceiving of the semiotic, or communicative, property of language as the "storehouse"[118] that can open an access to the mimetic, or magical, element of language. The Fall of the spirit of language means not so much a loss of the true language but, rather, a change in its mode of representation: instead of starting from a "revealed unity of essence," one must assume "multiplicities of essence" in which essence is being represented and articulated in the empirical world.[119]

This reflection points toward a thought figure whose fundamental importance for Benjamin's thinking can hardly be overestimated. It stamps his medial concept of language as much as his concept of experience. Against the Kantian restriction of experience, Benjamin insists "that most essential contents of existence are capable of stamping their imprint on the world of things, indeed that without such imprinting they are incapable of fulfilling themselves."[120] Benjamin's remark (as reported by Scholem), that "a philosophy that does not include the possibility of soothsaying from *coffee grounds* cannot be a true philosophy,"[121] makes the same basic point. This applies also to the programmatic formula that Benjamin uses in the essay

"Goethe's *Elective Affinities*" in order to check his epistemology and his philosophy of language against his philosophy of art: "The truth content emerges as that of the material content."[122]

In the preface—written in 1921—to his translation of the *Tableaux parisiens,* Benjamin's reflections on the theory of language were given their first public expression. "The Task of the Translator,"[123] however, is not so much concerned with language as such but, rather, with concrete forms of language in a historical context. Yet even so, the essay presupposes the medial, or magic, conception of language as much as the universal concept of translation that is based on this conception. "In the appreciation of a work of art or an art form, consideration of the recipient never proves fruitful."[124] Hence, the translation of a work of art is intended neither to transmit the work's meaning nor to serve a reader who does not understand the language of the original. Rather, it tests the original's "translatability."[125]

According to Benjamin, translation is to be understood "with an entirely unmetaphorical objectivity" as a form of the original's "continued life."[126] Just as, for example, the living language is subject to historical change that in later times becomes apparent in the archaic tone of certain phrases, so the works of art also have a natural life, to which their fame testifies, of which criticism is a part, and in which they attain their latest unfolding in translation. As great works of poetry first stand the test of time in the historical permutations of the original's language, so in translation they transcend the circle of their own language "for the purpose of expressing the innermost relationship of the languages" to each other.[127] It is in the hypothesis of a convergence of all languages, through which their kinship has been determined a priori, that Benjamin's theory of translation attains its vanishing point. In particular, the "suprahistorical kinship between languages consists in this: in every one of them as a whole, one and the same thing is meant. Yet this one thing is achievable not by any single language but only by the totality of their intentions supplementing one another: the pure language."[128]

By focusing on the one true language as integrating many tongues, the task of the translator comes into contact with that of the philosopher. When Benjamin sees "the divination and description" of the true language as "the only perfection for which a philosopher can hope,"[129] he defines the philosopher's task as propaedeutic and as one of critique. Together with the epistemological implications of the universal concept of translation, the essay also adopts that fundamental thought figure, which understands the communicative dimension of language as the inventory through which its mimetic, or magical, side is being expressed more or less secretly. In this way, the constant transformation of languages reveals itself to be the peculiar representational mode of pure language. Whereas "these languages continue to grow . . . until the messianic end of their history," it is the task of translation to ever anew make use of "the eternal life of the works and the perpetually renewed life of languages" in "putting the hallowed growth of languages to the test" of how far their hidden meaning is removed from revelation, how close it may be brought—in the knowledge that this remoteness is there.[130]

The proximity of this statement to the theses "On the Concept of History" (1940) is as obvious as the danger that they also "would be a perfect recipe for enthusiastic misunderstanding,"[131] a misreading, at any rate, that Benjamin foresaw for "On the Concept of History." Yet his interpretation of Genesis through his theory of language does not yield a theologically inspired view of history as a process of decay. Likewise, his statements on the growth of languages do not establish reasons for a speculation about the messianic end of history. Exactly like the concept of revelation, that of messianic growth serves to make structures understandable: the structure of language as well as the structure of history. And indeed, the task of discerning the metaphysical structure of history in the interest of gaining knowledge of the present is an objective that Benjamin had set for himself as early as in "The Life of Students."

## CHAPTER THREE

# Art Criticism and Politics, 1919–25

## 1. Romantic Philosophy of Art and Its Contemporary Relevance

Even though the development of Benjamin's philosophical ideas had "reached a crucial stage," as he wrote in a letter to Scholem of March 30, 1918, he realized that he had to "leave it at its current level" until he had completed all of his examinations. Only then "would he be able to devote himself to it completely and with complete freedom."[1] It was in the interest of academic requirements that the young student, who had been exempted from military service, moved to Switzerland where, in October 1917, he matriculated at the University of Bern. He had chosen Bern after exploratory visits to the universities in Zürich and Basel had proven unsuccessful. This search, motivated as it was by purely pragmatic considerations, was not focusing on one kind of academic teacher in particular, but on the choice of a professor who would agree to serve as his dissertation advisor. He wanted an official mentor less to inspire than not to impede his work. Benjamin at last found such a person in Richard Herbertz (1878–1959), the chairman of the philosophy department. Despite the impression that he kept the greatest possible distance from the routine of academic life, an impression Benjamin himself cultivated, the doctoral candidate, as recently discovered documents prove, did experience much inspiration during his two years as a student in Bern after all. Beyond that, he was given support in his attempt to start an academic career, a prospect that came to a definitive end only in 1925, when his *Habilitation* thesis was rejected.[2]

Moreover, Benjamin's own true interests turned out to be his guide at least partially when he was exploring topics for a dissertation, presumably at a distance from academic routine. For example, the plan he pursued at first, namely, to work on Kant and history,[3] is obviously closely related to the philosophical "Program" he wrote in Bern in 1918. Even after this project had come to naught when his study of the primary texts proved disappointing, his continued critical exploration of Kant remained decisive for his definitive choice of a topic. In a letter Benjamin outlined the issue his dissertation was to deal with:

> Only since romanticism has the following view become predominant: that a *work* of art in and of itself, and without reference to theory or morality, can be understood in contemplation alone, and that the person contemplating it can do it justice. The relative autonomy of the *work* of art vis-à-vis art, or better, its exclusively transcendental dependence on art, has become the prerequisite of romantic art criticism. I would undertake to prove that, in this regard, Kant's aesthetics constitute the underlying premise of romantic art criticism.[4]

Given its decided accent on philosophy, Benjamin's treatise *The Concept of Criticism in German Romanticism* has only tangential contacts with the research interests of professors in German departments, who, before and after the war, had increasingly emphasized the study of Romanticism. The book *Die romantische Schule* (1870; The Romantic School) by Rudolf Haym had cleared the way for such historical scholarship. More important, Wilhelm Dilthey (1833–1911) had traced the origins of his hermeneutics, which are guided by the concept of experience (*Erlebnis*), all the way back to Romanticism. Under Dilthey's influence, the Romantic movement assumed a place of significance equal to that of Classicism. Dilthey's essay collection of 1905, *Das Erlebnis und die Dichtung* (Experience and Poetry), had made this reorientation palpable most of all through the two important studies of Novalis and Hölderlin that follow the programmatic essay "Goethe and the Poetic Imagination." The central position he accorded Hardenberg/Novalis also meant an upgrading of early Romanticism. This revaluation extended even to Ricarda Huch's (1864–1947) *Blüthezeit der Romantik* (1899; The Blossoming of Romanticism), a work Benjamin listed in his bibliography. It was in the fragments of the early Romantics that Huch discovered the traces of an aesthetic and critical consciousness that, in the context of the incipient reception of Nietzsche, showed close connections to the "neo-Romantic" literature of the fin de siècle.[5] When Benjamin's dissertation was published in 1920, the Romantic era had definitely moved to the center of German literary scholarship. But the learned interests of professional Germanists now concentrated predominantly on *late* Romanticism, clearly at the expense of a devalued Classicism and in staunch opposition to the Enlightenment, as after the war the professoriate was striking a decidedly national note.[6]

There was hardly an academic study that failed to emphasize Fichte's importance for early Romanticism. His role in the formation of Romantic theory is the starting point for Benjamin's investigation as well. But Benjamin's reconstruction takes a turn that differs fundamentally from the work of literary historians, who follow a topos to be found as early as in Haym's work, according to which Friedrich Schlegel had carried Fichte's subjectivism to an extreme. This interpretation can also be found in Wilhelm Windelband's *Geschichte der neueren Philosophie* (first published 1878–80, 2 vols; A History of Modern Philosophy), a book that was important for Benjamin's understanding of Fichte. Windelband's conclusion saw the Fichtean concept of the productive imagination turning, in its interpretation by Friedrich Schlegel, into "the arbitrariness of the brilliant (*genial*) individual."[7] This verdict was also confirmed by Anna Tumarkin (1875–1951) in her study *Die romantische Weltanschauung* (The Romantic Worldview), which appeared the same year as Benjamin's dissertation. Benjamin had attended her lectures in Bern as well as those of Harry Maync (1874–1947), a specialist in modern German literature. Both scholars advocated the predominant yet vague opinion that early Romantic theorems depended on Fichte completely. Benjamin opposed this view by reconstructing the philosophical foundations of Romanticism on a conceptual level that had not hitherto been attained . This reconstruction led him to ground the theory of criticism of early Romanticism in an understanding of the concept of reflection that deviates from Fichte. The result is an approach that secures for his study the enduring attention of more recent scholarship on the Romantic era and, beyond that, intimates its proximity to postmodern theories of literature.[8]

Nevertheless, one should view with caution hasty attempts to attribute contemporary applicability to Benjamin's approach. Even though Benjamin wrote his dissertation mostly for academic purposes, it is obvious that his analyses are connected with issues he had discussed in earlier works and will raise again in later studies. Even before he had clarified the topic of his thesis, there was no doubt in his mind that "religion and history" are at the center of early Romanticism. Probably in accordance with the concept of tradition that already in his writings from the time of his early student years he had associated with a religiously elevated ideal of community, he described Romanticism as the last movement that kept tradition alive one more time, making tradition necessary. Therefore, in its decline, it had to resort to making use of *Catholic tradition* more than to any other. Its effort, premature in its own era and sphere, aimed at the Eleusinian-orgiastic disclosure of all secret sources of tradition that was expected to overflow, undesecrated, into all of humanity.[9]

Even though direct connections are impossible to prove, the proximity of this idea to Georg Lukács's interpretation of Romantic vitalism (*Lebensphilosophie*) in his Novalis essay in *Soul and Forms* (1911) is amazing. To Lukács also, early Romanticism appears as an attempt to create a new, harmonic, and all-inclusive culture that contains religious characteristics and that he describes as a yearning for the great synthesis. When it failed, it finally became reality only in art and thus at the expense of life.

In his dissertation, Benjamin expressed his understanding of Romanticism as centered in religion and history inconspicuously. That is to say, his references to Romantic messianism, while hidden in footnotes,[10] are nonetheless emphatic. In a retrospective letter he credits his study specifically with having pointed to "the heart of Romanticism, that is, messianism."[11] The Romantic metaphysics of history, while not made an explicit theme in the study itself,[12] established nevertheless the hidden point of reference in Benjamin's analysis, whose purpose it was to show how the perception of art and nature in early Romanticism adapted and reshaped the concept of reflection.

It is against this background that the concept of the "medium of reflection" is to be understood. Benjamin defines this concept structurally as a "fulfilled infinity of connectedness,"[13] and relates it to an understanding of infinity in which both the concept of a "progressive universal poesy" and history represent progress as "an infinite process of fulfillment, not a mere becoming."[14] Art, the way the early Romantics conceived of it, is to be understood on the basis of its philosophical premises as defined in Fichte's theory of knowledge, his *Wissenschaftslehre*. Hence, art is to be perceived as a medium of reflection. By basing his discussion on this concept, Benjamin succeeds in explicating the central concepts of the Romantic perception of art with great precision and conclusiveness. This concept of the medium of reflection provides early Romanticism with the theoretical premise both for establishing the autonomy of the artwork and for defining the theory of art criticism. In this way, the creative work can be apprehended as a center of reflection that finds its necessary supplement in criticism, that is, which in the medium of art finds a means to accomplish its completion.

Thus Benjamin arrived at an objective understanding of the Romantics' philosophy of art that was quite in contrast to the prevailing accusation that Romanticism was guided by subjectivistic arbitrariness. For Benjamin, this philosophy was characterized not least by its proximity to Kant's *Kritizismus*, of which the Romantics were well aware when they set out to establish the criteria for their own art criticism. Just as Kant in his theory of knowledge had been concerned with overcoming epistemo-critical dogmatism and skepticism in equal measure, so, Benjamin states, the Romantics had, in matters of art criticism, been intent on taking up a position both against Rationalism's concept of rules and the aesthetics of genius as espoused by Sturm und Drang. Friedrich Schlegel "secured, from the side of object or structure, that very autonomy in the domain of art that Kant, in the third *Critique*, had lent to the power of judgment."[15] As Benjamin recognized that the insistence on autonomy was the lasting accomplishment of Romanticism, he also wasted no time excluding the current practice of criticism from this insight and rebuking contemporary critics for their subjectivity and lack of orientation.

It was not in criticism but in contemporary literature that Benjamin found his assurance for the current relevance of early Romanticism. At the same time he found in recent literature a confirmation for his reconstruction of the foundations that underpin the Romantic philosophy of art. When the early Romantic theory of art, in a consistent outgrowth of its reflective conception of art, saw prose as art's highest form, and when the ideas of sobriety and technical calculation (*Kalkül*) were pushing traditional notions of inspiration and beauty into the background, then, he said, the spirit that guides the development of art had not allowed these Romantic ideas to fall into oblivion. Benjamin points to French Romanticism and German neo-Romanticism[16] as he summarizes his argument: "If one wanted to extract the basic principles of the theory of art in so eminently conscious a master as Flaubert, or in the Parnassians, or in the George Circle, then one would surely find among them the principles expounded here."[17]

Beyond that, it is fair to assume that Benjamin's own preoccupation with Baudelaire has something to do with Romantic principles as he understood them. In the spirit of the early Romantic conception of art, he had in his dissertation brought "criticism and translation close to each other."[18] Consequently, his theoretical interest in criticism went hand in hand with his practical work of translating. During the winter semester of 1917–18, when he attended the lecture course by the Romanicist Gonzague de Reynold (1880–1970) "Charles Baudelaire, le critique et le poète" in Bern, he purchased several volumes of Baudelaire for his library. He also bought Stefan George's poetic versions (*Nachdichtungen*) of the *Fleurs du mal*, first published in 1901.[19] Moreover, immediately after his oral examination he returned to his own Baudelaire translations, which he may have started as early as the winter of 1914–15.[20] That Benjamin did not, however, turn into a spokesman for the unbroken validity of Romantic principles becomes apparent not only in the theory of translation with which he prefaced his Baudelaire translations—a theory that is based on his very own premises for a theory of language. The dissertation itself also contains reservations that support this claim.

The "cardinal principle of critical activity since the Romantic movement—that is, judging works of art by immanent criteria"—is a tenet that Benjamin elaborated in his doctoral thesis. But it is a postulate that he had already made his own in his early critical studies. Yet for these early essays and for future work dealing with issues of art theory as much as for his attempt to formulate his own concept of criticism, a complementary insight is of paramount importance: Benjamin had come to realize that the theories of the Romantics had provided his conviction of the necessity and immanence of criticism with a justification "which in its pure form certainly would not completely satisfy any contemporary thinker."[21] In the concluding chapter of his study he argues that the philosophical premises of criticism cannot be limited to the theories of the Romantics alone. Rather, these premises must be based on the status "of German philosophy of art around 1800 as represented by the theories of Goethe and the early Romantics." Only then is it possible to describe the philosophical premises of criticism in a way that is "legitimate even today."[22]

He claims to have written the final chapter of his dissertation, "The Early Romantic Theory of Art and Goethe," as an "esoteric epilogue" for those readers with whom he "would have to share the dissertation as *my* work."[23] He emphasizes the importance of this appended section in the work itself,[24] in his public self-announcement in *Kant-Studien*,[25] and finally in private letters. The study of Goethe's theory of art and, even more, of his writings on natural science had occupied Benjamin intensely as early as his preliminary work. It is, moreover, usually overlooked that he has prefaced his dissertation with a Goethe motto in which "the analyst" is admonished "to train his eye, to see whether he has really found a mysterious synthesis or is only dealing with an aggregate, a juxtaposition, . . . and to see how this all might be modified."[26] Benjamin's own study is obviously far from a synthesis. Rather, the exceptional importance of its last chapter in juxtaposing

Goethe's theories of art and those of the Romantics consists of opening a perspective on the central problem of art criticism: the "problem of the criticizability of the artwork."[27]

Whereas the central part of the dissertation seeks to elucidate the theoretical premises for the Romantics' conviction that artworks are, in principle, criticizable, the corresponding section that would have to justify Goethe's contrary position turns out to be extremely brief. This part culminates in the question of how to adequately understand the relationship of the pure content or, in Goethe's terminology, the primal phenomena (*Urphänomene*) and the individual works. The commensurate problem, which the Romantic philosophy of art had defined exclusively in reference to form, had been solved there through the theory of the medium of reflection. Benjamin, in the first footnote of his last chapter, deferred a more detailed analysis of Goethe's art theory to a discussion "elsewhere."[28] This note and also the intensive revision of the textual passage in question,[29] written for a desired second edition of his dissertation, testify to the fact that he had planned to continue explicating the problem of art criticism as the status of German philosophy of art around 1800 had bequeathed it to him. "Goethe's *Elective Affinities*," by resuming, among other inquiries, the discussion of how to define the status of the primal phenomena, became Benjamin's attempt to use the debate with Goethe in order to mold the concept of art criticism into a truly contemporary shape.

## 2. Exemplary Criticism: "Goethe's *Elective Affinities*"

Benjamin had completed all preparatory work for his dissertation by the fall of 1918, and barely five months later he submitted his doctoral thesis for evaluation. He passed his oral exam summa cum laude on June 27, 1919. His principal academic advisor, Richard Herbertz, thereupon suggested, much to Benjamin's surprise, that he should pursue work on his *Habilitation* thesis in Bern. But this prospect confronted him with money problems, since his father's financial circumstances had been severely reduced due to inflation. Emil Benjamin refused to keep paying indefinitely for his son's academic pursuits, which, soon after the latter's return to Berlin in the spring of 1920, brought about "a total split"[30] with his parents and the departure of the young couple from the parental villa in Grunewald.

Little is known about the precise circumstances relating to his work on the important essay about Goethe's novel *Elective Affinities*. The writing itself, he reveals in a letter, is moving along "*very* slowly."[31] It probably extended from the fall of 1921 until the summer of 1922. Pieces of textual evidence document that he paid extremely close attention to linguistic precision and formal stylization. The captions that introduce the different sections of the essay show a thematic outline of equal stringency. (These captions[32] have been retained in the manuscript, but probably in the interest of preserving an overall impression of hermetic cohesion, were eliminated from the printed version.)

Two pieces of biographical data are relevant to an understanding of Benjamin's personal circumstances at the time he wrote the essay. In the spring of 1922, his marriage had reached a point of crisis that eventually destroyed it. Marital discord had been provoked by a constellation that corresponded to that depicted in Goethe's novel. Benjamin's decision to dedicate the manuscript version of his essay to Jula Cohn testifies to this private context. It may also suggest a reason for his choosing this particular topic. But the intellectual demands that the essay makes on its readers, as well as its underlying purpose, far exceed such personal motivation. Jula Cohn (1894–1981) was a friend from the time of Benjamin's involvement with the Youth Movement who had contacts in the George Circle. She had introduced Benjamin to the poet Ernst Blass (1867–1938), the editor of the journal *Die Argonauten*, which was published in Heidelberg by Richard Weißbach (1882–1950), and in which two of his short essays—"Dostoevsky's *The Idiot*" and "Fate and Character"—had appeared in 1921. During a sojourn in Heidelberg, Benjamin visited her while he was exploring opportunities for proceeding with his *Habilitation* there. He also established a close rapport with Weißbach, who agreed, first of all, to publish his Baudelaire translations and then offered him, with Blass's consent, the editorship of *Argonauten*. When Benjamin declined the offer, his publisher persuaded him to start a journal of his own. Its prospective editor, proudly and full of high ambitions, titled this venture *Angelus Novus* after a drawing by Paul Klee that he had recently acquired. The periodical in which his critique of *Elective Affinities* was scheduled to appear never advanced beyond the planning stage, however.[33]

The extant "Announcement of the Journal *Angelus Novus*" defines Benjamin's purpose as "redoubled efforts to restore criticism to its former strength"[34] and provides a first indication of what kind of criticism he wanted to see practiced in both its philosophical and its artistic contributions as the journal's public commitment. The "Announcement" (written in 1922) specifically emphasizes the exemplary value of *Athenäum* (1798–1800), the critical journal of early Romanticism. Benjamin states that this publication, more than anything else, lived up to its claim of manifesting the spirit (*Geist*) of its time without making any concessions to the public's taste or succumbing to the pull of what was currently deemed relevant. Once more borrowing locutions from his speech "The Life of Students" (1915), he further refines his journal's claim to "true contemporary relevance" by stating that "the universal validity of spiritual (*geistig*) utterances must be bound up with the question of whether they can lay claim to a place within future religious orders."[35]

The preeminent role Benjamin's "Announcement" assigns to criticism is to some extent based on his insight that such religious systems of order are not foreseeable at the present time. It is the task of criticism to discover in the works of art how things yet to come are already "working" an effect on the present and to do so without betraying them to the present. It is surely no coincidence that in this context he speaks of "seeking." It is "seekers" (*Suchende*) that Nietzsche, in the first of his *Untimely Meditations* (1873), had identified as the advocates of a genuine culture—in contrast to the "cultural philistines." Thus he had introduced a catchword that Hugo von Hofmannsthal also was to use prominently, for example, in a speech given at the University of Munich in 1927 and titled "Das Schrifttum als geistiger Raum der Nation" (Literature as the Spiritual Domain of the Nation). Aside from Rang's recommendation, it was no doubt also a certain spiritual proximity to Benjamin that Hofmannsthal intuited—quite rightly when seen against this background—that persuaded him to publish the essay on *Elective Affinities* in his *Neue Deutsche Beiträge* (New German Contributions) of 1924–25.

The "Announcement" gives no indication that the connection between Romanticism and Modernity, as analyzed in his dissertation, had lost any of its validity for Benjamin. By now, however, he is already looking at Stefan George's influence and oeuvre from a historical perspective. Beyond that, he denies that the poet's epigones have any importance whatsoever, unless it be, as he puts it maliciously, the "vigorous exposure of the limitations of a great master." The origins of his concept of criticism, to which *Angelus Novus* accords a place of dominant importance, should also be traced back not so much to early Romanticism as to Benjamin's dissertation. When he insists in the "Announcement" that it must be the task of positive criticism, "even more than it was for the Romantics," to "concentrate on the individual work of art" and "to recognize its truth by immersing itself in these works,"[36] he is recapitulating arguments he had worked out in this earlier study. At the same time, this shift in emphasis away from the conception of the Romantics hints at significant premises underlying his critique of *Elective Affinities.*

Benjamin wanted to have his essay understood as "an exemplary piece of criticism"[37]: exemplary is its choice of a subject, Goethe's "classic" novel; exemplary is the self-reflection and self-justification of criticism as made apparent through this particular work; and finally, the study is exemplary in its tacit polemical proximity to Friedrich Schlegel's critique of another Goethe novel, *Wilhelm Meister's Apprenticeship.*[38] In retrospect, Benjamin called his essay an attempt to elucidate a work of art "by confining my attention purely to the work itself."[39] In this way he emphasized the absolute validity of the Romantics' cardinal principle of immanent criticism along with the stronger concentration on the individual work as he had demanded in the "Announcement." As Schlegel had used *Apprenticeship,* so Benjamin used *Elective Affinities* to explicate the theoretical foundations of criticism through the medium of criticism. He introduces each of the three sections of his treatise, which refer to one another as thesis, antithesis, and synthesis, with short passages that demonstrate how the tenets of immanent criticism relate to commentary, biography, and finally to philosophy.

In terms of both content and theory, Benjamin's critique of *Elective Affinities* focuses on the objection toward which the very compact discussion of Goethe's theory of art had led him in the concluding chapter of his dissertation. It had been Goethe's endeavor, he had written there, to grasp the idea of nature in the primal phenomena (*Urphänomene*) and thereby make them into the archetypes of art.[40] This tenet provides the grounding for Goethe's conviction that criticism of a work of art is neither possible nor necessary. It is a tenet that, in the final analysis, rests on a latent ambiguity inherent in his concept of nature because this conception is due to a contamination of the pure and the empirical domains and favors an idolatry of sensuous nature.[41]

Consequently, it is the mythic as the material content of the work that provides the starting point for Benjamin's critique of *Elective Affinities.* He notes that the novel's plot (as much as Goethe's life) is replete with hints that signal the workings of mythic forces of nature. These powers, with their fateful portents and entanglements, cast a spell as much on the work as on the author. But myth, he emphasizes, does not have the final say in this novel. Rather, Benjamin wants to read Goethe's book as a transitional work, one that testifies to the poet's struggle for freedom from the clutches of mythic forces. As proof of this the essay offers its interpretation of the contrastive function of the novella titled "The Curious Tale of the Childhood Sweethearts" in the novel's structure, as well as its analysis of Ottilie. In the beauty of this figure, according to Benjamin's central thesis, myth itself becomes the subject of the novel. A metaphysical-speculative theory of "schöner Schein" (beautiful semblance/luster), delineating the boundary of the beautiful vis-à-vis the sublime, sets up the final conclusion according to which the novel, through the position the narrator assumes toward his female protagonist, escapes from the mythic spell cast by "schöner Schein." In the epigrammatic summary at the very end of the essay, "Only for the sake of the hopeless ones have we been given hope,"[42] it is left to the last of the "Primal Words Orphic" ("Urworte. Orphisch"), to "ELPIS, Hope," to express the work's sum total.

Focused on content, these explications are flanked in the tight-knit structure of the essay's arguments by digressions on the theory of criticism. In choosing *Elective Affinities*, Benjamin opted for a novel on whose "classic" stature all contemporary literary scholarship and readers were in agreement. Given the fact that editions of classic authors proliferated and considering the series of Goethe biographies with a positivistic orientation that were published at the turn of the century, one might even think that the essay was written as a comprehensive commentary. By contrast, Benjamin emphasized the critical intent of his investigation, the historical distance separating the essay from the subject of its analysis presenting not an obstacle to criticism but serving as a touchstone.

In Benjamin's reflection on the relationship of commentary and criticism in the first part of the essay, the concept of duration assumes a key position. A work *is* not a classic, but in the course of time it *becomes* a classic. In other words, the artwork becomes not only all the more important but also all the more enduring, the more inconspicuously and intimately its validity is bound up with its material—in Benjamin's terminology, the more its truth content coheres with its material content. His "basic law of literature,"[43] according to which the "truth content emerges as that of the material content,"[44] is confirmed by the history of the respective works. Benjamin's justification of criticism, more strongly than that of the early Romantics with its foundation in the logic of reflection, explicitly goes back to deliberations that are grounded in a philosophy of history.

A different emphasis prevails in the introductory section of the essay's second part, titled "Criticism and Biography" in the outline. Its external cause was Benjamin's confrontation with the heroizing image of the poet as propagated by the George Circle and exemplified by the Goethe book of Friedrich Gundolf (1880–1931), published in 1916 and welcomed enthusiastically at first by both the feuilletonists and the academic public. Within the carefully thought-out composition of the essay, the polemic against Gundolf for which Benjamin made use of earlier notes[45] attains an importance that far surpasses its immediate occasion.

Benjamin also develops his theory of art criticism in accordance with

a dialectical logic of thesis, antithesis, and synthesis that defines the sequence of the essay's several parts. Poetry's claim to truth, ascertained at
the beginning of the essay in the name of criticism, is confronted in the
second part with the assertion that poet and work are rooted in myth, an
irreconcilable revocation of this claim.

In fact, no work seems to confirm the legitimacy of Gundolf's mythi-
cizing approach more persistently than *Elective Affinities*. And did not
Benjamin himself declare the mythic to be the material content of the novel[46]
and in an expansive description call attention to the ubiquitous presence of
mythic powers even in Goethe's personal life?[47] Consequently, the refutation of Gundolf in Benjamin's critique becomes the *experimentum crucis*
of isolating that "layer in which the meaning of that novel autonomously
reigns," because where "the existence of no such special domain can be
proved, we are dealing not with a literary work of art but solely with its
precursor: magical writing."[48]

The liberation of art from myth, as Benjamin sees it, was not a historically singular process limited to antiquity. On the contrary, criticism concerns itself anew in every work of art that it analyzes with the problematic
relationship of art and myth. It is only through the entanglement of art with
myth in beautiful semblance (*Schein*) that criticism becomes necessary; and
only the irreconcilable tension of both aspects in the work of art makes
criticism possible.

While the first part of the essay, in its commentating explication of
the material content, had shown the significance of the mythic world, and
whereas its second section had disputed myth's autocratic rule, the concluding third part, with its examination of the poetized (*das Gedichtete*),
turns toward the work's truth content.[49] Consequently, this final section
of the essay begins with a reflection on the relationship of criticism and
philosophy. Later and with explicit reference to this paragraph, Benjamin
spoke self-critically of certain obscurities that impair the essay. The reason
for this is not to be found in a lack of theoretical stringency but in the terse
presentation of his thoughts within the essay's confines.

It is necessary to proceed from the fact that for Benjamin the task of
art criticism results from that all-inclusive epistemo-critical problematic
whose solution he, in his unpublished notes, had tried to find via reflections
on the linguistic essence of cognition. The demand, formulated in the early
essay on language, that one understand the artistic forms as languages,[50]
had defined the function of art criticism as principally philosophical. In his
critique of *Elective Affinities*, Benjamin specifies this tenet by saying that
art and philosophy coincide in the problem of how to represent truth.

Philosophy, to be sure, holds the ideal of a solution to this problem in the concept of system. But, as he had already done in the "Program of the Coming Philosophy," Benjamin treats the concept of system as, strictly speaking, problematic. The "unity of philosophy," conceived of "as the ideal of the problem,"[51] is relegated to the various philosophical endeavors analogous to the way pure language relates to the various individual languages. It is through this analogy that the stated affinity of philosophy toward the works of art becomes apparent. The law that Benjamin reclaims, according to which "the ideal can represent itself solely in a multiplicity,"[52] is, in the final analysis, implicitly prefigured in his medial concept of language.

In regard to terminology, however, this idea proceeds from the formulation of the basic problem of art criticism in the final chapter of his dissertation. The concepts that Benjamin had used there to describe the opposing viewpoints of the Romantics and Goethe—immanence and harmony on the one hand, multiplicity and the artful (das Musische) on the other—now are used together to spell out his own theory of art criticism.

The work of art does not, however, depict a philosophical problem. Rather, the work of art as a form of language is a medium of truth and, in this sense, it is philosophical. For this reason, "in every true work of art an appearance of the ideal of the problem can be discovered."[53] According to the essay's fundamental thoughts on the relationship of criticism and philosophy, the philosophical dignity of art is expressed by the very fact that works of art are representations not of truth but of its unattainability. For this reason, "in the face of everything beautiful, the idea of unveiling becomes that of the impossibility of unveiling." Thus, "the task of art criticism is not to lift the veil but rather, through [nothing but] the most precise knowledge of it as a veil, to raise itself to the true view of the beautiful."[54]

When, therefore, the beautiful presents itself to criticism as something "secret," it is being described by criticism according to its essential function. This means that, in Benjamin's understanding, the third aspect ("Moment") in Kant's analysis of the beautiful—relation[55]—has, with its negative relation to truth, advanced to being the sole definition of the beautiful. In the context no longer of a critique of (aesthetic) judgment but of a critique of language, the concept of revelation, understood in terms of the philosophy of language, takes the place held in Kant's logic of reflection by subjective purposiveness without any purpose.

Also, Benjamin's reference to that ingredient of beauty that derives from a philosophy of history[56] remains within the logic of his revision of criticism as derived from the philosophy of language. What criticism makes apparent about a work of art is the structure of its content in which the metaphysical structure of history becomes perceivable in model form. Even the remotest detail of historico-philological insight reveals the philosophico-critical knowledge of this distance from the state of perfection.

After the failure of the *Angelus Novus* project, the publication of the extensive and—stylistically no less than theoretically—demanding essay proved difficult and protracted. In the end, it was through Florens Christian Rang's intercession that contacts were established with Hugo von Hofmannsthal, who was so strongly impressed with the essay that he requested it for the *Neue Deutsche Beiträge.* There the essay was printed in two issues at the turn of 1924–25. Rang had already subjected Benjamin's dissertation to a critical reading that paid close attention to details, his objections exerting some influence on Benjamin's conception of criticism in his Goethe essay.[57] While Hofmannsthal's interest in Benjamin's work never went beyond a respectful distance, a close friendship grew between Rang and Benjamin. Even considerable objective differences that the prospective editor of *Angelus Novus* expressed about his prospective contributor's articles did not spoil their closeness. Benjamin believed that he detected characteristics of Rang[58] in Hofmannsthal's Munich speech mentioned above, while Hofmannsthal himself probably had Benjamin in mind at this juncture. The intellectual proximity of Benjamin's work to positions espoused by conservative cultural criticism seemed evident not during these years only. As late as 1938 he read with annoyance that, in regard to the *Elective Affinities* essay, he was "presented as a follower of Heidegger."[59]

## 3. The Problematic of Art: Criticism and Allegorical Artwork

As is true for Benjamin's dissertation, so also his *Habilitation* thesis, "Origin of German Tragic Drama," shows that, in spite of the book's academic purpose, veiled references to contemporary issues and arguments directly connected with his own theoretical interests found their way into this work. In choosing seventeenth-century tragedy as his topic he did, to be sure, turn to a special area of German literary history that had not been given much scholarly attention at that time. But the experience of the recently ended war created the condition for feeling close to the era of confessional wars and its attitudes about life as expressed in literature and the other arts. As a result, both academics and a wider reading public were receptive to anything "Baroque."

As early as in his "Prologue" Benjamin emphasizes that the current interest in the literature of the Baroque, when it relies on something more than diffuse emotions, is predicated on an aesthetic paradigm shift. He observes

that this interest owes its existence to a revaluation that Expressionism—
"which was, perhaps, affected by the poetics of the school of Stefan
George"[60]—had helped to bring about. Every unprejudiced insight would
have to proceed from this conclusion. In the treatise itself, Benjamin, using
his dissertation as evidence, expressly places the Baroque side by side with
Romanticism, claiming that like Romanticism the Baroque represents a
"sovereign opposite of classicism." Moreover, both orientations "are concerned not so much with providing a corrective to classicism, as to art
itself," where the Baroque "offers a more concrete, more authoritative, and
more permanent version of this correction."[61] The far-reaching implications
of this conviction are not discussed further. But Benjamin may be pointing
in the same direction when, in the prologue, he attributes the "remarkable
analogies to present-day German literature"[62] which currently give reason
for immersing oneself in the Baroque to that "artistic will" on which "the
relevance of the Baroque after the collapse of German classic[ist] culture"[63]
is based.

Following the art historian Alois Riegl (1858–1905), from whom he borrowed the term "artistic will" (*Kunstwollen*), Benjamin sees the Baroque
no less than his own present as a time of decline. But neither Riegl nor
Benjamin turn this observation into a value judgment. Rather, the concept
of artistic will is meant to make an understanding of such epochs of art history possible in which not the conclusively rounded work but the unfolding
of an art form per se is the center of attention. Yet the current relevance of
the Baroque that Benjamin established under the sign of the artistic will is
modified by the decisive point that, given all the analogies, it is necessary
to remember a significant difference: whereas literature in the seventeenth
century had been a determining factor in the nation's rebirth, the "twenty
years of German literature referred to here in order to explain the renewal
of interest in the earlier epoch, represent a decline, even though it may be a
decline of a fruitful and preparatory kind."[64]

When Benjamin calls it the purpose of "Origin of German Tragic Drama"
to engage in a "critical examination of the form of the *Trauerspiel*,"[65] historical and current interests coincide in the concept of criticism as they
had done in his earlier studies. He explicitly emphasizes the principle of
immanence that he had attributed to early Romanticism and had modified
in his exemplary criticism of *Elective Affinities.* Criticism, he writes in the
prologue, does not evolve "in response to external comparison, but [it takes]
shape immanently, in a development of the formal language of the work
itself, which brings out its content at the expense of its effect."[66] According
to another passage in "Origin of German Tragic Drama" that harks back

to the terminology of the Goethe essay, it is the object of philosophical criticism "to show that the function of artistic form is as follows: to make historical content, such as provides the basis of every important work of art, into a philosophical truth."[67] Benjamin even invokes Novalis's dictum again—referred to in the essay on Hölderlin—about "the *a priori* character of works of art as their immanent necessity *to be there*" to characterize his theoretical self-understanding.

Benjamin introduced both his dissertation and the published version of his *Habilitation* thesis with a motto taken from Goethe, and in his dedication dated the time during which his second thesis was prepared back to 1916. This was a year in which he had written, aside from the study on language, two essays, "*Trauerspiel* and Tragedy" and "The Role of Language in *Trauerspiel* and Tragedy,"[68] that touch on the topic of the book. One should also count the essay "Fate and Character"[69] among those preparatory works that directly anticipate arguments central to his theory of tragedy. Add to this a study of Calderón and Hebbel.[70] The circumstances under which this essay came about—in 1923, according to Benjamin's editors—remain unexplained. But its proximity to the book on the Baroque is immediately evident, as numerous intellectual motifs and the theory of drama of fate indicate—material that Benjamin carried over from the earlier into the later work.

Benjamin had originally submitted his book on German tragic drama as a *Habilitation* thesis for evaluation by the Division of Humanities (Philosophische Fakultät) of Frankfurt University, though in a version that can be reconstructed only insufficiently on the evidence of the printed book. That he finally settled on Frankfurt after unsuccessful explorations at Heidelberg and Gießen may to a considerable degree be due to the mediation of his granduncle, mathematician Arthur Moritz Schönfließ (1853–1928), who had served this university as an *Ordinarius* (senior full professor) and for a time as a dean until his retirement in 1922. Schönfließ established contact with Franz Schultz (1877–1950), the *Ordinarius* for literary history and during the decisive year of 1925 also the dean of humanities. In addition, Benjamin found a committed and intimate spokesman in behalf of his academic interests and concerns in Gottfried Salomon-Delatour, a *Privatdozent* (unsalaried lecturer) of sociology. It was Schultz with whom Benjamin arranged, in the fall of 1923, to write "a work on the form of *Trauerspiel*, with special emphasis on the drama of the Second Silesian School,"[71] his aim being the *venia legendi*, the authorization to teach as a full professor at a university, in his case, German literature.

Until May 1924 Benjamin stayed in Berlin, engaged in the necessary

study of original sources at the State Library. The final organization of his
material and the writing of the book's first version took place during a sojourn on Capri from May until October 1924. On his return to Berlin, he
announced the completion of a final draft, and in April 1925 he reported from
Frankfurt that he was dictating the final copy and submitting its first two
sections to Schultz. His official petition for *Habilitation* is dated May 12,
1925.[72] This application, however, was preceded by the withdrawal of his
advisor: Franz Schultz had declared himself in favor of the candidate being
transferred to the discipline of aesthetics. Thus it was left at last to his col-
league Hans Cornelius (1865–1947), the *Ordinarius* in charge of aesthetics,
to set the final act of this academic tragedy in motion—according to an
evaluation prepared by his assistant at the time, Max Horkheimer.[73] The
whole procedure was brought to an end with a strong recommendation that
the candidate should withdraw his application to forestall its rejection by
the faculty. As the transcript of the faculty meeting of October 12, 1925
indicates, Benjamin agreed to this request after some hesitation.

Contributing to this decision was an increasing inner resistance to the
*Habilitation* and an academic career, which Benjamin had mentioned in
letters to Scholem—who in the fall of 1923 had emigrated to Palestine—as
early as after the completion of the book's final draft. His reticence had been
motivated in part by his "conversion to political theory,"[74] which his encounter with the Latvian Bolshevik Asja Lacis in the fall of 1924 during his
stay on Capri had given a decisive first push. Inner reasons that were turning "the academic world for him into something irrelevant" are mentioned
in a letter to Salomon-Delatour, in which he is weighing the faculty's preference that he rescind his petition. If he had not nourished these reasons,
he continues,

> the effects of the treatment inflicted on me would have been destruc-
> tive for a long time to come. If my self-esteem were at all dependent on
> those comments, the irresponsible and thoughtless manner in which the
> authority in question treated my case would have given me a shock from
> which my productivity would not soon have recovered. That nothing of
> this—unless [it is] its exact opposite—has happened, remains my private
> business."[75]

But the wreck of his academic prospects did not also mean the end of
his book on Baroque drama. After a preprint of the chapter on melancholia[76]
had appeared in Hofmannsthal's *Neue Deutsche Beiträge* in August 1927,
the *Origin of German Tragic Drama* was at last published by Rowohlt in

January 1928. It is to this version of the study that Benjamin added the epistemological section of the prologue,[77] an introduction that makes the highest demands on the reader's comprehension. On the other hand, the absence of this section from the version presented to his academic evaluators also meant losing the theoretical justification of the concept of origin whose fundamental importance is indicated by the otherwise highly misleading title of the study. When Cornelius, charged with rendering an official evaluation of the thesis, asked for additional clarification, Benjamin submitted an outline,[78] in which he emphatically singles out the dominant theoretical importance that the concept of origin has for the structure and conception of his study. In this he goes back to formulations that appear verbatim in that part of the "Epistemo-Critical Prologue" that he had initially excluded.

But the version that finally appeared in print also remains fragmentary when measured against its author's plans. A final section, intended in the original outline to deal with "methodical ideas on 'criticism,'"[79] is nowhere to be found in the book version. The theoretical demands the book makes are at times oppressively high and are evident both in its complex architectonics and in its linguistic style: both aspects require of its readers an extreme degree of concentration. In the first edition, the resulting impression of hermeticism is further underlined by the graphic design the author had requested.

There is some truth to Benjamin's retrospective statement of 1932 that "the Baroque" had been the "right little horse, and I was just the wrong jockey, given the fact that the best Baroque specialist, *Privatdozent* Richard Alewyn in Berlin, has been appointed to Gundolf's chair at Heidelberg."[80] Alewyn (1902–79) was one of the scholars from whom Benjamin, after the demise of his academic ambitions, had hoped to receive a professional appraisal of *Origin of German Tragic Drama* that would do justice to its significance. Even if his assertion "that not a single German academician has deigned to review" his book[81] is not quite accurate, the attention it was given by Germanists working on the Baroque did indeed remain marginal.

Even today, the canonical appreciation of the Baroque book among Benjamin experts contrasts with a rather tepid recognition of its achievement by the current generation of scholars with a special interest in the literature of the seventeenth entury. In terms of the history of German studies, Benjamin's book on tragic drama is part of that break with the strictly philological self-definition of the discipline which in the 1920s made the Baroque a field of experimentation for the most diverse methodological approaches. Aside from a sense that his own time was defined by war and revolution, leading to the realization that this age has close affinities with the "antithetical sense of life" (Arthur Hübscher) of the seventeenth century, the rediscovery of the era of the Counter-Reformation by literary historians was given a decisive push by the rehabilitation of the Baroque in art history (Heinrich Wölfflin). Benjamin's treatise approaches the era from a perspective that sees language and genre structures as arising from their epochal context, which was characterized by theological and political issues, and revaluates allegory within the framework of a broadly conceived cultural and historical archaeology of this form of expression. As a result, his study contributed in no small measure to a reorientation of more recent scholarship, which uses the term "Baroque" no longer to designate an expressive style but an epoch. It was the merit of this view, which prevails to this day, that helped to bring about the recognition that the age between the Renaissance and the Enlightenment is an era in its own right and with its own distinct character.

Benjamin understands the *Trauerspiel*, mourning play, of the Baroque as secularized Christian drama. That, to be begin with, makes the "mourning play" fundamentally different than tragedy. This contrast—disregarding it was a major reason for the long-prevailing misperception of Baroque drama—is explicated in his treatise with the help of a table of categories for both art forms. This chart lists oppositional pairs and is ultimately based on factors derived from the philosophy of history. Its underlying insight is that the decisive precondition for tragedy is found in myth, whereas that of *Trauerspiel* is history. From this, Benjamin deduces his understanding of the ancient hero: no equivalent among the dramatis personae of *Trauerspiel* corresponds to his function in ancient tragedy. The theory of tragedy advanced in *Origin of German Tragic Drama*—a theory that begins with a critical discussion of Nietzsche's *Birth of Tragedy*—owes decisive stimuli to Florens Christian Rang and over many pages refers approvingly to Franz Rosenzweig's *Stern der Erlösung* (1921; trans., *The Star of Redemption*, 1971/2005) as well as to Lukács's essay on the "Metaphysics of Tragedy" in *Soul and Forms*.

As a secularization of the mystery play, the *Trauerspiel* of the Baroque is characterized by its "turning away from the eschatology of the sacred [*geistig*] plays." Where the medieval play and the Christian chronicle "present the entire course of world history as the story of redemption,"[82] Christendom, having disintegrated into the quarrel of the confessions, has lost its confidence in the process of redemption. In its place, the dramatists of the Baroque attempt to find, in a reversion to a bare state of creation, consolation for the renunciation of a state of grace. . . . Whereas the Middle Ages present the futility of world events and the transience of the creature as stations on the road to salvation, the German *Trauerspiel* is taken up with the hopelessness of the earthly condition.[83]

This representation of time "in terms of space,"[84] which is what Benjamin means by secularization, is the cause for the immanence of Baroque drama. But the "increasing worldliness," which the Counter-Reformation forced on both confessions, did not also cause "religious aspirations [to lose] their importance: it was just that this century denied them a religious fulfillment, demanding of them, or imposing on them, a secular solution instead."[85] One could say with but a touch of exaggeration that in Benjamin's understanding the Baroque overcompensates for the loss of the medieval perception of the world as the historical process of redemption with an apocalyptic worldview that has been held back in the secular.

Benjamin's book can be understood as an attempt to reveal the representative art form of the Baroque as the adequate expression of the era's theological situation. For this reason, the philosophical analysis of the linguistic form used both by the dramatis personae and in the plays' most important formal characteristic, allegory, remains strictly within the era's theo-logic. This is also the context in which the analysis of princely sovereignty is to be situated, an issue in connection with which *Origin* uses earlier work by Carl Schmitt (1888–1985), an expert in constitutional law who became a sympathizer of National Socialism. Benjamin mailed his book to Schmitt together with a short accompanying letter.[86] The editors of the first collection of Benjamin's letters found the mere fact so scandalous that they suppressed it.

With reference not least to the confessionally determined aesthetic particularities, especially regarding the conception and use of allegory, Benjamin states at the end of his study that the German, Protestant *Trauerspiel* is aesthetically insufficient. Hence, in its numerous excursuses, his study presents itself as a far-reaching prolegomenon toward a "theory concerning the 'origin' of *Trauerspiel* that is not to be limited to German and to the Baroque."[87] In Shakespeare, he says, the "foundational work," and in Calderón "the crowning"[88] of the new form of drama can be observed. Its historical metamorphosis takes shape, according to Benjamin, in Sturm und Drang drama as well as in the Romantic tragedy of fate. In the classicist historical plays of Schiller it celebrates an apocryphal resurrection.

For the construction of content, however, the medieval prehistory of the *Trauerspiel* proves to be of paramount importance. It is in the medieval Christian confrontation with the world of the ancient gods as part of a theology of evil that the conception of allegory is given the contours that define the Baroque. The same can be said as well for the theory of mourning (*Trauer*), in which posterity possesses nothing less than a "commentary on the *Trauerspiel*."[89] Also here, the ancient perception of *melencolia illa heroica* was adapted in accordance with theological premises: They make the Baroque concept of melancholy readable as a secularized theological concept that, in confrontation with its origin in the theological doctrine of *acedia*, is revealed to be a mortal sin.

In this way the critic recognizes in the work of art, as Benjamin wrote about his study of the Baroque in a curriculum vitae of 1928, "an integral expression of the religious, metaphysical, political, and economic tendencies of its age,"[90] resulting in an inclusive orientation that makes *Origin* exemplary for later works also. At the same time, the "Epistemo-Critical Prologue" renews, through its connection with the critique of epistemology as developed in the early essay on language, the fundamental claim of his philosophy of language that it comprises politics, history, and art in equal measure. Within the frame of this theory of ideas, the theory of the decline of true language serves Benjamin as a model for explicating the category of origin. Accordingly, the relation of the "essential unity" of the true language to the "essential multiplicity of the many languages" can be considered a "relationship of origin." In a peculiar middle position between a purely logical and a purely historical designation, "origin" designates the mode of "representation and articulation" of an essence—or of an idea, as *Origin* puts it—in the empirical sphere: "The essential unity reigns over a multiplicity of essences in which it manifests itself, but from which it always remains distinct."[91] Like the conception of language in the early essay on this topic, the category of origin therefore describes a medial-discontinuous representation.

In his discussion of the titular category in *Origin*, Benjamin connects the problem of how truth emanates from a work of art with the theory of the continued life of the artwork. For the "life of the works and forms" does not mean an unfolding, not a connection established by the real historical process but rather "a natural history."[92] The purpose behind Benjamin's "idea of natural history"—a point that Theodor W. Adorno took up in his address to the Kant Society in Frankfurt in 1932—is to define "origin" as the locus where the singularity of historical phenomena enters into a union with repetition that is typical of natural processes. Singularity and repetition determine the rhythm with which in the form of origin "an idea will constantly confront the historical world, until it is revealed fulfilled, in the totality of its history."[93]

It is the task of criticism to comprehend the appearance of the idea in the works and forms of art. For the book, the cardinal principle of immanent criticism is precisely expressed by the anti-Nietzschean formula of "the birth of criticism from the spirit of art," which Benjamin used in the outline he wrote for Cornelius. Like the definition of criticism as "mortification of the works," it summarizes the conviction that "the allegorical work of art carries its own critical dissolution, as it were, within itself."[94] Thus *Origin* uses allegory as the principal object for a philosophical art criticism—but hardly as its instrument and even less as a reference to the presumable root of criticism in theology or even in the Kabbalah.

Allegory proves helpful to criticism by anticipating the process that takes place inside enduring works. What interested Benjamin here, as he wrote in a letter to Rang that uses a locution he repeats in *Origin*, is "the specific historicity of works of art,"[95] which can be revealed not in art history but only in criticism. Transformed in the course of time into objects of historical-philological knowledge, the connection of the works among each other is no longer created by history but through the philosophical interpretation of their material contents. It is not this critical knowledge but rather the insistence on theological knowledge and, based on this, a rigorous reservation toward beautiful semblance (*schöner Schein*) that defines what Benjamin understands to be the fundamental characteristic of Baroque allegory. Whereas in classicist art the symbol transfigures its material object into beauty, this object presents itself to the allegorical worldview of the seventeenth century as a connection of equivocal cross-references that does not want to be enjoyed aesthetically but must be comprehended in the light of divine wisdom. Insight into the way this form of expression has been conditioned by history and theology reveals to the critic the access to the material content of Baroque *Trauerspiel*.

In this, the critical mortification of the works shows itself to be the precondition of their philosophical "rebirth."[96] For this mortification applies only to the historically singular form in which the works achieved their desired effect and then passed into oblivion. In the critical description, however, they awaken into a new life, insofar as they are no longer being given over to the arbitrary course of history but are being understood as necessary components of a configuration in which an idea represents itself through the sequence of its historical exemplifications. The critical mortification of the works is thus to be seen, in Benjamin's terminology, "as a transformation of the work of art into a new, philosophical domain."[97] Criticism, by enacting this metamorphosis of the works and thereby making the legitimate forms of their historical return recognizable, becomes itself an aspect of the continued life of these works. Indeed, the concept of metamorphosis employed to denote this process suggests itself as easily as the concept of origin (*Ursprung*, as used in the title) and, not by accident, alludes to the concept of *Urphänomen*. The motto from Goethe's *Geschichte der Farbenlehre* (The Theory of Color) that introduces Benjamin's book evokes not only its author's intensive preoccupation with Goethe but also confirms the significance of the concept of criticism that he had defined in this discussion in a way he considered binding.

It is, therefore, not vague analogies at all but critical insights that the expansive excursuses of *Origin* , ranging from the medieval mystery play to the Expressionist drama, bring together to constitute "an idea developed to its concrete fullness"[98] about German tragic drama. And it is most of all a lack of philosophical-critical reflection that in Benjamin's view discredits the contemporary "sentimental"[99] immersion in the Baroque. In contrast to the fashionable attempts by Expressionists to imbue the Baroque with current relevance, Benjamin perceives a topicality—one that does justice to the term "Baroque" as designating an epoch in terms of a philosophy of history—in the fact that both historical periods experienced their era as a time of crises, which includes the "consciousness that art had become problematic." According to a retrospective view Benjamin expressed in a later work, this consciousness had become for him an acid test in the debate about the fate of art, which he sees entering its decisive stage after the end of the world war.[100]

## 4. Paul Scheerbart and the Concept of the Political

While he was still working on his book on German drama on Capri in the fall of 1924, Benjamin sent out those "Communist signals"[101] to Scholem in Palestine that mark as deep a break in his intellectual biography as the encounter with Asja Lacis meant for his personal life. Most often this "conversion to political theory," as he himself called it in this context, has been judged a programmatic rejection of the hitherto dominant direction of his thinking: its metaphysical orientation. By contrast, his letter to Scholem does not speak of a rupture but of his intention to no longer "mask the actual and political elements of my ideas in the good old, homely German way" but to "develop them by experimenting and taking extreme measures."[102]

A first impetus to think seriously about politics had come to him from Ernst Bloch, whose *Geist der Utopie* (1918; trans., *The Spirit of Utopia*) he had read while he was still in Bern after he had taken his degree in the fall of 1919. Bloch had come to Switzerland in 1917 in order to prepare an inquiry into the country's pacifist ideologies for the *Archiv für Sozialwissenschaft und Sozialpolitik* (Archive for Social Sciences and Social Policy), edited by Emil Lederer, Ernst Jaffé, and Max Weber. Even though he found "enormous deficiencies" in Bloch's *Spirit of Utopia*, he considered it "the only book" on which, "as a truly contemporaneous and contemporary utterance, I can take my own measure"—in the area of politics, that is. In his attempt to formulate his still inadequate ideas about politics, as Benjamin wrote in a letter, the author's "companionship was even more useful than his book, because in conversation he so often challenged my rejection of every contemporary political trend that he ultimately forced me to immerse myself in these matters, which somewhat I hope was worthwhile."[103]

A critique of *Geist der Utopie* that Benjamin had written at Bloch's request must be considered lost. In an epistolary comment Benjamin conceded that this book in some important discussions agrees with his own convictions, but he emphasized at the same time that it "is diametrically opposed"[104] to his idea of philosophy. A similar ambivalence can be detected on closer analysis in a formulation included in the "Theological-Political Fragment"—the title was added by Adorno—which may be datable to this time, not the least by the fragment's reference to Bloch. There Benjamin considers it "the greatest merit" of Bloch's *Spirit of Utopia* "to have denied the political significance of theocracy with full determination."[105]

In point of fact, however, Bloch's position in this respect is anything but unequivocal. "Theocracy," the relationship of politics and religion, is a theme that also plays a central role both in the political pamphlet *Zur Kritik der deutschen Intelligenz* (1919; trans. *Critique of the German Intelligentsia*) by Bloch's friend Hugo Ball (1887–1927) and in Salomo Friedlaender's review of *The Spirit of Utopia* that appeared in Kurt Hiller's *Ziel* yearbook in 1920 under the title of "Der Antichrist und Ernst Bloch." Benjamin knew both texts, and he held Friedlaender (1871–1946) in especially high esteem, both as a philosopher in Nietzsche's footsteps and as the author of grotesques that he published under the pen name of Mynona, an anagram of Anonym (anonymous). Friedlaender's behest that Bloch should abandon his priestly ministrations and become sober and profane[106] provided the decisive cue for the "Theological-Political Fragment."

When Benjamin himself denies the political importance of theocracy in this extended note, he does so only in order to assure himself of its religious sense. The Kingdom of God, which, he wrote, could not be "the telos of the historical dynamic," not its "goal" but at best its "terminus (Ende),"[107] is confronted in the fragment with the order of the profane. Benjamin calls this order "profane" for two reasons. First, because it specifically does not refer to the Messianic as its telos but is sustained by the "idea of happiness." In this definition, "profane order"—which will have to be explained in detail—is identical with the political. And second, he calls this order "profane"—and emphatically: a "profane order of the profane"[108]—because it not only opposes the Messianic but in this opposition is also connected to it. Accordingly, politics conducts the business of the Messiah where it totally and absolutely commits itself to the earthly pursuit of happiness. "Seek for food and clothing first; then/shall the Kingdom of God be granted to you," and be granted without further effort from you (von selbst). Quite obviously Benjamin found his own conviction expressed in Hegel's inversion of the New Testament message that he quotes to introduce the fourth of his theses "On the Concept of History."[109] In the fabric of ideas comprising his "mystical conception of history,"[110] as presented in the "Theological-Political Fragment," everything earthly is ultimately connected with the Kingdom of God solely at the cost of its own demise. The goal of politics is happiness; its method, however, as he writes in conclusion, is called "nihilism."[111] Whenever politics sets itself goals, it has to limit these goals to the order of the profane. But inasmuch as politics limits itself to the profane, the goals it sets for itself are ultimately of no value (nichtig).

In this way Benjamin moves happiness to the center of his conception of politics, in the context of which it is part of the order of the profane, as is politics itself. Yet for Benjamin happiness is a political category in the narrower sense not merely due to its being part of the order of the profane. Rather, the subject pursuing happiness is not the individual human being but the individual as part of humanity. This reading of the fragment is suggested by a number of uncompleted occasional writings that are part of its orbit.[112] Their center is a peculiar metaphysics of the body (Leib) whose intellectual design reveals far-reaching influences of that philosophical tradition that extends from Romanticism through Nietzsche, the Expressionist reception of Nietzsche (Kurt Hiller, Erich Unger, Salomo Friedlaender, Paul Scheerbart), and the philosophy of vitalism (Henri Bergson, Ludwig Klages) all the way to Theodor Fechner's Psychophysik and the epistemological discussion within neo-Kantianism that followed in its wake. Benjamin had encountered the latter in Bern in the person of Paul Häberlin (1878–1960), the *Ordinarius* for philosophy with special emphasis on psychology and pedagogy, whose lectures on the "psychophysical" problem he had attended in Bern. These lectures were published in 1923 under the title of *Der Leib und die Seele* (Body and Soul).[113]

The time in Bern and the intended review of Bloch's *Spirit of Utopia* also stimulated his preoccupation with writing a major work on politics, a project that is frequently mentioned in letters. From the "arsenal" of his political writings that Benjamin surveyed in January of 1925, only some fragments and the essay "Kritik der Gewalt" (Critique of Violence)[114] have come down to us. The extant documents suggest that he had planned an extensive study, divided into three more or less independent parts. The book was to begin with an investigation titled "Der wahre Politiker" (The True Politician), after which was to follow a second part titled "Die wahre Politik" (True Politics), comprising the two chapters "Abbau der Gewalt" (Dismantling Violence, possibly identical with "The Critique of Violence") and "Teleologie ohne Endzweck" (Teleology without a Final Purpose). The concluding section was to be the philosophical critique of Paul Scheerbart's (1863–1915) utopian novel *Lesabéndio* (1913), in which Benjamin would also have wanted to respond to Friedlaender's review of Bloch.

From the time when Benjamin was working on this project a note with his "definition of politics" has been preserved. This note defines politics as "the fulfillment of unintensified humanness" (*die Erfüllung der ungesteigerten Menschhaftigkeit*). When seen in its proper context, this perplexing definition becomes readable as a formula directed against Nietzsche. That is to say that Benjamin, in the fragment "Kapitalismus als Religion" (Capitalism as Religion),[115] understands the conception of the *Übermensch,* the culmination of the doctrine of the death of God, as an attempted "breaking open of the heavens by an intensified humanness."[116] The tragic heroism of Zarathustra, which Nietzsche had good reasons to invest with a religious aura, is decoded in the fragment as the most radical and grandiose fulfillment of capitalism's religious essence, capitalism in Benjamin's description being a cultic religion dominated by guilt and debts. The critical turn of the fragment against Nietzsche, all in all, is not contradicted by the high degree of probability that Benjamin owed his initial intuition to an insight of Nietzsche, who had insisted in the *Genealogy of Morality*[117] that "the main concept 'Schuld' ('guilt') descends from the very material concept of 'Schulden' ('debts')."

In all six sections of "Outlines of the Psychophysical Problem" the metaphysics of body ("Leib" as the opposite of "soul") serves as the central theme. By proceeding from it, one can pin down the three points of view that are basic to Benjamin's political philosophy. Together with his focusing on the collective as the subject of political actions—a focus grounded in the metaphysics of the *Leib*—it is, secondly, the tension-filled separation of the political from religion but also from justice and morality that proves to be fundamental. By emphasizing this demarcation, Benjamin appropriated Max Weber's doctrine that Modernity is a system of values that is defined by pluralism.[118] And by limiting the political to the domain of the profane and to humanity as the subject of politics, he designated the goal of politics to be happiness, making it the quintessence of corporeal life. In the third part of these "Outlines," finally, he concentrated on "technology,"[119] placing it in the persistent center of his reflections on politics.

The coordinated interplay of these fundamental ideas can be traced in the extensive essay "Critique of Violence," published in 1921. Insofar as Benjamin shows that in legal justice (*Recht*) the existing structures of power rest on violence and remain under its domination, violence becomes the focus of the political question, now defined in a more specific sense: under what circumstances are societal agreements possible? Posing the question in this way, the essay takes up arguments advanced in Georges Sorel's (1847–1922) *Réflexions sur la violence* of 1906 (trans. *Reflections on Violence*, 1999). Also in the background of Benjamin's thoughts is philosopher Erich Unger's (1887–1950) book *Politik und Metaphysik* (Politics and Metaphysics) of 1921. Unger was a disciple and close friend of Jewish philosopher of religion Oskar Goldberg (1887–1952), whose theories Unger utilized in his doctrine of the reality-creating power that archaic rituals exert on the idea of founding a national community.

"Critique of Violence" cites the concept of the proletarian general strike as an example that "nonviolent resolution of conflicts" is possible.[120] In the proletarian general strike, he says, the spell of violence is anarchically broken in that this kind of strike "not so much causes as consummates" the upheaval.[121] This idea becomes clearer when one reads it in conjunction with Sorel's definition of "general strike." For Sorel, it is a "myth," which he defines as "a body of images capable of evoking instinctively all the sentiments which correspond to the different manifestations of the war undertaken by socialism against modern society."[122]

Myth, which Sorel understands by resorting to Nietzsche's perception of myth and to Bergson's theory of intuition, brings about the intuitive formation of the revolutionary mass. This mass is less the cause of the upheaval

than, in the very process of forming itself, it functions as the agent that carries it out. Benjamin prefers, to be sure, to make a strict distinction between
the proletarian general strike and "the incidence of actual violence in revolutions."[123] But ultimately the legitimacy of revolutionary violence rests
for him (quite as it does for Sorel) on the fact that this violence destroys
the existing order, which is founded on legal force (*Rechtsgewalt*), in an act
in which a different kind of force, one that is free of any legal force, manifests itself. The archetypal form of this violence, which is the opponent of
mythic lawmaking, is justice as "the principle of all divine endmaking."[124]
Through the use of revolutionary violence as "the highest manifestation of
unalloyed violence by man," a "new historical epoch is founded."[125] This
epoch, he says, would no longer bear the marks of a community founded on
the law but of one based on justice. The precarious question, however, if in
particular historical situations violence was indeed a manifestation of this
kind—"to decide when unalloyed violence has been realized in particular
cases"[126]—the essay surrenders to a final *non liquet*. With this nondecision
Benjamin restricts the jurisdiction of politics, in this essay as much as in the
"Theological-political Fragment," to the order of the profane.

In "Critique of Violence" Benjamin credits technology—the term used
here in its broadest sense—with being a technique of "non-violent civil
agreement."[127] This is an idea that would presumably have been elaborated
in the philosophical critique of Scheerbart's "asteroid novel" *Lesabéndio*,
which was to round off the projected work on politics. Benjamin's scattered
remarks about Scheerbart make it possible to reconstruct his arguments
with some degree of certainty. The planet on which the plot of the novel
takes place turns out to be "the best of all worlds,"[128] because it exempli-
fies the successful interaction of man and technology. The allusion to the
theodicy formula is justified when it is seen against the background of the
early notes on anthropology and their metaphysical interpretation of pain,
notes that Benjamin here makes use of again. The experience of pain, which
the titular hero goes through and which the other inhabitants of the planet
share to the extent that they participate in transforming their planet by
realizing Lesabéndio's construction projects, becomes the measure of their
success and of their transformation into a different species. The "spiritual
(*geistig*) overcoming of the technological,"[129] for which Benjamin praises
Scheerbart, expresses itself through the conviction that the inhabitants of
the planet try out in practice during the work of reconstructing their star.
The theme of this creed is that technology does not exist for the expropria-
tion of nature but that technology, by liberating humanity, also liberates all
of creation in a brotherly way.[130] By obviously extending his speculations on

signals from Capri clearly reveal his attempt to see how his early meta-physical speculations will henceforth hold up in an experiment conducted under Marxist premises and in new historical contexts. Hence he now re-formulates his reflections on the psychophysical problem as the question of how theory and practice are related, an issue that becomes the center of his confrontation with Communism. For this reaccentuation, the question of a practical political commitment in favor of Communism—an option he considered quite seriously—is of considerable importance for Benjamin's personal development; in the evolution of his theories it is not more than a secondary factor.

In this respect Georg Lukács's *Geschichte und Klassenbewußtein* (1923; trans. *History and Class Consciousness.* 1971) was at least as important as the impetus Benjamin owed Asja Lacis, who suggested that he should read that book. He took from it the philosophically grounded conviction that in Communism "the problem with 'theory and practice'" appears to be that "any insight into theory is precisely dependent on practice."[137] Especially the exuberant conception of revolutionary practice, which Lukács in retro-spect found necessary to denounce as "messianic utopianism" and which he saw further discredited through its intellectual proximity to Georges Sorel's philosophy, had during the 1920s secured Benjamin's interest in Lukács's work. In this way the problems raised in Benjamin's earliest notes, in which he oriented his politics along the psychophysical problem, retained their importance for him even in the images and reflections of his latest works. Within the framework of what in the *Arcades* and elsewhere is discussed under the rubric of "anthropological materialism," technology continues to occupy its place of central importance. True politicians know that mankind possesses "in technology not a fetish of doom but a key to happiness."[138] And they know that true politics is not embodied in the politician but as-sumes corporeal form in mankind's revolutionary ecstasy of happiness.

## CHAPTER FOUR

# Journalistic Commitment and Essayistic Work, 1925–33

## 1. Profane Illumination: Surrealism and Politics

Even before the Frankfurt faculty turned down his *Habilitation* request, Benjamin had confessed in a letter written in May 1925 to Scholem in Palestine that "for a thousand reasons, it is becoming less and less likely that I will enter upon a university career."[1] And even before he submitted his thesis, he had established contacts with publishers and journals, thereby laying the foundation for his future remarkable journalistic career. For example, the letter to Scholem announces the publication of the essay "Naples," written in collaboration with Asja Lacis, in the weekly *Literaturblatt* (Literary Review) of the newspaper *Frankfurter Zeitung*. With support from Siegfried Kracauer, the feuilleton editor of *Frankfurter Zeitung* since 1924, Benjamin was able to place numerous reviews and, in 1931, the great essay on Karl Kraus in one of the Weimar Republic's most respected daily newspapers. A number of smaller pieces, among them the essay on Julien Green, appeared in *Neue Schweizer Rundschau* (New Swiss Review), edited by Max Rychner (1897–1965).

It was, however, Benjamin's contributions to the weekly journal *Die literarische Welt* (since 1925 edited for Rowohlt Verlag by Willy Haas and later appearing independently) that proved to be of paramount importance. As he had reported to Scholem, he was involved in that journal, "as the contributor of a regular column on recent French art theory."[2] His contacts both to Rychner and to Rowohlt had been facilitated by Hugo von Hofmannsthal. *Literarische Welt*, which had quickly become the leading German literary review of the 1920s, published his essays on Keller, Proust, Valéry, and Surrealism as well as "Little History of Photography," to name but the most important of his well over one hundred contributions. These established

Benjamin's self-understanding as a critic and essayist before political events put an abrupt end to his journalistic career in Germany.

This picture would not be complete, however, without the option that underpinned Benjamin's plans as outlined in the letter quoted above: If it should turn out that he had no luck with his journalistic and book-publishing ventures, he wrote, "I will probably hasten my involvement with Marxist politics and join the Party—with a view toward getting to Moscow in the foreseeable future, at least on a temporary basis."[3]

As the focal point of this consideration one may single out three pieces, written between 1925 and 1927, that are closely intertwined thematically. They illustrate and vary the plans and options he had sketched in the letter: the image of a city, "Moscow," the essay on Surrealism, and the slender volume of aphorisms titled *One-Way Street*.

Before *One-Way Street* was published by Rowohlt Verlag in 1928 simultaneously with *Origin of German Tragic Drama*, excerpts from it had appeared as early as 1925 in *Berliner Tageblatt* (Berlin Daily). This collection of aphorisms serves as the most visible evidence of the reorientation taking place in the years after the failure of Benjamin's academic ambitions and of his attempt to position himself inside the politically leftist critical intelligentsia. At the same time, the publication of an extract from the book, an early version of "Imperial Panorama," documents his endeavor to be counted among the contemporary artistic avant-garde. This text was printed in 1927 in a Dutch translation in the Constructivist *International Revue I 10*, edited by Arthur Lehning (1899–2000), a short-lived periodical (1927–1929) that was close to the artists of the G-group around Ludwig Mies van der Rohe and Hans Richter.

The essay "Moscow," published in 1927, looks back to a journey to Moscow that Benjamin undertook at the turn of 1926–27. Even though he did not join the German Communist Party before or after his trip to the Soviet Union, and even though his sojourn in Moscow was motivated not least by important private reasons, his report nonetheless gives evidence if not of his engagement in party politics, then of a specifically political perceptiveness.

The same can be said about Benjamin's "*Sürrealismus*" essay, an analysis that points the way for his later works in several respects. He submitted it two years later to *Literarische Welt* as its correspondent for recent French art theory. He had taken notice of the Surrealists and their circle even earlier than that: in 1924, when André Breton's *Manifesto of Surrealism* was published, he had translated a short text by Tristan Tzara on photography[4] for the periodical *G. Zeitschrift für elementare Gestaltung* (Journal for Elementary Design), coedited by Richter and Mies van der Rohe. Before

*Literarische Welt* printed this important essay, it had published excerpts from Louis Aragon's *Paysan de Paris* (The Nightwalker) that Benjamin had translated into German, and in 1927 the renowned *Neue Rundschau*, published by S. Fischer Verlag, had printed his "Gloss on Surrealism."[5]

In December 1924, Benjamin mentioned a "brochure" (in French, a *plaquette*) "for friends," in which he intended to collect his "aphorisms, witticisms, and dreams."[6] Even its later title, *Einbahnstraße*, implicitly signals the book's French roots, its proximity to Surrealism, but not without giving it a bit of a slant that the dedication to Asja Lacis clarifies. As an engineer who has cut this street through the author,[7] she has determined its irreversible, that is, its political direction. The book's title and theme indicate a program that finds its indirect expression in its content as well as in its graphic design and intellectual structure.

The first aphorism, "Filling Station," not only connects with the book's title but takes up a key metaphor of the Surrealists. In his *Paysan de Paris* of 1926, a foundational text of Surrealism, Aragon celebrated the gas pumps ("distributeurs d'essence") as idols of Modernity. Along the roadways that serve "the principle of acceleration regulating travel nowadays,"[8] they have replaced the stations of the cross that formerly lined the *via crucis* of the pilgrims. Through them Modernity worships that blind power of the machines that have emancipated themselves from their creators and have long lived a life of their own beyond any form of usefulness. Hence they turn into objects of that phenomenology of the quotidian that reveals itself only to imaged thinking and that Aragon imagines under the rubric of a "modern mythology."[9]

Already in the gloss "Dream Kitsch" Benjamin had emphasized this objective and outward-turned significance that dreams and fantasies have for Surrealism. Whereas the dreams of the Romantics blazed the trail into the fantastic, dreams are for the Surrealists "a shortcut to banality" in which "technology consigns the outer image of things to a long farewell." In Friedrich von Hardenberg's (Novalis's) unfinished novel *Heinrich von Ofterdingen* (1802), the young protagonist dreams of a blue flower, an image that appeared to signify the Romantics' captivation by nature. Later in the nineteenth century it became a metaphor for an indistinct longing, a mental attitude that was identified with Romanticism per se. Benjamin wanted to see it replaced by "historical illumination."[10] His objective understanding of the work of dreams at the same time entails his differentiating the Surrealists from psychoanalysis by crediting them with being "less on the trail of the psyche than on the track of things."[11]

Accordingly, the first aphorism of *One-Way Street* establishes the primacy of facts over convictions so that this maxim, which he owes to this particular moment in history, can immediately be used to foster a new understanding of the writer's activity. Benjamin states that "literary effectiveness can come into being only in a strict alternation between action and writing." But that effectiveness is not being served by "the pretentious, universal gesture of the book." Rather, it is necessary to exert influence through "the inconspicuous forms" of "leaflets, brochures, articles, and placards."[12] *One-Way Street* gathers its author's aphorisms, witticisms, and dreams pursuant to the decisive insight, he writes in another aphorism, "that the book in [its] traditional form is nearing its end."[13] He makes Mallarmé, who in *Coup de dés* was "the first to incorporate the graphic tensions of the advertisement in the printed page,"[14] the first ancestor of this insight. But Benjamin could just as well have pointed to its grandson, Aragon, in whose *Paysan de Paris* advertising leaflets, bulletin board posters, and lists of drinks are part of the text. Or he could have mentioned André Breton, whose *Nadja* (1928) makes photographs of faces, locales, and objects replace long-winded descriptions. But the Surrealists not only opened Benjamin's eyes to the world of everyday things. They also showed him how limited is the view that glances over them. This balancing act between consent and criticism will become the dominant theme of the essay on Surrealism, which was published two years after *One-Way Street*.

In *One-Way Street*, Benjamin describes this medial change through the book's central metaphor. As streets and roadways bring to mind acceleration as a principal experience of Modernity, so topicality and advertising formulate their claim to be taken seriously by intellectuals. Speed alters not only perception but also the function and self-understanding of the writer. Because Karl Kraus refuses to accept this fundamental experience, Benjamin sees him as stuck in a hopeless position, fighting a losing "battle with the press."[15] As Benjamin notes, it has long been irrelevant to trust in the critics' carefully considered judgment or to lament its decline when it fails to materialize, because "its day is long past."[16] Against the horizon of the new media—Benjamin singles out photography and film and in a speculative aphorism imagines even the invention of the personal computer[17]—criticism has lost its legitimacy. Its place is being taken by "the critic as the strategist in the literary struggle"[18] whose task Benjamin describes not by chance as a technical one. Instead of insisting on critical distance he seeks closeness in polemics and considers the loss of objectivity compensated more than enough by the gain of the potential for influence.

In order to understand the presumed contradiction of this stance to Benjamin's previous conception of criticism, it is necessary to read his reflection in the light of the letter explaining to Scholem his turn toward the topical and political elements in his thoughts. This means that "the literary exegesis of German literature will now take a back seat. This exegesis is at best essentially meant to conserve and to restore what is genuine in the face of Expressionistic falsifications. As long as I do not manage to approach texts of a totally different significance and magnitude from a stance that is appropriate to me, that of commentator, I will generate a 'politics' from within myself."[19] It appears that at least for a time Benjamin considered the possibility that he might find texts of this significance in the Hebrew-Jewish tradition. But he did not go through with his plan to travel to Palestine, a plan he pursued rather half-heartedly in 1928–29, though with Scholem's support, and not least for this purpose.[20] On the other hand, a curriculum vitae written around 1928 mentions "the plan of a book on the three great metaphysical writers of our day: Franz Kafka, James Joyce, and Marcel Proust."[21] At any rate, the years to come show that Benjamin's political orientation again and again entered into a productive tension with the stance of a commentator he had called a function appropriate to him.

Even without Party membership, Benjamin's assessment of the political situation in *One-Way Street* reveals an unorthodox position on the extreme left of the political spectrum. He saw the bourgeoisie as doomed, the only question being "whether its downfall will come through itself or through the proletariat." If its "abolition is not completed by an almost calculable moment in economic and technical development (a moment signaled by inflation and poison-gas warfare), all is lost."[22] This apocalyptic prognosis is contrasted in the work's final section, "To the Planetarium," with the vision of reconciliation between man and nature, which takes place on a planetary scale and is made possible by technology. It is a vision that once more assembles all the motifs of his political thinking. Its center is defined by the metaphysics of the collective body, the "measure of its convalescence" being determined by the "power of the proletariat."[23]

No part of this fundamental position changed, even when Benjamin confronted the postrevolutionary situation in the Soviet Union. But his sojourn of two months in Moscow at the turn of 1926–27 came about primarily for a private reason: his love relationship with Asja Lacis. The trip turned into a disappointment for him, as his *Moscow Diary*, one of the few extant private notebooks, documents with heart-wrenching candor. These diary notes also form the basis of the essay "Moscow," which Benjamin published in 1927 in the journal *Die Kreatur*, edited by Martin Buber.

In a letter written to Buber he outlined his intentions, which are relevant not just for this text. He intended "to present a picture of the city of Moscow as it is at this very moment. In this picture, 'all factuality is already theory.'"[24] His reference to Goethe—he borrowed the quote within a quote from *Maxims and Reflections* on *Naturwissenschaft im Allgemeinen* (Natural Science in General)—does indeed reflect epistemological principles. Well into the time of his exile writings, Benjamin will be occupied with developing an epistemology of history whose theoretical foundations bring his early critique of Goethe into contact with his critical reception of Surrealism. The point Benjamin makes with his Goethe quotation in his letter to Buber involves its application to a historical topic. For this reason, it is significant that Benjamin begins his essay with an emphatic reminder of the "fact of 'Soviet Russia,'" which indicates, if not constitutes, a "turning point in historical events."[25] In other words, the actuality that in Russia a Bolshevik revolution has taken place is the irreversible fact that gives the visitor the key to understanding what presents itself to his eyes.

When Benjamin traveled to Moscow, the October Revolution had taken place ten years before. In January 1927, the third anniversary of Lenin's death was being observed. Lenin's "New Economic Policy" had afforded the country a phase of relative internal and economic stability, to be sure, but at the price of high unemployment, especially in the cities, and the emergence of a new bourgeoisie. It was hardly possible to claim a victory for socialism. Whereas the personality cult surrounding Lenin seemed to secure the Bolsheviks' popularity among the populace, a fierce struggle for power took place behind the public scenes. Trotsky's ouster from power by Stalin showed the first consequences: two months before Benjamin's arrival in Moscow in December 1926, Trotsky had been removed from the Politburo, and at the Fifteenth Party Congress of the Communist Party of the Soviet Union in December 1927 he was expelled from the Party. Two years later he would be expelled from the Soviet Union.

With scant knowledge of these events and without venturing any kind of prognosis, Benjamin shows his remarkable sensitivity for the country's upheavals. The "new optics"[26] gained in Russia give a first suggestion of the premises underlying his report: when looked at from Moscow, Berlin is a "deserted city."[27] This observation proves the revolutionary fact that "Bolshevism has abolished private life."[28] The reorganization of housing arrangements reflects not only the workaday world of labor but also contributes decisively to shaping the appearance of streets populated by the masses.

Benjamin had already been alerted to this connection years before in Naples. There, housing circumstances such as the revolution had produced in Moscow had arisen, fostered by the climate of the Italian South, as a consequence of poverty and wretchedness. The dissolution of a life in privacy that one could observe in the streets and in the slum neighborhoods reminds one not only of a precivilized, collective state of domestic cohesiveness, but also points ahead toward a situation in which the bourgeois separation of living room and street has been done away with.[29] Benjamin decodes this interpenetration of archaic and modern forms of human habitation as the signature of a historical upheaval that requires an architecture attuned to the needs of the collective. As he noted in a review in 1929,

> the cult of 'dwelling' in the old sense, with the idea of security at its core, has now received its death knell. Giedion, Mendelssohn, and Le Corbusier are converting human habitations into the transitional spaces of every imaginable force and wave of light and air. The coming architecture is dominated by the idea of transparency—not just of space but also of the week, if we are to believe the Russians, who intend to abolish Sundays in favor of leisure-time shifts.[30]

It is this both historical and historic experience that Benjamin encountered in the writings of the Surrealists, and this is exactly what he meant by "profane illumination," the key concept of his essay. The hope to which the two implications of the title of Breton's *Nadja* allude—a woman's name and, in Russian, "the beginning, but it's only the beginning of the word *hope* [nadiezhda]"[31]—is not the least directed toward clarifying the search for one's own identity, an enigma introduced at the beginning of the narrative. To get closer to it, Breton writes, he continues to live in his glass house, where sooner or later he will be able to see who he is.[32] His reader Benjamin, well familiar with the author of *Glasarchitektur* (1914), Scheerbart, could not have been given a more appropriate cue. "To live in a glass house"—so his essay takes up its cue—"is a revolutionary virtue par excellence."[33] To Scheerbart he owes the insight that "architecture will be the canon of all creations and products."[34] In the same way that Benjamin takes Breton's metaphorical writing by its literal word, he is intent on saving the historical experience of Surrealism and with it also its revolutionary nucleus from misapprehending itself as an aesthetic revolt.

Benjamin is convinced that this is a misapprehension from which the German observer of the presumably more progressive French avant-garde is protected. In his essay on Surrealism, he notes that "as a German he has long been acquainted with the crisis of the intelligentsia, or, more precisely, with that of the humanistic concept of freedom." He knows of the intelligentsia's frenetic determination "to go beyond the stage of eternal discussion and, at any price, to reach a decision." Whoever has personally experienced their exposed position "between an anarchistic Fronde and a revolutionary discipline" will not be deceived by what appears to be a merely superficial awareness,[35] Benjamin writes in the second paragraph of the essay—a passage in which he is quoting himself from his review of the conservative cultural critic Julien Benda's sensational manifesto *La trahison des clercs* (1927; trans., *The Great Betrayal*, 1928). Benda had seen the political commitment of contemporary intellectuals as a betrayal of their originally nonpartisan, humanistic mandate. Benjamin, on the contrary, recognized this politicization as indicative of the irreversible "decline of the independent intelligentsia," which he considers to be "the result if not solely, then decisively of economic factors."[36] It is this vanishing point that Benjamin has in mind when he subtitles his essay "The Last Snapshot of the European Intelligentsia."[37]

Benjamin reads the writings of the Surrealists against the grain, as it were. Their belief in the "omnipotence of dream,"[38] as proclaimed in Breton's "Manifesto of Surrealism" of 1924, and their apotheosis of fantasy and intoxication, which the Surrealists picked up where the Romantics had left off, do not manifest for him a new literary movement at all. Rather, these slogans announce a specific experience, the significance of which the theories of the Surrealists themselves have, however, penetrated only insufficiently. Benjamin understands this experience, in contrast to narcotic intoxication or to religious ecstasies, as a "profane illumination." But this profane illumination did not always find the Surrealists equal to it, or to themselves. He claims that already Lenin had brought these two factors together by calling religion "the opiate for the people."[39] This quote of course does not derive from Lenin but from Marx. Benjamin, furthermore, does not quote accurately—"Opium des Volkes" (opium of the people) is what Marx in the introduction to the *Critique of Hegel's 'Philosophy of Right'* (1843) calls religion.[40] But the thrust of Benjamin's idea is quite clear. The encounters that the Surrealists experience in the metropolitan cities and that in their writings turn into witnesses of an environment radically transformed by technology, has to be converted, he postulates, "into revolutionary experience, if not action."[41]

As early as 1929, Benjamin was able to detect clear indications that Surrealism would follow in the direction to which he had pointed. Pierre Naville, quoted affirmatively in several places in the essay, had already joined the Communist Party of France (CPF); Breton and Aragon were soon to follow him. But Benjamin's essay was written for German readers, and joining the Party, which he could not get himself to do, did not necessarily seem to provide the answer to every question after all. The program of an "anthropological materialism," which the essay's conclusion advocates and in support of which he refers to the earlier experience of "Hebel, Georg Büchner, Nietzsche, Rimbaud"[42] and before them once again to the "well-ventilated utopias of a Scheerbart,"[43] would in the final analysis have to be reconstructed not by way of Marx or Lenin but from Benjamin's own early writings. His becoming conversant with the basic texts of Historical Materialism will remain a desideratum well into the late 1930s.

## 2. The "Strategist in the Literary Struggle"

The strategy Benjamin pursued in the literary struggle of the Weimar Republic was determined by the decline of the independent intelligentsia that he had repeatedly diagnosed. The symptoms of this crisis can be observed on the one hand in the crisis of art and of the literature business, and on the other in the crisis of education and its most important institution, the university. Accordingly, between 1926 and 1933, Benjamin reviewed relevant new literary publications with an emphasis on France but also a considerable number of selected scholarly books.

In a letter written to Max Rychner dated March 7, 1931, he wrote that he had not been led to the materialistic approach through Communist propaganda but under the impression of the representative works that had recently emanated in his discipline of literary history and criticism. The "basic metaphysical tendency" of his research, if nothing else, had removed him quite far from bourgeois scholarship. His *Origin of German Tragic Drama* demonstrated just "how far strict adherence to genuine academic research methods leads a person away from the contemporary stance of the bourgeois and idealistic enterprise." Proof of this "is borne out by the fact that not a single German academician deigned to review it."[44] As early as *One-Way Street* Benjamin had seen the contemporary relevance of scholarship warranted not in presumably modish themes, but in the critical reflection of its methods and techniques. Between the index cards of the researcher and the scholar's filing system, the book is today already "an outdated mediation."[45] In this manner, scholarship basically anticipates the insight that the book in its traditional form is nearing its end. This needs to be taken into consideration when dealing with the topics science and scholarship raise.

In his critique of *Wissenschaft*, Benjamin, whom innumerable academic fashions were posthumously to invoke as their predecessor, presented himself circuitously as a conservative. In his own time he saw the rise of a type that is even more prevalent nowadays, that is, "that of the young university teacher who believes he is fostering the 'renewal' of his discipline by blurring its borders with journalism."[46] There is nobody in the humanities who "is willing to continue its traditions from a lecture podium."[47] In a section that was not included in the printed version of One-Way Street he expressed the conviction that research and teaching in the humanities have by necessity to be esoteric and that the laws and forms of scholarship in the humanities must in the end appear to the great scholar "as theologically determined." But this conviction refers less to a worldview than to an attitude concerning the dignity of scholarly and scientific work, which culminates in the vision of an elitist institution in which "the practice of the seminar as a *privatissimum*" is the rule and in which research support is unrestricted: "In America, where things that escape the destruction imposed on the inventory of Central and Western Europe will seek refuge, one surmises that one will find the origin of such academic constitutions."[48] Benjamin's laconic remark, jotted down under the experience of the hyperinflation of 1923, appears equally relevant today.

Benjamin detected two tendencies in the appointment to professorships in the humanities. There are the sectarian aesthetes, who without any sense of responsibility hope to enjoy the pursuit of their private interests at the university, and the *condottiere* types, who occupy chairs as the most propitious places to exert influence in the interest of their mission.[49] This is a diagnosis Benjamin saw confirmed at the beginning of the 1930s: "In ten years, university chairs will have been completely divided up between the charlatans and the sectarians. The conquest of chairs by the George School was the first symptom."[50]

The pattern just described recurs in roughly the same form in Benjamin's reviews of scholarly publications. Hence, two critiques deal with important studies by members of George's circle. Both the review of Gundolf's *Gryphius* (1928) and the comprehensive discussion of Max Kommerell's *Der Dichter als Führer in der deutschen Klassik* (1928; The Poet as Leader in German Classicism) make a critique of methodological premises their central concern. Against Gundolf he draws attention to the fact that access to Baroque poetry can be gained only by studying the world of its poetic forms and linguistic structures, whereas the figure of the poet, from which Gundolf proceeds, is alien to the Baroque.[51] While in the refutation of Gundolf it is the *Drama* book that provides the foil for Benjamin's critique, the review of Kommerell mobilizes decisive insights from his dissertation. "Every dialectical analysis of George's poetry"—and, must be added, of its conception of the poet—"will have Romanticism at its heart, while every orthodox hagiography will be best advised to downplay Romanticism as much as possible."[52] By stylizing the poet as leader, modeling him on the example of the ancient hero ("Heros"), Kommerell (1902–44) construes "Classicism as the first canonical German insurrection against time—a holy war of the Germans against the century, of the kind George himself later proclaimed."[53] In this manner, Kommerell's book (on which Benjamin bestows the attribute of being in its own way a masterpiece) turns into "a salvation history of the Germans."[54] As a kind of Magna Carta of German conservatism, it remains under the spell of vision and refuses to engage the present time.

Besides Heinz Kindermann (1894–1985), who was to have a splendid career in the Third Reich, Benjamin saw Oskar Walzel (1864–1944) as a representative of the second type of successful university professor whose publications are driven by the ambition "to demonstrate that they are as well informed as the midday edition of any metropolitan newspaper."[55] On the one hand, his polemic here is directed against the concept of both "experience" (*Erlebnis*) and "empathy" (*Einfühlung*). On the other, it attacks the orientation of literary historiography toward universalizing syntheses, for which Walzel, following the example of Fritz Strich, went back to the formal "basic principles" that the art historian Heinrich Wölfflin (1864–1945) had developed to describe art historical styles. What is being revealed in this manner is "not poetic literature but a way of writing and talking about it."[56] A literary-historical construction of this kind is, however, ultimately erected on a concept of culture shaped by neo-Kantianism, in the center of which Rickert and Windelband had anchored the concept of value. In its "profligate drive toward totalities"[57]—an inevitable consequence of this premise—Benjamin recognized the misfortune of this approach both in Walzel's *Wortkunstwerk* (1926; The Literary Work of Art) and in the essay collection *Philosophie der Literaturwissenschaft* (1930; Philosophy of Literary Scholarship), edited by Emil Ermatinger, to which also the Frankfurt *Ordinarius* Franz Schultz contributed. In "this quagmire, the hydra of scholastic aesthetics is at home with its seven heads: creativity, empathy, freedom from time, imitation, sympathetic understanding, illusion, and aesthetic enjoyment."[58] It is against this hydra that Benjamin aims his salvos.

A better alternative, he reminds his readers, is the practice of an earlier generation of German literary scholars who refused "to regard the literature of their own age as a suitable subject for research." It had been their ascetic professional maxim to serve "their age directly by attempting to do justice to the past."[59] Elsewhere, Benjamin refers explicitly to the Brothers Grimm and sees the slogan about the "veneration of the insignificant," originally directed polemically against the founding fathers of *Germanistik*, as expressing the "spirit of true philology" and hence paraphrasing his own concerns.[60] How little this has to do with the philological ethos of the Grimms, but how much more with his own approach as practiced especially in his book on Baroque drama, is made clear when he singles out the works of Konrad Burdach and the scholars associated with the Warburg Library as exemplary models that influenced it.

Benjamin also has this context in mind when he repeatedly demands that certain "works and forms" should, selectively, be treated in monographs,[61] and that scholarship should concentrate on the "radical singularity of the artwork."[62] His reason is that a genuine commitment based on a love of art should turn to what he calls art's "inside as that of a monad."[63] Only "the investigation of individual works"[64] shows scholarship a way of penetrating to the concrete ground for what these works had been "in their [own] historical past." This would also guarantee that "research never misses the real concerns of its time."[65] According to Benjamin, this direction had not been pointed out, however, by Wölfflin's *Kunstgeschichtliche Grundbegriffe* (1915; trans., *Principles of Art History*, 1932) but by Alois Riegl (to whom he had already paid tribute in his book on Baroque drama), whose study *Die spätrömische Kunst-Industrie* (1901; trans., *Late Roman Art Industry*, 1985) had overcome the "conventional universal history with its so-called 'high points' and 'times of decline.'"[66] Benjamin claims that today's reader can sense in Riegl's book the subterranean forces that were to come to the fore in Expressionism.

Following Riegl's precepts, Benjamin's critique of contemporary academic practice leads to the initial stages of reception theory. This critical paradigm should not be confused, however, with a more recent analytical approach by this name because its concern with *literary* history is rather marginal. When Benjamin demands that one should consider the individual work within its historical circumstances, its reception by contemporaries, its translations, its fame,[67] he does so because he has no interest in portraying "literary works in the context of their age, but to represent the age that perceives them—our age—in the age during which they arose."[68] This is an idea that will remain fundamental to his philosophy of history. It is expressed also in his, at first sight, surprising demand for a separation of research and teaching in academic work. Teaching should be centered around the most recent additions to the canon that suggests what it means to be educated. But the value of its content "is perhaps a matter less of renewing teaching through research than of renewing research through teaching."[69]

Without saying so directly, Benjamin measures not only the routine of contemporary academic busyness by the standards and insights he had

himself attained in the *Habilitation* thesis, which had not been accepted
by representatives of this very routine. As seen from the vantage point of
his own present, the relevance of the Baroque had become apparent to him,
because that era had been aware of the "problematic of art." Contemporary
criticism needs to account for this awareness that a crisis exists. It is not by
chance that Benjamin attributes this awareness to a critic who had committed himself in his writings to a theological way of looking at things. This
connection establishes the starting point for his review—published in 1931
in *Neue Rundschau*—of a collection of essays by Willy Haas. In these essays, he writes, Haas clears his "approach to the work of art by demolishing
the doctrine of 'art's domain.'" The basic motif of Haas's view, he continues, is his conviction that the "theological illumination of the works" is at
the same time the genuine interpretation of determinants equally political
and modish, economic and metaphysical." By turning destructively against
art in this manner, Haas's theological attitude confronts the attitude of historical materialism with a radical insistence "that makes one the opposite
pole of the other."[70] For Benjamin, Haas stands at that crossroads that had
brought him to his own realization that there does exist a mediation, however strained and problematic that relationship may be, from the perspective
of his particular stance on the philosophy of language to the way dialectical
materialism looks at things. "But there is absolutely no bridge from [my]
position to the complacency of bourgeois scholarship."[71]

    This position is also the starting point for Benjamin's frequently po-
lemical and at times very severe controversies with representatives of the
left-wing bourgeois intelligentsia of the Weimar Republic. In their writings
he discovered a "very specific attitude," one whose ironic admission of the
intellectual's hopeless situation contains "a touch of irresponsibility."[72]
To put it bluntly: "The position of a humanistic anarchism is lost beyond
help."[73] Just as illusionary, he says, is the idea that one can be so emancipated as to stand between or above the classes. Benjamin denounces left-
radical writers of the stamp of Erich Kästner, Walter Mehring, and Kurt
Tucholsky as "the decayed bourgeoisie's mimicry of the proletariat."[74] In a
prominent place—in *Die Gesellschaft* (Society), a monthly edited by Rudolf
Hilferding, which was close to the Social Democratic Party (SPD)—Benjamin
accused the bourgeois left of having been agents of all intellectual booms,
from Activism via Expressionism to the New Objectivity. Their "political
significance, however, was exhausted by the transposition of reflexes (insofar
as they arose in the bourgeoisie) into objects of distraction, of amusement,
which can be supplied for consumption."[75] He called the melancholy of
Erich Kästner's (1899–1974) poems a reflex of an "attitude to which there

is no longer, in general, any corresponding political action," because it is "to the left of what is generally possible."[76] In a similar vein, Kurt Hiller, the principal representative of Activism, in whose periodical *Das Ziel* Benjamin's essay "Life of Students" had appeared, is accused of advocating an image of power "that is totally devoid of any political sense, unless it is to reveal how even the degraded bourgeoisie is unable to let go of certain ideals from its days of glory."[77]

For Benjamin, an idea is political not if it subscribes to an idealistic-utopian aim but succeeds in "setting the masses in motion"[78] on historical territory. Brecht, whose maxim about "the art of thinking in other people's heads" Benjamin quotes in this context, provided him with a counter image not for the Hiller review alone. Whereas the be-all and end-all of Mehring's poems and songs is the effect, Brecht's chansons have emancipated themselves from cabaret and, by gaining transformative power, from décadence.[79] While Kästner's poetry does not go beyond smugness and fatalism, Brecht's poems create "consciousness and deed" and thereby fulfill the "task of all political" verse.[80]

Benjamin's critique of the left-radical bourgeois intelligentsia found an important ally in Siegfried Kracauer, whose study *Die Angestellten* (1930; trans., *The Salaried Masses*, 1998) he dealt with twice: in an extensive essay in *Gesellschaft* and in a notice in *Literarische Welt*. Benjamin's text in *Gesellschaft*, titled "Politicization of the Intelligentsia" by the editors against the author's objection (as a note in his own copy indicates), was published as part of a debate about the situation of the intellectuals that had been initiated by Karl Mannheim's *Ideologie und Utopie* (1929; trans., *Ideology and Utopia*, 1936) and by his thesis of the "free-floating intelligentsia." He explicitly considers Kracauer's investigation "a milestone on the road toward the politicization of the intelligentsia, in sharp contrast to the fashionable radicalism of the writings of the latest school."[81] The reason for this is to be found not only in the political stance of its author but even more in the methodological premises that justify this position. As Kracauer himself put it, he had tried to penetrate "the true structure of reality" instead of issuing his decrees from on high, as radicalism does. Because how was the workaday world to change, he asked, "if even those whose vocation is to stir it up pay it no attention?"[82]

When Benjamin observed that Kracauer's pictorial wit ends in "those composite Surrealist images that not only characterize dreams (as we have learned from Freud) and the sensual world (as we have learned from Paul Klee and Max Ernst), but also define our social reality,"[83] he implicitly lays claim to Kracauer for a program that he himself will pursue during these years in a critical argument with Surrealism in his unfinished *Parisian Arcades*. With respect to its immediate merit, however, Benjamin credits Kracauer's work with "a constructive theoretical schooling that addresses neither the snob nor the worker, but is able to promote something real and demonstrable—namely, the politicization of the writer's own class. This indirect impact is the only one a revolutionary writer from the bourgeoisie can aim at today. A direct effect can proceed only from practice."[84]

The two programmatic essays about Kästner and Kracauer flank his no less fundamental discussion of the collection of essays *Krieg und Krieger* (1930), edited by Ernst Jünger (1895–1998). It is a book that Benjamin analyzes in 1930 also in *Gesellschaft* in an article titled "Theories of German Fascism."[85] Clearly, his skirmishes with the left-wing intelligentsia did not keep the strategist in the literary struggle of the Weimar Republic from mounting the necessary counterattack against the consolidating array of right-wing conservatism.

Benjamin also recognizes that also the writers around Jünger cannot deny their origin in décadence. In their experience of the First World War, the decisive factor that shaped their political stance and to which their writings give testimony, Benjamin detects "an uninhibited translation of the principles of *l'art pour l'art* to war."[86] But the authors of the volume in question can aestheticize the experience of war and turn it into the cult of heroism resigned to fate only because they overlook as a bit of an irritation the technological aspect of war, an aspect that confronts them with the anonymous death of millions in the new warfare that is defined by technology and materiel.

This is precisely where Benjamin's critique comes in. The technological means that, being restricted by circumstances of private ownership, find no adequate exploitation in everyday life, justify themselves in war. The destructions of war, he says, provide "clear evidence that social reality was not ready to make technology its own organ, and that technology was not strong enough to master the elemental forces of society."[87] By contrast, the heroic stylization of the war experience guarantees that such a stance can be carried over into the time of peace and will in this manner remain loyal to the, in the double sense of the word, "lost" war.

Obedient to the technological necessities of their craft, Jünger's warriors as the war engineers of the ruling class form the counterpart of the chief executive officers in tuxedos. Benjamin in fact unmasks "the dependable fascist class warrior,"[88] who appears in the guise first of the war volunteer and then of the postwar mercenary. Thus the decisive opportunity that this war had offered in reality has been missed. It is the one, terrible, last chance "to correct the incapacity of peoples to order their relationships to one another in accord with the relationship they possess to nature through their technology."[89] As always, Benjamin considered technology not as a "fetish of doom but a key to happiness."[90] But more than ever, this central category of his political theory is connected now, three years before Hitler's assumption of power, with his prognosis of an inevitable civil war.

### 3. The Task of the Critic

In a letter to Scholem sent from Paris in January 1930, Benjamin avows self-confidently that it is his purpose "to be considered the foremost critic of German literature," admitting at the same time that he had not as yet reached this goal. In subsequently referring to Rowohlt's promise to publish some of his essays as a book, he apparently thought that he may be moving significantly closer to realizing this ambitious intention. His plan, however, faced objective difficulties: "to be relevant in criticism, that, basically, means creating it as a genre."[91] While most of the essays to be included in this volume had either been completed already or were to be finished at a later time, the treatise "on the current circumstances and theory of criticism,"[92] which was to serve as an introduction, shared the book's fate: it was never written. As the extant publisher's contract shows, an essay about "the task of the critic" was to open the book, and the essay "The Task of the Translator" (1921)[93] was to close it. Various notes on the topic of criticism—they can be dated to 1929 through 1931—most probably were not meant to relate to the volume of essays in question only. They also refer to a different project.

This project was a journal Benjamin first mentioned in October 1930. It, too, was to be published by Rowohlt but edited in conjunction with Brecht. The title they had chosen was *Krisis und Kritik*.[94] As early as February of the following year, however, after Benjamin had read the first manuscripts submitted for publication, he informed Brecht that he was resigning as coeditor.[95] Not a single issue of *Krisis und Kritik* appeared. But even so, Benjamin's preparatory work on these two unrealized projects documents a continuity of central concerns in his thinking that go back to his early theory of art criticism. This continuity is all the more instructive given the changed context in which he was developing these reflections.

Benjamin was convinced that criticism as a genre had to undergo a fundamental transformation before it could reverse its current decline. The cause of this atrophy, he said, was the "irrelevance of the reviewing business," which, "once it had been taken over by journalists, had devastated criticism."[96] The reverse side of a supposed obligation to inform the public and to please it with value judgments was for him a firm attachment to traditional, purely aesthetic standards. By contrast, moderation would be the first step toward a revival of genuine criticism. "Its essential characteristics: not to be dependent on books just published; to be applicable to scholarly works as much as to belles-lettres; to remain impartial toward the quality of the particular work in question." Its optimal capability: the coincidence of "cognitive usefulness" and "literary valuation."[97] Criticism, as he had written about his Keller essay[98] in his letter to Rychner (dated March 7, 1931) quoted above, must make its readers recognize "the true condition of our present-day existence." Every genuine perception is also evolving, on the part of the individual who perceives, into a form of "self-perception that is grounded in a philosophy of history rather than in psychology."[99] In accordance with this understanding of art, Benjamin's major literary-aesthetic essays and his numerous critical contributions to, for example, newspapers, should be seen as pursuing an identical goal. In either case, the critic reflects on what is, now more than ever, his noblest task: to "lift *the mask of 'pure art'* and show that there is no neutral ground for art."[100]

This statement has been read all too hastily as the formula for a changed concept of criticism, one henceforth characterized by political commitment. But, as Benjamin saw it, he had directed his efforts toward "opening a path to the work of art by destroying the doctrine of the territorial character of art"[101]—by which he means the doctrine of the autonomy of art—as early as in his *Origin of German Tragic Drama* (1927), a book presumably caught up in metaphysics. And so he reaches back in his notes to a theory about the continued life of artistic works that he had developed in the context of this work. This theory is defined by the "dominant idea" that "this continued life unmasks the territorial character of art as a sham."[102] The critical insight into the essential nature of art, gained through its great works, is the precondition for an understanding of their present fate. A type of criticism, however, that holds fast to the standards of a traditional aesthetic will do justice neither to the great works nor to its own present task.

It is against this background that one must see both the critic's self-image as a "strategist in the literary struggle"[103] and his demand that criticism must have a "program."[104] Program and strategy are not subject to any political doctrine. At the same time, however, Benjamin believes that the necessity of a politically revolutionary commitment is predetermined in the development of literature. This is the reason that he does not invalidate the cardinal principle of an immanent criticism in the notes of 1930–31, but continues to apply it consistently. In accordance with his exemplary critique of *Elective Affinities*, Benjamin demands that criticism must provide an explanation of "how the material content and the truth content of a work of art interpenetrate." It is only "inside the work itself, at the place where truth content and material content coalesce, that the art-sphere has definitively been left behind."[105] He notes that in the end the principle of immanence—which is to say, the conviction "that criticism is immanent to the work of art"—leads to the insight that "for its great works, art is merely a transitional stage. They had been something different (in the state of their genesis), and they will turn into something different (in the state of criticism)."[106]

The theory concerning the continued life of artworks is given its most radical formulation in the theory that deals with the change of art's function. The reader is being made aware of this connection—still within the context of traditional book reviewing—in the idea "that reading is only one of a hundred ways of gaining access to a book."[107] Like the collector—and Benjamin was a very passionate collector—so also the critic is not a reader in the true sense of the word. Though he is obviously still bound up with books as a medium, the critic tests the observation formulated in *One-Way Street* "that the book in its traditional form [i.e., as the Book of Books that, through Luther's translation, had become the people's property, *Volksgut*] is nearing its end."[108] These arguments anticipate the direction that Benjamin's theoretical discussions of photography and film will soon take; and so they also foreshadow both the originality and the limitations of his thinking about these genres.

The volume of essays to be published by Rowohlt Verlag and to be introduced by these reflections would have collected the important essays on Gottfried Keller, Johann Peter Hebel, Robert Walser, Kraus, and Proust on which Benjamin's rather modest reputation among the wider reading public was based during his lifetime. Among literary scholars today, his name is of course connected with these writers and with Surrealism as well as with Kafka and Baudelaire. Within this horizon, each essay also illustrates in its own way the experimental and extremely contrasting character of his thinking in the final years of the Weimar Republic. For Kafka and Proust, whom he occasionally referred to as "metaphysical writers of our day,"[109] he must have felt, on account of his own intellectual development, an especially close affinity. The basically metaphysical orientation of his research, however, had led Benjamin toward insights that do not deny this foundation but, under changed historical conditions, try it out in new intellectual constellations.

Among the studies he completed between 1926 and 1931, it is not only the important essay on Proust, however, that can be understood as an experiment in this sense. The essays are connected with each other subliminally through a number of recurrent themes and thought figures. The essay on Gottfried Keller (1819–90), published in 1927 in *Literarische Welt* and originally conceived to publicize the new critical edition of his works, focuses attention on the nineteenth century, for which Benjamin demands that "we would need to arrive eventually at a revaluation"[110] as an indispensable condition for an appropriate appreciation of Keller. The aspects Benjamin demonstrates as constituents of Keller's intellectual physiognomy are his hedonistic atheism, his melancholic materialism, his humor, and "the vision of happiness"[111] realized in Keller's prose. They suggest a secret vanishing point that is expressed in the formula "love of the earth,"[112] a phrase used by Conrad Ferdinand Meyer to characterize Keller on the occasion of his seventieth birthday. This Zarathustrian locution moves the called-for revaluation of the nineteenth century toward an "anthropological materialism" and toward the category of happiness that is central to Benjamin's critical debate with Nietzsche. Also Proust's fixation on the past century that dominates his work is likewise connected for Benjamin with his desire for happiness.

Humor, understood not only as an anthropological gesture but as a narrative attitude, connects Keller with another poetic writer of the century whom bourgeois literary historiography had neglected: Johann Peter Hebel (1760–1826), to whom Benjamin devoted an essay in 1926. In Keller's prose Benjamin had observed "the interpenetration of the narrative and the poetic."[113] He saw this as an indication of a tendency in the post-Romantic era that he will welcome in Döblin, Kafka, and in his essay on the storyteller Nikolai Leskov as the "restitution of epic narration." By contrast, the nineteenth century in accordance with the Romantic preference for the novel and with the era's dominant preoccupation with the idea of the nation, had been unable to appreciate Hebel the storyteller. He was a writer for the people, who found a source of inspiration in dialect and for whom, as for "all genuine, unintellectualized popular art (*Volkskunst*)," the provincial is not a contradiction of the cosmopolitan. The boundary line that separates his kind of narrative from the novel represents the one pole of Benjamin's theory of narration. The other pole is Hebel's stance on myth and fairy tale. This is what Benjamin alludes to when he characterizes the heroes of the Swiss novelist and storyteller Robert Walser (1878–1956) as people who have gone through insanity and left it behind. Theirs is an experience they share with fairy-tale figures, and this is the reason, according to Benjamin's claim in the essay he wrote for the periodical *Tagebuch* (Diary), that one has to understand Walser's prose as part of the "great profane debate with myth that the fairy tale represents."[114]

Interest in the nineteenth century as the prehistory of the present time remains dominant even in Benjamin's essays on contemporary authors like Julien Green, Karl Kraus, and Paul Valéry. Close examination confirms that his interest in the most recent past as part of a preoccupation with his own present corresponds to "a self-recognition in the one seeking cognition via a philosophy of history" of the kind that Benjamin demands of the critic. In the works of Julien Green (1900–98), but above all in Proust, Benjamin found a congenial interest in this epistemological concern that was to occupy him intensely in his later writings. It is their narrative method, he says, to approach the past not through reflection but through "actualization,"[115] or "making present."[116] In Green's work, defined as it is by theological motifs, remembrance is conjoined with creaturely suffering which as such is timeless. In this manner he fuses things past, the old-fashioned, with the primordial. No less than the method of "making present" does the concept of primal history (Urgeschichte) assume central importance in Benjamin's philosophy of history. It is certain, he wrote toward the end of the essay on Julien Green—published in 1930 in Neue Schweizer Rundschau—"that for every generation a piece of primal history is fused with the existence, the life forms, of the immediately preceding one; thus, for the generation alive now such a fusion takes place with the middle and end of the previous century."[117] This thought underpins the Arcades as much as Berlin Childhood around 1900—not to mention Proust's work, to which Benjamin is referring here explicitly.

Marcel Proust's (1871–1922) huge novel À la recherche du temps perdu, which appeared in seven parts between 1913 and 1927, had originally occupied Benjamin as a translator. In November 1925 he first translated its fourth volume, the following year during a sojourn in Paris together with Franz Hessel its second and third volumes.[118] The translation of volume 4 must be considered lost; the two others were published in 1927 and 1930, before the publisher cancelled the project. Even as he was working on the translation, Benjamin expressed his intention to write about Proust, a plan he did not realize until 1929, when he published the essay "On the Image of Proust"[119] in three installments in Die Literarische Welt.

The portrait he draws in this essay sees the monumental work of remembrance suffused with an elegiac desire for happiness that is directed at an eternal "once more." This marks the origin of Proust's "cult of similarity"[120] that links his novel to dream; it is also the point from which for Benjamin any synthetic interpretation of Proust has to proceed. As is well known,

Freud had recognized that similarity is one of the logical relations in the formation of dreams.[121] But as Benjamin does in his interpretation of Surrealism, so he also in his reading of *Recherche* attributes to dream an objective direction, one turned toward the world of things. It is not merely by chance that he perceives in Proust's homesickness "for the world distorted in the state of similarity . . . the true surrealist face of existence" breaking through.[122] The essay, after all, uncovers a different genealogy of similarity than that postulated by psychoanalysis, with Proust himself in his essay on Baudelaire giving a hint about it that Benjamin picked up. Proust had spoken there of a curious dismantlement of time "in which only the red-letter days are shown."[123] It is this time concept of "correspondences" that Proust's method of "making present" presupposes—and which later became the issue that starts Benjamin's critical dissociation from Proust. In 1926, in a letter to Hofmannsthal, Benjamin had spoken of the "profound and ambiguous impressions"[124] with which Proust filled him. When a good number of years later in the study "On Some Motifs in Baudelaire" he came to speak about Proust once more, his comment about the "inescapably private character"[125] of the concept of experience (*Erfahrung*), which *Recherche* grounds in *mémoire involontaire*, signals his reservations. In other words, where experience in the strict sense of the word predominates, "certain contents of the individual past combine in memory (*Gedächtnis*) with material from the collective past."[126] Even so, this note, which assumes its true meaning only in the context of Benjamin's own philosophy of history, presupposes a concept of time and remembrance that for Benjamin has taken representative shape in Proust's novel. It cannot be denied, after all, that the perspective of "the individual who is isolated in various ways,"[127] from which Proust has written his novel, does offer decidedly critical insights into the constitution of bourgeois society. In Proust's analysis of snobbism and in the role he accords to homosexuality, Benjamin sees the bourgeoisie reduced to nothing but the role of consumers. By the same means Proust unmasked the bourgeoisie's efforts to deny that it was built on a material foundation. Much of the greatness of *Recherche*, Benjamin says, "will remain inaccessible and undiscovered until this class has revealed its most pronounced features in the final struggle."[128]

It was not the essay on Proust, however, but the intellectually demanding and no less structurally difficult essay on Karl Kraus (1874–1936), which Benjamin singles out as exemplary of his thinking. It was this essay that provoked Scholem to accuse Benjamin of having fallen prey to Marxist self-deception.[129] Directions on how to read the titles of the text's three sections—"Cosmic Man" (*Allmensch*, lit., "the All-Human"), "Demon," and "Monster" (*Unmensch*, lit., "the In-Human")—can be found among the paralipomena. The essay on Kraus, he writes there, "defines the place where I stand and don't belong."[130] As early as in *One-Way Street*, Benjamin, who since 1918–19 had been a regular reader of *Die Fackel* (The Torch) and who certainly recognized in the thinker on language a kindred spirit, had maintained a distance from Kraus's campaign against the press. Scholem reproached Benjamin for betraying his intellectual origins by projecting insights he had gained in the pursuit of a theological method onto a materialistic terminology—a rebuke that is right at least in pointing out that Benjamin's debate with Kraus makes use, as is easy to see, of ideas he himself had developed earlier. But the cue words he used as section headings, which relate to each other as thesis, antithesis, and synthesis, emphatically refer to a more complicated connection than the one suggested by the philosophy of language that Scholem has in mind. The monster of part 3, a mirror reflection of Kraus's intellectual physiognomy, is conceived as the polemical opposite of Nietzsche's *Übermensch*, the superhuman.

Benjamin's debate with Nietzsche, which in the essay itself has a point of contact in Kraus's polemic against Nietzsche's art of the aphorism, is part of that early political shift of emphasis in Benjamin's thinking from which he forges ahead in the Kraus study and in all his other essays. What excessive demands this made on Benjamin's readers becomes apparent not least in Kraus's own reaction. In his response in *Die Fackel*, Kraus found the essay well intentioned and probably also well considered. But all he could find in it was nothing more than that it is dealing with him and that its author seems to know a goodly number of things about him of which he himself is ignorant. That may be psychoanalysis, was the concluding conjecture with which he sought to annihilate his opponent.[131]

It is as the symbol of destruction that the "inhuman" becomes the "superman's" antithetical counterpart. Benjamin may have seen Kraus here as a satirist in the tradition of Swift, who suggested using the children of the poor for culinary purposes. This may have induced Benjamin to attribute a cannibalistic streak to satire. But Kraus appears to him as the representative of a more real humanism. In contrast to classical humanism and its apotheosis of creativity, the destructive aspect of nature is the vital element of "real humanism," as represented besides Scheerbart and Kraus's friend Adolf Loos by Karl Marx.[132] In Klee's *Angelus Novus*, an image that advanced in the Kraus essay not for the first and not for the last time to the position of one of Benjamin's thought figures (*Denkfiguren*),[133] the *Unmensch* "as the messenger of a more real humanism"[134] has been given one of his multifarious embodiments. The message of the New Angel says "that the developing man actually takes form not within the natural sphere but in the sphere of mankind, in the struggle for liberation," and that, consequently, "there is no idealistic but only a materialistic deliverance from myth."[135] A paralipomenon explains this by stating that humaneness "must be abandoned on the level of individual existence so that it can come forth at the level of collective existence."[136] Benjamin touches on the connection between destructiveness and technology, his central issue, when he remarks in the essay that "the average European has not succeeded in uniting his life with technology, because he has clung to the fetish of creative existence."[137]

When seen against this background, the essay paints a portrait of Kraus that contains features of demonic ambiguity. The "strange interplay between reactionary theory and revolutionary practice that we find everywhere in Kraus"[138] is established as early as in the first section, *Allmensch*. This is made apparent through the journalistic commitment of the editor and sole author of *The Torch*, because Kraus does not, finally, succeed in extricating himself from his entanglement with newspapers. Kraus's fight against the empty phrases of media jargon, against a language distorted by the press, is both "the expression of and the struggle against" this entanglement.[139] By contrast, Benjamin recognizes in the empty phrase the combination of language and technology, and in journalism he sees the "expression of the changed function of language in the world of high capitalism."[140] Because of his insufficient understanding of this situation, which is determined not least by technology, Kraus's polemical formulas, which he uses in *The Torch* to wage his campaign against the press, "are the kind that tie up, never the kind that untie."[141] A different formulation of this passage clarifies what Benjamin means by a successful "untying" of the empty phrase: "its transformation into watchwords."[142]

Even more than the Kraus essay, his essay on Paul Valéry (1871–1945) requires the reader to read between the lines. In a letter of 1925, Benjamin had directed Scholem's attention to "the splendid writings" of Valéry and had contrasted them to "the dubious books of the Surrealists."[143] The essay, published in *Literarische Welt* on the occasion of Valéry's sixtieth birthday in 1931, is a testimony, if nothing else, to the continuing validity of Benjamin's early high esteem. Its significance is indicated even more strongly, however, by the Valéry quote that he used as the motto for the third version of his theses in "The Work of Art in the Age of Its Technological Reproducibility."[144] In Valéry's alter ego, Monsieur Teste, Benjamin discovered another harbinger of the inevitable "reign of the dehumanized"[145] in the present age. As the personification of pure intellect, he is a figure not only of that inquisitorial reflection on his productivity that Valéry demanded of the writer, but even more so of his renunciation of the idea of creativity, the concomitant of this demand. The artwork is not to be understood as creation but as construction, because in the realm of pure spirit, art and science form a continuum.

These convictions, which Valéry gained from studying the method of his beloved Leonardo da Vinci, led him to the conception of *poésie pure.* This methodically reflected and, as it were, Constructivist manner of proceeding that Valéry demanded of the lyric poet, the basically technological attitude toward his work, Benjamin claims, he put to good use at least in a preparatory way to arrive at an understanding of technology in the word's narrower sense. Not in the essay of 1931, but in the extensive study he wrote three years later for *Zeitschrift für Sozialforschung* (Journal for Social Research), "The Present Social Situation of the French Writer,"[146] did Benjamin point out the limits Valéry had imposed on this idea. He states that Valéry had "failed to extend the idea of planning from the realm of art to the sphere of the human community. That threshold he did not cross; the intellectual remains a private person."[147]

Among contemporary writers it is Bertolt Brecht who, in both his work and self-understanding, has crossed this threshold in an exemplary way. To be sure, a piece on Brecht is not mentioned in the contract for a collection of his essays Benjamin had signed with Rowohlt. But he did bring together the most important motifs he discussed in the essays intended for this volume in the various studies—some short, some longer—he wrote on Brecht's work between 1930 and 1939. In Brecht's character of Herr Keuner, for example, Benjamin recognized—in a radio lecture on Brecht broadcast in 1930—a distant relative of Valéry's Monsieur Teste,[148] who reflects Brecht's conception of art in his own particular way. As had Valéry, so also Brecht had broken with the fetish of the artwork. Brecht's programmatic *Versuche* (Attempts), appearing between 1930 and 1933, reveal, according to Benjamin, a technological understanding of his activity that extends also to the technological means of his production—"the theater, the anecdote, the radio"[149]—and that includes their transformation.

As the quintessence of Brecht's intended transformations, the epic theater has risen "to the level of technology." Its forms "correspond to the new technological forms, those of film and radio."[150] Through its "literarization of the theater," meaning its interspersing of "material being given shape" with "material already formulated,"[151] that is, through the use of billboards and intertitles on the stage, the epic theater establishes a connection with other institutions of intellectual activity such as the book and the newspaper, thereby promoting the "literarization of the circumstances of life" and hence a comprehensive politicization of society. By questioning the conventional character of the theater as entertainment, the epic theater invalidates traditional aesthetic standards and at the same time threatens the privileged position of professional critics. Inasmuch as the effect evoked by the theater is no longer based on empathy, which is aimed at the individual spectator, but considers it the task of a performance "to organize a mass of listeners," criticism "in its present forms no longer has an advantage over this mass but lags far behind it."[152]

These observations do not, however, prevent Benjamin from assigning the epic theater a place in literary history. In turning away from dramatic theater, which develops its plot successively in a sequence of scenes, the epic theater is based on the retardatory principle of interruption. Because of its representation of familiar episodes or "circumstances" and because of its "untragic hero," Benjamin sees the political-didactic theater of Brecht in proximity to the mystery play and to Baroque *Trauerspiel*. In these forms of drama, as in Brecht's epic theater, not the action of the plot but the representation of creaturely suffering occupies the center of the untragic stage events.[153] Both types of plays are driven by a didactic (in the case of the Baroque drama by a theological-didactic) intent. The situation that the epic theater lays open in this manner is what Benjamin refers to as "dialectics at a standstill."[154] Snatched from the movement of the plot as well as from the course of time, the state of affairs so displayed presents itself, like a flash of lightning, to astonishment: "Dialectics at a standstill is its true subject matter."[155] With these ideas Benjamin revolves around a set of issues that he will try to utilize also for his theory of historical cognition.

I suddenly robbed of the very basis of my existence as an independent re-searcher and writer. I also—though a dissident and not a member of any political party—was no longer sure of my personal liberty."[4]

In his letter to the Danish Aid Committee for Refugees from Abroad, Benjamin pointed out that, while he had no ties to a political party, his political commitment was the principal reason for his flight. He made no special mention of the fact that as a Jew in Germany his existence was en-dangered. But he had mentioned as early as 1932 in a letter to Scholem that the boycott of his writings had been motivated by anti-Semitism.[5]

The works he wrote during the first years of his exile in France are a direct reflection of his extremely precarious economic situation, but they also indicate that he was trying to account intellectually for the new politi-cal realities. During the entire time of his exile, the Frankfurt Institute for Social Research—with Max Horkheimer as its director since 1930—proved to be Benjamin's only halfway dependable source of income. Even before 1933, Horkheimer had established branch offices in Geneva, later in Paris and London. In this way he had not only seen to the Institute's continued existence but had also made sure that its *Zeitschrift für Sozialforschung*, which he had been editing since the fall of 1932, would be published. It is this periodical that, since the beginning of Benjamin's exile, printed, with few exceptions, all of his more important works. Since he depended on fi-nancial support from the *Zeitschrift*, he repeatedly found himself obligated to coordinate his plans for work with the ideas of the Institute and occasion-ally to carry out work on commission. The journal that published his essays had declared its task to be twofold: to work out "a theory of contemporary society as a whole" and thus to formulate "a theory of the historical course of the present epoch."[6] This offered Benjamin sufficient opportunities to pursue his own theoretical approaches within an established framework.

The first study he wrote for *Zeitschrift für Sozialforschung*, an exten-sive essay on "the sociology of French literature,"[7] he had agreed on with Horkheimer while he was still in Germany. It was written under the most difficult circumstances on Ibiza, where he had almost no recourse to pri-mary source material. Although he referred to the result of this effort, the essay "The Present Social Situation of the French Writer" (1934)[8] as "sheer fakery,"[9] he credits it with providing insight into connections "that until now have not been brought out so clearly."[10] However directly subject to the circumstances of its origin, the essay offered Benjamin an opportunity to revise the theoretical positions he had developed in his earlier critical essays on literature. In the spotlight of the political development that drove him into exile, his debates with Surrealism, with Green, Proust, and Valéry were now assuming sharper contours. In the essay of 1934, Benjamin excerpted longer passages from his earlier essays and integrated them into the new context so that the respective sections would now comment on one another.

It is not only against this background that Benjamin's irritated reaction to Scholem's provocative question—whether his essay is meant as a "Communist credo"— becomes understandable. In his answer Benjamin insisted that the essay contains nothing substantially new and that his political stance had not changed. He was astonished, however, about the insinuation that his Communism could find an appropriate expression in the form of a credo, insisting that his writings have always conformed to his convictions and that he has "only seldom made the attempt—and then only in conversation—to express the whole contradictory grounds from which those convictions arise in the individual manifestations they have taken." Referring to his earlier letter to Max Rychner, he justified his Communist sympathies as "absolutely nothing other than the expression of certain experiences I have undergone in my thinking and in my life."[11]

As the starting point for this survey of contemporary French literature, Benjamin selected Guillaume Apollinaire's (1880–1918) gloomy vision in his *Le Poète assassiné* (The Assassinated Poet, 1914) of a "pogrom against poets,"[12] which seems to have lost nothing of its topical relevance. As in the essay on Surrealism, Benjamin sees Apollinaire's book as raising the question of what function the bourgeois intelligentsia is prepared to assume—by now in "the social climate of imperialism."[13] What is at issue here for Benjamin is already indicated by the fact that his essay's title speaks of the "writer" (*Schriftsteller*) and not of the "poet" (*Dichter*). The social position of an author was revealed immediately by the terminological alternative that offered itself to him when he tried to explain his self-understanding. This alternative, Benjamin is convinced, has now become irrelevant. The stages in the development that this insight fixates lead from Futurism through Dadaism to Surrealism, which has already taken the work of art beyond the threshold of poetry.

It is against this background that Benjamin accuses Julien Green not only of having succumbed in his novel *Épaves* (1932; lit., flotsam, trans. *The Strange River*, 1932) to social conformism, but also of being old-fashioned in questions of novelistic technique.[14] It comes as a surprise that Proust serves as the opposite example. In going back to his earlier essay, Benjamin emphasizes more than the social-critical dimension of the *Recherche*. The fact, previously mentioned rather descriptively, that Proust's work "combines poetry, memoir, and commentary,"[15] defines him now as a writer who by fusing literary forms has also expanded the possibilities of his craft beyond its traditional boundaries. When seen from this aspect—Benjamin calls it the "technical dimension"—Proust joins Valéry who "has reflected on the nature of technique in writing like no one else."[16]

As Proust made the activity of the writer perceptible throughout his novel by making himself available to the reader at any time with comments and justifications, so Valéry has admired Leonardo because as an artist he nowhere in his work renounced "his claim to give the most precise account possible of his activity and his methods."[17] But even though Valéry's technical-Constructivist conception of poetry marks the most advanced position, he is nonetheless incapable of transgressing the aesthetic boundaries his theory of *poésie pure* has set for him, as Benjamin's crucial objection (briefly mentioned before) has it.

This step, inherent in the concept of authorship, not only toward a self-reflection of literary technique but also toward a social and political commitment has been taken, aside from Aragon and Emmanuel Berl (whom Benjamin's essay quotes extensively and with approval), by André Gide. But even as a traitor to his own class, the bourgeois intellectual does not automatically represent the interests of the proletariat. As he had done previously in his Surrealism essay, Benjamin denounces anarchism, terrorism, and nihilism as failed attempts by bourgeois intellectuals to connect with the proletarian masses. The rhetorical question he had raised earlier, that is, whether the conditions of revolution are to be located in the changing of attitudes or of external circumstances[18] aim at making the writer aware of his social function, with which the control over certain means of production is connected. The Surrealists, he writes, "found a place for the intellectual as technologist." Now it is necessary that he put his technology at the disposal of the proletariat, because it alone "depends on technology at its most advanced" level.[19] The concept of literary technique (*Technik*) that is connected with this idea will be the focal point of Benjamin's address "The Author as Producer." The position of this technique vis-à-vis the new technological media of photography, radio, and above all, film will also take up a function of art he had mentioned in passing in "The Present Social Situation of the French Writer" (1934): the possibility of using art as "a key to the psychoses"[20] that originate not the least in the threat to workaday life posed by technology.

Part of Benjamin's attempts to secure a foothold as an exile in France was his plan for a series of lectures about the "*avantgarde allemande,*" which he conceived as a counterpart to the essay that had appeared in *Zeitschrift für Sozialforschung.* The cycle, in which Benjamin intended to deal with the novel, the essay, theater, and journalism, using Kafka, Bloch, Brecht, and Kraus as his examples,[21] was to be financed by subscription. Even though this venture did not materialize, certain aspects of it are of interest beyond the issues it promised to discuss. The lectures were to take place in the private residence of the physician Jean Dalsace, who was close to the Communist Party of France and entertained connections to the Institut pour l'étude du fascisme. The makeup of its collaborators, which included German emigrants as well as members of France's liberal bourgeoisie and Communists, anticipated first steps toward the formation of a popular front, which the internal political controversies in France had placed on the national agenda.[22] According to a note on the manuscript—it is extant among Benjamin's papers—he delivered his address "The Author as Producer" before the members of this institute on April 27, 1934. The desire to make this text accessible to a larger public by having it published in its original format in the exile periodical *Die Sammlung*, edited by Klaus Mann, remained unfulfilled. It was not printed during Benjamin's lifetime. In letters to Adorno[23] and Brecht[24] he referred to it as a companion piece to his old work on epic theater, in which he also "comments on current questions of literary politics."[25]

More even than in the case of the essay on contemporary French literature, the title of this address is to be understood as expressing a program. And as that essay did, so the address makes use of sections from earlier works. In this way it demonstrates the continuity of central themes and at the same time subjects them to the demand for a constant reexamination of one's own position,[26] which is what Benjamin expects of the contemporary writer. The author as a producer is being seen as the owner of specific means of production. In this manner, Benjamin believes, he is able to bypass that unproductive alternative according to which the "quality" of a work, as guaranteed by its autonomy, is usually to be seen as incompatible with a "tendency." Instead, he would like to prove "that the tendency of a literary work can be politically correct if it is also literarily correct."[27] This literary tendency, however, "can consist either in the progress or in a regression of literary technique."[28]

But this is not to be understood inevitably as the demand to give up the art of poetic literature in favor of an activity committed to practical work the way Sergei Tretyakov (1892–1936) had done as "an operative writer" under the conditions of Soviet Russia. This example shows, however, that "we have to rethink our conceptions of literary forms or genres in view of the technical factors affecting our present situation."[29] Benjamin first mentions the newspaper as a paradigmatic instance and then points to photography as part of illustrated reportage and, with emphasis on Brecht, to radio and film as examples of the new media that demonstrate that literary forms are historical forms of expression and as such subject to transformation. There have not always been novels, not always tragedies. In the "mighty recasting of literary forms"[30] that Benjamin observes, even those forms that testify to the continued life of the works of art—the commentary and the translation—have their place.

The productive confrontation with the technological media, but also within their own framework, opens up the opportunity to imbue the traditional literary forms and means of expression, once they have been blasted out of their old contexts, with a new purpose. The newspaper, for example, in which Kraus had been unable to see anything but the arena of literary confusion, to Benjamin proves to be the place where "the literarization of the conditions of living"[31] is being set in motion in prototypical fashion. In the newspaper, the disappearance of conventional distinctions between the genres also does away with the distinction between the writer (Schriftsteller) and the poet. And beyond that, the introduction of letters to the editor columns has helped to suspend even the separation of author and reader. That this observation is marked, with respect both to the bourgeois press and to the broadcasting networks of Benjamin's own time, by limitations that are imposed by circumstances of private ownership, only confirms its political timeliness.

In essence, in quoting his earlier material, Benjamin's address follows Brecht, whose epic theater is introduced as the model of how to use literary technique in an up-to-date manner. Besides the "organizing function,"[32] for which Benjamin credits the particular stylistic character of Brecht's theater, there is a complementary idea that he will pick up again in the film theory of the "Work of Art" theses. The technique of montage, Benjamin says, on the one hand advances through alienation the reasoned insight into the unreasonableness of the existing circumstances; on the other, through its interruption of the "action" (Handlung), this technique knows all about habitual reaction,[33] taking its cue from the existential experiences of people who, in a workaday world dominated by technology, are permanently subjected to tests and evaluations.

What Benjamin focuses on in these two works that are concerned with topical issues of literary politics he will later describe in an expanded theoretical context as the "changing function of art"[34] that must be grasped in its historical importance. A decisive step in this direction is the extensive essay, commissioned by Zeitschrift für Sozialforschung, about the Social Democratic cultural historian Eduard Fuchs (1870–1940).

In a letter to Benjamin of January 28, 1935, Horkheimer had written that it "has for a very long time been a personal wish of ours to see a good report on Fuchs in the *Zeitschrift*."[35] Fuchs lived, as did Benjamin, in exile in Paris until his death in 1940. As the trustee of his friend Felix Weil's fortune, Fuchs played a very significant, behind-the-scenes role in establishing the Institute, with which he continued to maintain a close association.[36] Benjamin made no secret of his aversion to this task, which he postponed again and again. Even though Benjamin had agreed to the request in May 1934, his text, titled "Eduard Fuchs, Collector and Historian," did not appear until the fall of 1937, after a delay of more than three years. Other interests, which delayed completion, proved in the end to be extremely fruitful for its conception.

In May 1935, Benjamin interrupted work on the essay in favor of an exposé of the *Arcades Project*, for which he had been able to secure the initially rather noncommittal interest of the Institute. His intention of writing a study about the Parisian arcades originated as far back as 1927, when he was in the French capital working on his Proust translation. Under completely diverging premises he returned to this plan in the fall of 1934, while he lived in Paris in exile. Closely connected with this project, which was to occupy him until his death, are the "Work of Art" theses, which he wrote down in October 1935. In a letter he outlined the epistemological context that ties these two studies together. Knowledge of the situation of today's art, which is his concern in the theses, is predicated on an understanding of the fate of art in the nineteenth century. With this insight he claims to have realized the epistemological theory of the *Arcades Project*, "which has crystallized around the very esoterically applied concept of the 'now of recognizability,' . . . in a very esoteric fashion, . . . using a decisive example."[37]

When seen against this background, "the feeling of contempt"[38] Benjamin increasingly was trying to suppress while he was occupied with Fuchs's writings, proved to be a highly productive affect. It allowed him to use his inevitably critical discussion of Fuchs's method as an opportunity for deriving from his oppositional discussion "positive formulations concerning historical materialism."[39] The fundamental significance of these critical comments is to be gauged not the least from the fact that he made use of them again both in the *Arcades Project* and in "On the Concept of History."

In the essay itself, Benjamin's ambivalent attitude toward his subject is expressed by the duality he posits between the collector and the historian, which he sees as defining Fuchs's intellectual physiognomy. The relationship of these two aspects to one another is prefigured in Benjamin's title, that is, in a formulation that suggests that the collections of the cultural historian are "the practical man's answer to the aporias of theory."[40]

The challenge to which Benjamin responds in his essay in accordance with this maxim consists of the difficulty involved in taking "account of the recent past,"[41] in which Fuchs participated both subjectively and objectively as a materialist historian of art and as an active socialist who was close to the German Social Democratic Party. After a rather extensive quotation from a letter by Friedrich Engels to Franz Mehring of July 14, 1893, Benjamin comes to the conclusion that the history of art is not an autonomous area of history. This insight, he is convinced, constitutes the guiding principle for any materialist conception of history. The frequently quoted aphoristic comment that Benjamin makes in this context and repeats verbatim in "The Concept of History" that "there is no document of culture which is not at the same time a document of barbarism,"[42] is, however, a variation on an insight of Nietzsche.

For Nietzsche there is no doubt "that slavery belongs to the essence of culture" and that "cruelty [is] at the heart of every culture."[43] If this conviction is "the source of that hatred which has been nourished by the Communists and Socialists as well as their paler descendants, the white race of 'Liberals' of every age, against the arts, but also against classical antiquity,"[44] then for Nietzsche this aversion testifies all the more in favor of art as a stimulant of life and forever against the enemies of art who raise their voices in the name of justice, equality, and compassion. Benjamin's pointing out that culture and barbarism belong together is not simply concerned, however, with the opposite evaluation of the same insight. Rather, he carries out a "revaluation" that is fully in accord with Nietzsche's genealogical approach to history. The place that the concept of life or of power had occupied for Nietzsche, Benjamin gives to the concept of politics. Benjamin was convinced that only "genuine—that is to say, political—experience"[45] is capable of demolishing the fetishistic conception of culture that has attached itself both to its products and to the process of its transmission. In this sense he declares it to be the task of a materialistic historiography "to brush history against the grain."[46] In the Fuchs essay he buttresses his critique of the concept of cultural history in a footnote with a quote from Marx. But its more detailed explication in the text is given by his resorting to the concept of origin in *Origin of German Tragic Drama*[47] and to the idea, likewise developed in earlier writings, of the continued life of artworks.

The Fuchs essay honed the idea that a work of art can be grasped adequately only in the context of its prehistory and afterlife by urging that one "become conscious of the critical constellation in which precisely this fragment of the past finds itself with precisely this present."[48] As a consequence of thus directing the conception of history toward the present, the "now of recognizability," history is no longer thought of as a process. The place of its narrative, or "epic," representation, predominant in conventional descriptions, has been taken over by a dialectical presentation of history that contains a concurrently destructive and constructive element: Any particular epoch is being blasted "out of its reified 'historical continuity' "[49] and placed in a relationship with the present. This conception of history has no place for the category of progress, as does the view of the historian Fuchs, whose faith in technological progress, whose notion of "cultural heritage," and whose deterministic perception of the course of history as inevitably carrying along the victory of the proletariat, show him to be deeply rooted in the nineteenth century.

To Benjamin's mind, these convictions had been discredited even before the victory of Fascism forced him into exile. Rather, he discovered in the figure of the passionate collector Eduard Fuchs certain leanings toward a materialistic theory of art and history that, together with the collector's interest in the material aspect of art, show up the flaws in the historian's theoretical insights. Hence, for example, Fuchs the cultural historian developed en passant, as it were, a theory of orgies that refutes his own apotheosis of creativity; and hence, at the intersection of his historical, social, and cultural interests, it is fashion with its own particular way of measuring time that becomes the subject of his writings. Toward the end of his essay, Benjamin praises Fuchs the collector's preoccupation with Daumier, whose works he had been one of the first to collect, as a pioneering deed. By perceiving caricature as a mass art—according to Benjamin—Fuchs was led "necessarily to the question of the technological reproduction of the work of art"[50]—and thus to a thematic complex that he himself was investigating in "The Work of Art in the Age of Its Technological Reproducibility."

One more text, which has been rather neglected by Benjamin scholarship, is part of the theoretical context in which he connects the idea of the changing function of art with the conception of history as relating to the present. Even as he was working on the final corrections of the Fuchs essay, he reported to Horkheimer the discovery of a treatise that "he had read with great excitement."[51] It was an essay titled "The Regressions of Poetry" and first printed in 1828, by Carl Gustav Jochmann (1790–1830), a writer placed between the Enlightenment and Romanticism and forgotten by literary historiography. Excerpts from this text selected by Benjamin together with his introduction were published in Zeitschrift für Sozialforschung in 1939–1940. Jochmann, as Benjamin explained in his introduction, was one of the literary men who vouch for that tradition of revolutionary-democratic thinking in the German bourgeoisie, for whom Paris, according to Nietzsche, was the capital of the "good Europeans." This is the tradition, interrupted only by "the establishment of the Prussian Reich,"[52] to which Benjamin refers also in his collection of letters titled *Deutsche Menschen. Eine Folge von Briefen* (1936; German Men and Women. A Sequence of Letters), a short anthology on which he had started working in 1931. Benjamin himself claimed that he had come across Jochmann's essay during the preparatory work on this collection. After the publication of the text, however, he became involved in a controversy with the poet and essayist Werner Kraft (1896–1991) about who had first made this discovery. It is a dispute in which Benjamin did not cut a good figure.[53]

The reasons Benjamin gave for his proposal to have this text published in *Zeitschrift für Sozialforschung* make it clear that he considered it a further model case of a concept of history whose point of reference is the present. His formulation that this text "has today become untraceable and had yesterday been incomprehensible"[54] places it in very close proximity to the "Work of Art" theses which he had announced in a similar locution, seeing the earlier text connected with them through the "motif of the decay of art's aura."[55] Jochmann's reflections "on the historical boundaries that humaneness could impose upon art"[56] speak to the function of art from a secular perspective, a view that Benjamin had likewise advanced in his theses. The contemporary relevance of Plato's conviction that poetry is "harmful, superfluous—in a *perfect* community"[57] is a point he had already made in his address "The Author as Producer." The Soviet state, Benjamin had said, will not banish the poet as Plato's republic would, but it will assign him other tasks than "to display in new masterpieces the long-since-counterfeit wealth of a creative personality." This function has, rather, become "a privilege of Fascism."[58] By contrast, Jochmann had come to the point of affirming the Platonic "edict of banishment." But Jochmann does remain undecided, according to Benjamin, how the reader might imagine a more creative employment of the imagination that has been liberated so that it can be used more productively. Jochmann seems to offer the vision both of "a more humane form of political economy" and of "a rebirth of the 'poetic spirit.' "[59]

Benjamin's introduction seeks to illustrate the contemporary relevance of Jochmann's speculations by highlighting the specific view of history to which his insights are beholden. Jochmann's thinking is the opposite of that of the Romantics because for him the past is not a fetish that needs to be preserved for the present through empathy and imitation. On the contrary, its present relevance is evident only to a persuasion that makes "human beings more keenly aware of their own history and capable of learning things from it."[60] And this is what the introduction praises Jochmann's text for, both in terms of its subject matter and in its theoretical premises. Following the lead of the formula from his *Drama* book about "the consciousness of the problematic of art," Benjamin places the essay in a tradition that in the more recent past had been represented by the architect and cultural critic Adolf Loos (1870–1933) and his fight against ornament (*Ornament und Verbrechen*, 1908; trans., *Ornament and Crime: Selected Essays*, 1998). In the most recent past, however, it is Benjamin himself with "his attempts to formulate a materialistic theory of art" in his study about "The Work of Art in the Age of Its Technological Reproducibility,"[61] who speaks on behalf of this tradition.

Benjamin's early work is present in this outline in yet another way. In a variant,[62] his text points to Erich Unger's treatise *Gegen die Dichtung* (Against Poetry), which had captured his interest as early as 1925, the year of its publication. Unger was convinced of the reality of myth and believed in the archaic power of the imagination, whose force could will the existence of the god, and in which Nietzsche is as strong a presence as are the speculations of Unger's mentor Oskar Goldberg. These ideas had served Benjamin as critical points of reference in his cogitations on the concept of the political, which go back to the early 1920s. Unger saw the reality of myth as a precondition for a program he hoped to see realized as a theocratically constituted Jewish state. In other words: like Jochmann, Unger had the political use of the imagination in mind. And, as it were, his ideas proved to be timely. In his introduction to Jochmann's "Regressions," Benjamin sees Unger's study as defining the stridency of the contemporary debate about the value of everything aesthetic, which the totalitarian regimes claim as their own "in order to sanction even their bloodiest accomplishments."[63]

## 2. The Work of Art in the Age of Its Technological Reproducibility

The study to which Benjamin called attention in October 1935 in letters to Gretel Adorno and Max Horkheimer in similar locutions that emphasize its importance has for a long time been perceived if not as his most significant, then as his most controversial, piece of writing. He himself saw it as a decisive advance "in the direction of a materialistic theory of art," basing his claim above all on its paradigmatic character as a philosophy of history. Its issue, he wrote to Horkheimer, was to locate the precise place in the present to which his construction of history in the work on the Parisian arcades will refer as to its vanishing point:

> If the pretext for the book is the fate of art in the nineteenth century, this fate has something to say to us only because it is contained in the ticking of a clock whose striking of the hour has just reached *our* ears. What I mean by that is that art's fateful hour has struck for us and I have captured its signature in a series of preliminary reflections titled "The Work of Art in the Age of Its Technological Reproducibility."[64]

Nowhere did Benjamin mention in the letters that film would be at the center of these reflections. In the exposé of the *Arcades Project* he had hinted only vaguely that the panoramas, popular in the nineteenth century, had, beyond photography, anticipated film and sound film.[65] In accordance with the theses, however, he notes in the *Arcades*[66] "that all problems of contemporary art find their definitive formulation only in the context of film."[67]

It makes good sense nonetheless that Benjamin's theses are first concerned with the technological reproducibility of the work of art and in this context begin with photography and then go on to film. As *One-Way Street* proves with its aphorisms on book printing and newspapers, Benjamin had noticed connections relating to the theory of media in earlier years. Moreover, it is not unimportant that his first documented interest in photography grew out of a Surrealist context: in 1924 he had translated a short text by Tristan Tzara about Man Ray's technique of photographing without a camera, the so-called "Rayography."[68] In the essay on Surrealism itself he acknowledged the role of photography in Breton's *Nadja*[69] as a medium to provide profane illumination of the quotidian. Beyond that, he had gratefully accepted the observation of a friend from the days of his youth, Alfred Cohn (1892–1954), with whom he kept in touch by mail even after the latter's emigration to Spain. Cohn had recognized the continuity of this new work, which appeared in print in 1936, with his friend's earlier studies "in spite of its new, and surely often surprising, tendency."[70]

This continuity, which Benjamin above all saw "grounded in the fact that, over the years, [he] had tried to achieve an increasingly precise and uncompromising idea of what constitutes a work of art,"[71] goes beyond the description of the aura as contained in the formula, taken from the essay on *Elective Affinities*, about "the object *in* its veil."[72] Rather, this continuity also includes his attempt—a foray at times into the area of art history—to comprehend the essence of the artwork within the frame of a theory of perception, as he had done in the *Drama* book in connection with Riegl's conception of *Kunstwollen*. In thesis 4, Benjamin explicitly insists that his work is a critical continuation of preliminary work done by the Viennese School, Riegl and Wickhoff, who, as he put it in a later formulation, "have examined the historical variables of human perception."[73] In this way he regains for aesthetics a horizon that had been lost by the fixation of eighteenth- and nineteenth-century philosophy of art on the Classical-Romantic canon. He has this context in mind when in the penultimate thesis he demands that one recognize film as "the most important subject matter, at present, for the theory of perception," which, in accordance with the word's original meaning, "the Greeks called aesthetics."[74]

Thematically, the theses directly continue the account of "The Little History of Photography" (1931), which had appeared in three installments in *Die Literarische Welt*. What connects these two works in terms of theory, furthermore, is the variously controversial concept of aura and the thesis of its decay as the decisive event in the development of nineteenth-century art. Given the central significance of this thesis for both works, it is at first sight far from obvious what, in view of so much undeniable continuity, constitutes the new and surprising tendency of the more recent work, to which Benjamin attaches such great importance. Even so, it is possible to identify the seam where the theses pick up the reflections of the "Little History of Photography" and develop them further.

Just as Benjamin believes that he can prognosticate the future development of art only against the background of its position vis-à-vis the conditions of production, so he sees the history of photography substantially determined by its industrialization. The contemporary "convulsion of capitalist industry," he writes, makes us look back "to the pre-industrial heyday of photography," thereby providing an opportunity for grasping its essence. As a consequence of this historical construction, the commercial utilization of photography turns out to be a temporary phenomenon. If in the course of industrialization other possibilities that are an inherent part of technology have remained unutilized, then they are now as a consequence of the present crisis of capitalism "beginning to enter into consciousness."[75] This insight is obscured, however, by the debate about "photography-as-art," which accompanied its early phase and has even today lost nothing of its presumed relevance. Of very much greater relevance than the aesthetic debate, however, he considers the social fact of "art-as-photography," that is, the question of "the impact of the photographic reproduction of artworks . . . for the function of art."[76] Photography as a reproductive technology, he says, makes it possible to perceive a painting, a sculpture, or a building more easily and differently than in reality, "mechanical reproduction [being] a technique of diminution that helps people to achieve control over works of art."[77]

In Benjamin's understanding, photography is, to begin with, a technique. This makes the aesthetic debate misleading not only because it does not recognize this fact but because in the name of creativity it also advocates a philistine conception of art that is "a stranger to all technical considerations."[78] With this, the "Little History of Photography" makes use of a decisive idea from Benjamin's writings on literary theory. In the case of photography, the relevance of the new technology becomes apparent when it is applied to the observation of nature. Photography, in other words, is an instrument of perception. But in the border region of magic and technology, the early photographs (*Lichtbilder*, light pictures) testify to the fact that "it is another nature which speaks to the camera than that which speaks to the eye." In photography "a space informed by human consciousness gives way to a space informed by the unconscious." And it "is through photography that we first discover the existence of this optical unconscious, just as we discover the instinctual unconscious through psychoanalysis."[79] A person's way of walking, for example, his posture at the fraction of a second as he takes a step, becomes known to him only through the technological devices of photography.

As such an exploration of the optical unconscious with the aid of a camera, Benjamin also praises the plant photographs of Karl Bloßfeldt (1865–1932), whose *Urformen der Kunst* (1928; trans., *Art Forms in Nature*, 1929) he had reviewed enthusiastically as early as 1928. In his preface to this volume, the editor and gallery owner Karl Nierendorf had emphasized that it is technology "that nowadays makes our relationship with nature more intimate than ever and with the help of its devices allows us insights into worlds that had heretofore been closed to our senses."[80] This is the idea Benjamin took over. According to his review, it is to Bloßfeldt's credit that he contributed more than his share to "that great stock-taking of the inventory of human perception that will alter our image of the world in as yet unforeseen ways."[81]

If, therefore, it is a specific form of perception that is being expressed in the early photographs, then this form is substantially defined by the interplay of the new technology with its object. The concept of the aura is Benjamin's attempt to pinpoint the particular nature of this interplay. The famous formula, repeated verbatim in the "Work of Art" theses: "A strange weave of space and time: the unique appearance or semblance of distance, no matter how close it may be,"[82] describes the aura by implicitly following

Kant's analysis of sensual perception in his transcendental aesthetics. As a space-time phenomenon, the aspect of uniqueness in early photography was due not least to technological reasons. The as yet underdeveloped technology of the camera that necessitated an elaborate procedure before a picture could be taken had its concomitant aspect in a distancing "shyness before the camera"[83] on the part of the person to be pictured. Moreover, the low photosensitivity of the lenses with their extremely long exposure time required of the model to hold still patiently. In Benjamin's words, "everything about these early pictures was built to last."[84] That is to say, the early photographs were not only products of a time-consuming and distance-creating procedure. They were also documents confirming the claim to durability of the person captured in the picture. Each photograph existed in one copy only and was preserved as part of a family's possessions.

It would nonetheless be a mistake, Benjamin emphasizes, to see the aura merely as the product of a primitive camera. "Rather, in this early period subject and technique were as exactly congruent as they became incongruent in the period of the decline that immediately followed."[85] In the second half of the nineteenth century, high-speed lenses made the auratic photograph technologically obsolete. If processes are now being developed for the purpose of artificially creating the aura on the photos, then Benjamin sees this as betraying "the impotence of that generation in the face of technical progress."[86] In the age of imperialism, the bourgeoisie had lost confidence in technology to which, as to a promising encounter of man and technology, the aura of the early photographs had borne witness.

In the history of photography it is Eugène Atget (1857–1927) who for Benjamin marks a new stage. His photos of Paris, taken between 1898 and 1927, he considered "forerunners of Surrealist photography,"[87] which the Surrealists themselves had been among the first to recognize. In June 1926, three photos by Atget were for the first time printed publicly in the seventh issue of *Révolution surréaliste.* Atget, insisting that his pictures are documents and nothing else ("c'est du document et rien d'autre"), had given the photographer Man Ray (1890–1976), who had discovered him, permission to print them only on the condition that he would remain anonymous. Atget's 1912 photo of people observing an eclipse of the sun (*Avant l'éclipse, place de la Bastille*) appeared on the cover of the periodical and was subtitled "Les dernières conversions." Without any kind of commentary and as part of a regular column where the journal printed dreams, there followed the photo of a display window with corsets (*Corsets, Boulevard de Strasbourg, 10e arr., 1921*). Finally, the last pages included a photo titled "Versailles," on which a young woman is pictured before a row of houses. Atget had indeed taken this photo in Versailles; but it shows what the caption in the *Révolution surréaliste* does not mention, a brothel (*Maison close, Versailles, 1926*).

To Benjamin's way of thinking Atget deserves special credit for having liberated the object from the aura, thereby having raised the question of a genuinely contemporary function of photography. This notion the Surrealists put to the test in their own way of placing photos, in the style of a montage, into a strange context. According to Benjamin, Atget's photos document a change in perspective whose dominance has become all-pervasive at the present time. In its space-time structure, this perception is the opposite of the auratic perception. The place of the magic of distance has been taken over by the closest proximity, that of uniqueness and duration by transience and reproducibility.

> The peeling of the object's shell, the destruction of the aura, is the signature of a perception whose sense for the sameness of things has grown to the point where even the singular, the unique, is divested of its uniqueness— by means of its reproduction.[88]

It is obvious that the photographic reproduction of artworks represents one possibility of satisfying a need thus transformed. But even in the early years of photography one had been persuaded to see it as a rival of painting not least because of its unsurpassable capability to make good on the latter's claim of representing reality. When contemporary photography keeps this task in mind, then, Benjamin insists, it is necessary to grasp "the lessons inherent in the authenticity of the photograph."[89] The magic emanating from the early photographs is due also to the fact that the visual space opened by photography had been entered into with one's "innocence intact—or rather, without inscription."[90] It is only with the help of captions, he says, that photography can fulfill its modern—and for Benjamin that means its political and social—task. Where photographs in the Surrealistic montage do not go beyond the boundaries imposed by scandal, Benjamin would like to introduce them into the field of politics. Smaller and smaller cameras make it possible

> to capture fleeting and secret images whose shock effect paralyzes the associative mechanisms of the beholder. This is where inscription has to come into play, which includes the photography of the literarization of all circumstances of life and without which all photographic construction must remain arrested in the approximate.[91]

This idea of contextualizing is one of the starting points for the theses on "The Work of Art in the Age of Its Technological Reproducibility," which Benjamin took one decisive step further in connection with the specific condition of film: "The directives given by captions to those looking at images in illustrated magazines soon become even more precise and commanding in films, where the way each single image is understood seems prescribed by the sequence of all preceding images."[92] The shock effect produced by photography when photos are included in different genres of writing, for example, in an illustrated newspaper, is in Benjamin's understanding being put to propagandistic use. In film this shock effect, for example, what suddenly happens when a button is pushed, is employed to set free a different but no less political way of acting: that of living with these experiences as something quotidian, of getting used to them as part of a daily routine. The images reeling off on the screen, by permanently interrupting the spectator's concurrent associations, force him to capture and neutralize any shock effect thus created through "an increased presence of mind." Benjamin is convinced that film

> is the art form corresponding to the pronounced threat to life in which people live today. It corresponds to profound changes in the apparatus of apperception—changes that are experienced on the scale of private existence by each passerby in big-city traffic, on the scale of world history by each fighter against the present social order.[93]

The modern function that film must fulfill under these circumstances is "to train human beings in the apperceptions and reactions needed to deal with a vast apparatus whose role in their lives is expanding almost daily."[94]

Benjamin had mailed the theses to Horkheimer with the remark that through them he had tried "to give the questions raised by art a truly contemporary form," from the inside, to be sure, "avoiding any *unmediated* reference to politics."[95] This does not preclude that he attributed to his theoretical deliberations an undeniable political relevance. Moreover, he hoped that their publication might even have a political effect. His desire to publish the theses in *Zeitschrift für Sozialforschung* had to be aligned with Horkheimer's strategy to maintain the journal's claim to scholarly objectivity even under the conditions of exile, a strategy that is characterized by the "decision to refrain not only from any even halfway political activity but also from any collective or organized measure taken to provide explanations of the state of affairs in Germany."[96] This policy was adhered to even more stringently after the Institute had moved to the United States in 1934. The decision to which both sides agreed—to publish the text in *Zeitschrift für Sozialforschung* in French—did make the desired reception in France possible, to be sure, but their compromise had depended on Benjamin's accepting certain conditions. It was in Moscow that he hoped to be able to publish his theses without being hampered by concerns of this kind. He did not abandon this plan, which he had mentioned in his letters immediately after the completion of his manuscript,[97] even after the French version had been published, holding on to it with an obstinate, though in the end futile, determination.

Under these circumstances, not only the text itself but also the history of the publication and reception of "The Work of Art in the Age of Its Technological Reproducibility" turned into a political issue. During Benjamin's lifetime the theses were printed only in the French translation prepared by Pierre Klossowski in close cooperation with their author.[98] For reasons of political caution, the first thesis (identified also as "preface" [*Vorwort*] in other versions) and a number of important footnotes were deleted; likewise, all allusions to the contemporary political situation and the term "Communist" were consistently suppressed. The posthumous reception of this work was at first based on a textual version Benjamin had prepared from the printed French translation for its publication in the Soviet Union. The typescript of this version is extant.[99] It shows several distinctive differences from the manuscript preserved among Benjamin's literary estate. The translation into French was based on yet another version, which had for long been considered lost and had been made available for the first time in one of the two supplementary volumes of *Gesammelte Schriften*.[100] This is the version of the theses—expanded in a few important passages not included in the manuscript—that Adorno read. It is being used here as the one that Benjamin had originally wanted to see printed; an overview of all four versions is given in a synopsis prepared by the editors.[101]

In order to illustrate the new quality that film represents for the work of art in the age of its technological reproducibility, Benjamin first recapitulates his theory of the loss of the aura, now extending its relevance to the entire history of art. This turns the aura into a historical phenomenon in two ways: the origin of the aura is tied not only to the uniqueness and authenticity of the artwork but also to a form of transmission that takes the artwork's uniqueness and authenticity into consideration. The magic element of the aura Benjamin now attributes to the originally cultic function of art. Any artwork passed on from the past and of religious origin, as well as any other artwork, no matter how secular it may be, demands an attitude from its recipient that contains traits of cultic veneration. When the artwork lost its uniqueness in the age of mass reproduction due to the possibilities inherent in technology, the artwork emancipated itself from this context of its reception. Benjamin is convinced that as a result "the whole social function of art is revolutionized. Instead of being founded on ritual, it is based on a different practice: politics."[102]

It follows from this idea that the function of art we are aware of today is historically transitory and "may subsequently be seen as incidental."[103] This is basically a reformulation of the theory concerning the continued life of works that Benjamin had developed in his writings on the theory of literature. Already there he had seen the work of art as becoming independent of the domain of pure art through the practice of translation and criticism. The territorial character of art has conclusively been unmasked as a deception by the medial conditions that define the reception of art in the present era. The refusal to accept this insight means for Benjamin implicitly the appropriation of art in the service of ideological-political interests. On the other hand, his demand for defining the function of art in explicitly political terms is congruent with his conception of the political as outlined in the early 1920s, in the context of which technology plays a decisive role. In film as the "art form whose artistic character for the first time is entirely determined by its reproducibility,"[104] these points of view come together as in a focus.

As in the case of photography, so also the conception of film as art in the traditional sense leads to misunderstandings. Instead, the specifically technological character of art reveals itself retrospectively when art is seen from the vantage point of film. While in the service of magic, which Benjamin understands as a first technology still fused with ritual, the art of primeval times fulfilled altogether practical purposes aimed at the domination over nature. This primitive first technology must be distinguished from a second one, which seeks to influence nature by playful means that keep a distance from it. Benjamin sees film especially connected with this second technology.

In his eyes film is an art form that is determined throughout by a technological element, that is, reproducibility. This is true, on the one hand, in regard to the enormous production costs that for commercial reasons alone demand the mass distribution of films. On the other, the essence of film is based on the technical facility of reproduction. Film represents, as it were, the reproduction of reproduction. From shooting in a studio until the final cut it consists of separate parts that in turn are never unique but at any time are reproducible, improvable.

In this way, that is, by technological means, film becomes the faithful copy of a nature that itself is dominated throughout by technology. When

film comes about only through the montage of separate pieces of material
shot in a studio, then this process corresponds to the actor's accomplishment, which Benjamin compares to a test, divided into a multiplicity of individual tasks, in front of the recording equipment. In the role of a proxy, he
himself enacts the process of dealing with the world of the movie audience's
working environment. In accordance with Brecht's demand that an actor
has to show a thing and at the same time himself, Benjamin now applies a
central principle of the epic theater, the element of gesture, to that medium
whose new technical forms this type of theater had pointedly taken up. In a
movie house this display of the technique of film by an actor becomes the
"object of [a] simultaneous collective reception"[105] that gives the masses the
"means of organizing and regulating" themselves.[106]

It is not difficult to recognize in these reflections as well as in his speculations on the genesis of proletarian class consciousness, though these are
relegated to a footnote, the fundamental ideas of Benjamin's early political philosophy, which, with an eye on technology, moved the collective
into the center of political activity. The political reality of the 1930s did
not disprove them. Rather, the movies, dominated as they are by capitalist
interests, in the cult of the star put a form of reception to the test that could
under different social circumstances experience a "political utilization."[107]

But it is not fortuitous that Benjamin centered his theory of film around
the thesis of the aura's decay, thereby placing it into the expanded context
of a theory of perception. He believed that he may use film as the art form of
this era in order to draw conclusions from it about the contemporary "organization of perception,"[108] just as Riegl had reconstructed the then prevailing organization of perception from the relics of the late Roman art industry.
Where Riegl did not go beyond a formal description of the changed perception, Benjamin believed that he could point to its societal circumstances. It
is against this background that the comparison of camera technique and
psychoanalysis, in transferring the comparison to the collective, assumes its
crucial social significance. As psychoanalysis illuminates the instinctual unconscious, so the camera intrudes into the optical-unconscious and explores
the consequences that the spread of technology, which is experienced as a
threat, has on the fears and dreams of the masses. As much as this expansive
technology may harbor the danger of mass psychoses, this same process has
also created "the possibility of psychic immunization by means of certain
films in which the forced development of sadistic fantasies or masochis-
tic delusions can prevent their natural and dangerous maturation in the
masses." In Benjamin's opinion, collective laughter is one such preemptive
and beneficial way in which mass psychoses of this type come into the open,

"American slapstick comedies and the films of Walt Disney" providing the "therapeutic shattering of the unconscious"[109] that he envisioned.

Film realizes this function since it is the expression and agent of a manner of perception that diametrically opposes that which the traditional artwork requires of its spectator. Where the aura demands contemplation, film caters to the mass need for distraction. When Benjamin, in conclusion, describes this contrast by applying the antagonistic conceptual pair of "tactile and optical,"[110] he once more makes use of categories central to Riegl's theory of art in order to support his own thinking. The "tactile" shock effect of film turns film into an instrument of getting used to the impositions that modern technology has used in order to subjugate the workaday world to its purposes. At the apex of modernism, the theses reformulate the myth of Telephos as alluded to in the final moments of Richard Wagner's *Parsifal:* "The wound can only close/the spear that struck it." Only technology itself makes the means available that are needed to meet the challenges and threats it poses. But this task cannot be accomplished without social changes.

Shortly before the outbreak of the Second World War, Benjamin observed the tendency of Fascist states not to give the masses their rightful due but merely to give expression to them. This "aestheticizing of political life" he sees culminating in the mobilization for war. *"Imperialist war is an uprising on the part of technology, which demands repayment in 'human material' for the natural material society has denied it."*[111] Nietzsche was convinced that even "the *Greeks* could certainly think of offering their gods no more acceptable a side-dish to their happiness than the joys of cruelty" and that even in Homer the Trojan Wars at heart "intended to be *festivals for the gods and . . .* probably festivals for the poets, too . . ."[112] For Marinetti, who celebrated war as an aesthetic phenomenon, the self-alienation of humankind, according to Benjamin, had reached the point "where it can experience its own annihilation as a supreme aesthetic pleasure."[113] The famous final locution of the theses that counters the Fascist "aestheticizing of politics" with the Communist "politicizing of art" is not to be read as a fait accompli but rather as an imploring appeal addressed to the Communist opponents of Fascism.

In his epistolary critique of the theses, Adorno continued the series of intense critical debates with those of Benjamin's works he was able to read in manuscript form. Beginning with the essay on Kafka and the exposé of the *Arcades Project,* these responses will from now on accompany the publication of Benjamin's essays and often enough influence them considerably. With respect to the theses that make up "The Work of Art in the Age of Its Technological Reproducibility," Adorno's objections anticipate two aspects that have played a considerable role in the history of the study's reception. They can be summarized succinctly in two closely related re-monstrations: on the one hand, Benjamin is accused of underestimating the technical aspect (*Technizität*) of the auratic artwork and of overvaluing that of nonautonomous art, that is, that of the movies. On the other hand, Benjamin is reproached for the inappropriate confidence he has in the spon-taneity of the proletariat (in the form of the movie audience), which Adorno himself, referring to Lenin who was known to have assigned a leading role to the intelligentsia in the revolutionary mobilization of the masses, was unwilling to accept.[114] Adorno blamed the two opinions with which he found fault on what he saw as the dubious influence of Brecht, about which he lamented tirelessly in his later critical objections. The rejoinder that less an alien influence than a genuine component of Benjamin's own construc-tion of a theory is at issue here does not diminish the objective persuasive-ness of Adorno's criticism.

## 3. Reinstatement of Epic Narration

In December 1933, the exile periodical *Die Welt im Wort*, the short-lived successor of *Die Literarische Welt* edited by Willy Haas in Prague, published a short essay in which Benjamin draws up a kind of interim appraisal of his time. Even though it is not known when and for what occasion he wrote it, the stated concern of the article—"to introduce a new, positive concept of barbarism"—appears, in view of the events occurring in Germany at that time, in an uncomfortable and possibly embarrassing light, especially for today's reader. But precisely when seen against the background of the Fas-cist assumption of power, Benjamin's no doubt self-conscious provocation evokes the concluding formulation of the "Work of Art" theses. Just as the theses put an up-to-date revaluation of the concept of the artwork on the agenda, so the essay subjects the term "experience" to a critical revision.

Benjamin does not consider the result of this diagnosis—the fact "that experience has fallen in value" and that with the "tremendous development of technology" as witnessed during the First World War "a completely new poverty had descended on mankind"—a loss.[115] Given the new poverty of experience, what from the perspective of traditional standards cannot but appear to be barbarism now turns into a virtue. The emancipation from the ballast of an educational heritage that has become useless is opening the doors for constructive minds, for the geniuses of a new beginning and of starting from scratch. "A total absence of illusion about the age and at the same time an absolute commitment to it—this is the hallmark"[116] of the positive barbarian. Benjamin found paradigmatic pracitioners of this virtue in the works of Loos and Klee, in Brecht, and once again in Scheerbart. Glass as a construction material and the glass architecture of Scheerbart and Le Corbusier become his essential representatives of this constructive poverty. "Objects made of glass have no 'aura,'"[117] he writes in the essay and adds that transparency knows no secret. Whereas the bourgeois shields himself from the outside world in his *intérieur* and makes himself at home in private seclusion, in the glass house domesticity and property become a public affair.

The prospect of a posthumane humanity that the essay outlines around the model of the positive barbarian may be decoded as an image contrasting the vision of the superhuman whom Nietzsche imagines as a hero. Aphorism 900 in *The Will to Power* speaks of "another type of barbarian," who "comes from the heights: a species of conquering and ruling natures, in search of material to mold. Prometheus was this kind of barbarian."[118] From the perspective of technology, Benjamin's positive barbarism is conceived as antiheroic. In the last sentence of his essay he calls upon the individual that he should "from time to time . . . give a little humanity to the masses, who one day will repay him with compound interest."[119]

As a concept that is the opposite of the barbaric new beginning, "experience" in Benjamin's essay denotes the quintessence of continuity. Communicability, less as a form of knowing than as a form of passing on, is its distinguishing mark. Experience takes the shape of an apothegm that is being handed down to the next generation with the authority of advanced age or of a tale "that passes from mouth to ear."[120] In this form it is the formulation for a theory of epic narration that Benjamin developed in a fragmentary way in a series of essays written at the beginning of the 1930s. Their roots can be traced back to his plan, mentioned in a curriculum vitae of 1928, to write a study of the fairy tale,[121] and to his preoccupation with Hebel, praised by Benjamin in his essay of 1926 as a storyteller. Benjamin has occasionally moved his reflections on the art of oral narration and of its contrast to the novel—as outlined in notes he wrote down in 1928–1929—to a competing place with Lukács's *Theory of the Novel*.[122] Nevertheless, the conclusive formulation of these reflections during the 1930s took place in very close connection with the theoretical contexts that also occupied him at that time in his other studies.

His review of Alfred Döblin's novel *Berlin Alexanderplatz* (1929), published in *Die Gesellschaft* in 1930, makes this clear. Döblin (1878–1957), he wrote, has responded to the crisis of the contemporary novel by demanding an "emancipation of the epic narrative from the book" and in this way has confirmed Benjamin's conclusion that the "oral tradition, the stuff of epic narration" (*die Epik*), is "different in kind from what forms the stock-in-trade of the novel."[123] The place where the novel is born is the individual who seals his solitude in equal measure by participating in the hero's destiny and through the act of silent reading. In his latest book Döblin questioned this sense of comfort on the part of the reader, which shows him at the apex of his theoretical insights. Through his rediscovery of true language, not written but spoken, he testifies to "the reinstatement of epic narration (*das Epische*) that we now encounter everywhere, even in drama."[124]

In montage Benjamin had discovered the stylistic principle that shatters the structure and also the narrative mode of Döblin's novel and that "clears the way for new, very epic possibilities."[125] It is film, Benjamin writes, "film at its best moments," that has accustomed us to the material of montage, to "the autocracy of the authentic." To be sure, he compares the "Biblical verses, statistics, and texts of hit songs . . . that Döblin uses to confer authority on the narrative . . . to the formulaic verse forms of the traditional epic."[126] But in the context of the new media, the new epic potential Döblin had introduced is epic first and foremost in the Brechtian sense. His demand for "the emancipation of the epic from the book" does take place in his *Story of Franz Biberkopf* within the boundaries set by the medium of the book. But it is not this fact that Benjamin's review finds fault with. Rather, what he objects to is that Döblin's hero in the end quits being exemplary and, invested with a personal fate, at last turns into a character in a novel. In this way, however, the novel is not being shattered; on the contrary, the epic narrative is being subjected to the laws of the novel form. To Benjamin's mind, *Berlin Alexanderplatz* does indeed document the "crisis of the novel"—as the title of his review suggests. It does not, however, demonstrate how this crisis can be overcome.

When, at the beginning of 1936, Benjamin accepted a commission to write a study of the Russian poet Nikolai Leskov (1831–1859), he nonetheless felt little inclined to take this as an opportunity for thinking about Russian literary history. He would instead, he announced in a letter, "take one old hobbyhorse out of its stall" and try to push his "oft-repeated observations on the antithesis between *romancier* and storyteller and [his] old preference for the latter."[127] He wrote this essay on the storyteller Nikolai Leskov after an agreement with the Swiss theologian Fritz Lieb (1892–1970), with whom he had become acquainted in his Parisian exile and whose political position was on the far left. It was published in Switzerland in October 1936 in the journal *Orient und Occident*, which was coedited by Lieb. The essay does indeed contain the observations he mentions in his letter in the form of quotations from his own early notes as well as from "Experience and Poverty."

At least at first sight, the essay about the "storyteller" appears to strike quite a different note than one would expect in view of the "Work of Art" theses, which were published that same year. And it is true that these two near-contemporaneous and obviously so incompatible studies usually serve to confirm the perception of Benjamin's Janus-faced nature. Already Alfred Cohn had played off the "old and cozy tone" he heard in the "Storyteller"[128] against the "evil eye" of historical materialism he found predominating in Benjamin's other works. Benjamin, responding in a mood made both cheerful and pensive by this comment, wrote back that he had intentionally chosen this tone for his essay

> but surely not without the awareness that it has come at the expense of certain sacrifices. I believe that the essay's insights could in principle have been preserved even more incorruptible—only that for *me*, and for the time being these were my insights, this was not possible. It's specifically this high degree of incorruptibility with which I do wish, however, to credit the formulations of the piece on "Reproducibility."[129]

Hence it is the same insights that the two works formulate in different, though not equally unmistakable, ways. In a manner that is exemplary for the essay on Leskov, Brecht had expressed these insights in 1931 in one of his *Versuche*. The old forms of mediation, he wrote in *The Three-Penny Lawsuit*, "are not unaffected by the newly emerging ones nor do they survive alongside them. The film viewer reads stories differently. But the storywriter views films too. The technological advance in literary production is irreversible."[130]

Such a person watching a movie, "who reads stories differently," is Benjamin, who emphasizes at the beginning of his essay that depicting Leskov as a storyteller does not mean "bringing him closer to us but, rather, means increasing our distance from him," because it is only when viewed from a distance that "the great, simple outlines which define the storyteller stand out in him."[131] The diagnosis, repeated at the start of the essay, that the ability has been lost to exchange experiences by speaking about them marks the distance that separates the present age from the lifeblood of a story. But an oral tradition is the source even of storytellers who, like Leskov, have written their tales down.

That is to say, telling a story is not limited in Benjamin's opinion to telling it orally. Rather, even when written, the tale maintains the gesture of communicability, which at the same time distinguishes it fundamentally from the novel. Good counsel, the quintessence of what the storyteller communicates, likewise is of importance not per se but as a communication: "After all, counsel is less an answer to a question than a proposal concerning the continuation of a story."[132] Accordingly, storytelling is basically the art of keeping alive the process of the tales' unfolding. Because of this episodic structure, which transcends both the mode of its presentation and its generational circumstances, the story told becomes for Benjamin "the image for a collective experience to which even the deepest shock in every individual experience—death—constitutes no impediment or barrier."[133]

Whereas the novel captures the depiction of individual life within the barriers set by death, the storyteller's tale is based on the rhythm not of individual but of collective life, since it is relating not historical but creaturely happenings. The story/history which in the end all stories tell is the history/story of nature, is that of mankind. In this sense, the "first true storyteller is, and will continue to be, the teller of fairy tales."[134] According to Benjamin, the fairy tale

> tells us of the earliest arrangements that mankind made to shake off the nightmare which myth had placed upon its chest. . . . The liberating magic which the fairy tale has at its disposal does bring nature into play in a mythical way, but points to its complicity with liberated man. A mature man feels this complicity only occasionally—that is, when he is happy; but a child first meets it in fairy tales, and it makes the child happy.[135]

So far, so nostalgic—and thus easy to misunderstand, if reflections on the fairy tale in the "Storyteller" essay were not repeating the central idea of the "Work of Art" theses, meaning the idea that the technological medium of film makes possible the process of learning how to participate in "the interplay between nature and humanity."[136] It should be remembered also that Benjamin's reference to happiness takes up the key concept of anthropological materialism and hence politics. Not only this context suggests the necessity of developing "the transformation of epic forms,"[137] which had been perceived in "Storyteller" more out of an interest in an ideal type than from focusing on a philosophy of history, and of advancing it beyond the boundary observed there. Already in "Experience and Poverty," a variant the editors included in the critical apparatus indicates the direction this idea was to take. The new barbarism that Benjamin supports is said to be

akin in many ways to the barbarism of children . . . One can also tell them
fairy tales again in which the world is as new and clean as only children
can be. Best of all, fairy tales as movies. Who, after all, could have confirmed experiences of the kind that Mick[e]y Mouse makes in his films.
A Mick[e]y-Mouse film is perhaps at this time not understandable yet
to individuals, but an audience does understand. And a Mick[e]y-Mouse
film can rhythmically rule a whole audience.[138]

In posthumous notes from the context of "Storyteller," Benjamin chose
a starting point contrary to the essay and looks at the tale from a decidedly contemporary perspective. He states that there is every reason to fear
that the narrative forms that are thought to be eternal have long been dis-
avowed: "[T]he description by the television set, the hero's words by the
gramophone, the moral of the story by the next statistic, the person of the
narrator by everything one gets to know about him." Even so, the prognosis
reads: "Storytelling—it is bound to stay. But not in its 'eternal' form, in that
cozy, splendid warmth but in sassy, audacious [forms] of which we are as
yet unaware."[139] One of the possible forms of a future way of storytelling
had already been mentioned in the Döblin review. But beside the possibility
of an "interaction between the decay of storytelling and the new mode of
writing as practiced in novels"—the posthumous notes single out Döblin
and James Joyce—Benjamin looks at replacing storytelling with film: "Film
instead of narration."[140]

What Benjamin says about storytelling is true no less of experience.
As the quintessence of tradition, of the formal principle of communicability, experience is given a new form, one in keeping with the technological
media of the motion picture and radio and hence is up-to-date on account
of their new narrative principles, that is, their episodic character and the
structural principle of interruption. This kind of experience is subject to a
dialectics that conjoins it with the new narrative forms to the extent that
these, at the apex of modernism, renew the oldest promises given to mankind. The subject of this experience, however, is no longer the individual
but the collective.

This is also the context for Benjamin's preoccupation with Franz Kafka
(1883–1924), which is given its most significant expression in the essay
Benjamin wrote in commemoration of the tenth anniversary of Kafka's death.
Even before that, in a radio address occasioned by the publication of the
posthumous volume *Beim Bau der chinesischen Mauer* (1931; trans., *The
Great Wall of China, and Other Pieces*, 1933), he had characterized Kafka's

books as "stories pregnant with a moral to which they never give birth."[141] Benjamin had begun to take notice of Kafka rather early. A letter of July 21, 1925[142] suggests that he had read the story "Vor dem Gesetz" ("Before the Law") immediately after its publication in the volume *Ein Landarzt. Kleine Erzählungen* (1919; A Country Doctor. Short Stories). Among his unrealized plans for public comment on Kafka is an essay to be included in the volume negotiated with Rowohlt in 1928 and an address on the Prague writer to be given as part of the series of lectures proposed in Paris in 1934.

Both in talks with Brecht and in the correspondence with Scholem, Kafka was being mentioned repeatedly and in detail since the beginning of the 1930s. The commission to write a study for *Die Jüdische Rundschau* (Jewish Review) about the poet on the occasion of the tenth anniversary of his death (1934), Benjamin owed to Scholem's intervention with Robert Weltsch, the editor-in-chief of this biweekly journal. But only the first and the penultimate section of Benjamin's extensive manuscript appeared there, which was one reason why he thought of expanding the essay for publication as a book. Copious notes have been found among his posthumous papers that document a sustained and intensive interest. In part, these notes directly refer to the detailed epistolary discussions about the essay with Kraft, Adorno, and Scholem as well as to talks with Brecht.

The attempt, again undertaken with Scholem's help, to gain the support of Schocken Verlag for a book on Kafka to be written by Benjamin did not materialize when Schocken showed no interest in this project. (Schocken had published Max Brod's and Heinz Politzer's edition of Kafka's *Gesammelte Schriften* in six volumes, 1935–37.) This is the background to the letter of June 12, 1938,[143] which de facto is addressed to Scholem but which was implicitly meant for Salman Schocken. In this memorandum, which forms the capstone of his (as it turned out, fragmentary) analysis of Kafka, Benjamin outlines the basic direction of another (never written) book. This study was to dissociate itself polemically from Max Brod's recently published life-and-works description, titled *Franz Kafka. Eine Biographie. Erinnerungen und Dokumente* (1937; trans., *Franz Kafka, a Biography*, 1947 and 1960).[144]

The long-prevailing perception that Kafka had been largely unknown during his lifetime and immediately after his death has for some time been shown to be untenable: "When measured by the small number of his publications, the nearly complete absence of journalistic writing, his reputation was in fact rather extraordinary."[145] Those among Benjamin's acquaintances who contributed quite considerably to Kafka's posthumous renown include Willy Haas and Siegfried Kracauer.

Kracauer accompanied the publication of the three Kafka novels, which Max Brod edited—*Der Prozess* (1925; trans., *The Trial*, 1937), *Das Schloss* (1926; trans., *The Castle*, 1930), *Amerika* (1927; trans., *America*, 1938)—and of the volume of stories and short prose pieces (1931), which was also the occasion for Benjamin's radio lecture, with detailed reviews in *Frankfurter Zeitung*. They opposed the kind of theological interpretation advocated emphatically above all by Brod and his coeditor Hans-Joachim Schoeps, an orientation for which Brod, moreover, claimed vindication on the basis of his personal acquaintance with the poet. Kracauer, by contrast, accentuated the role in Kafka's novels[146] of a fear that is not to be falsely interpreted in psychological terms, and he pointed out a view, distorted in the manner both of fairy tales and dream states, that sees this world as abandoned by truth.[147] For Kafka's description of the world's condition as a waking dream, finally, the posthumous volume of 1931 provides him with the catchword of "the human organizations which are unfolding their menacing potential at the present time."[148] In his essay, Benjamin likewise referring to the story "Building the Great Wall of China," states that Kafka, using a variation of Goethe's well-known phrase about politics as the destiny of his time, could have defined "organization as destiny" because for him "the question of how life and work are organized in human society"[149] has become impenetrable.

Haas, who was personally acquainted with Kafka, saw to it that the poet became known quickly in Berlin literary circles. In June 1926, *Die Literarische Welt*, which he edited, devoted a whole issue to Kafka, Haas himself contributing one of his numerous studies. Benjamin was right to observe that the center of Haas's essay collection *Gestalten der Zeit* (1930; Contemporary Figures) were the texts dealing with Kafka and Hofmannsthal. But as the book's reviewer, he did not accept the theological critique, on which he found its essays to be based, without reservations, much as he sees the Kafka exegesis of the future "being shown its directions here by an interpretation that everywhere penetrates to the theological facts with the highest energy."[150] But his sympathy is engaged less by the theological analysis than by the consistent vigor with which the theological approach rejects the purely aesthetic one. Because of this destructive turn against art, Benjamin sees it allied with its opposite pole, the historical-materialistic stance. In his Kafka essay of 1934, Benjamin considers the theological and the psychoanalytic interpretation to be the two ways that are most likely to "miss the essential points"[151] of Kafka's writings. This verdict explicitly applies also to Haas, which did not, however, keep Benjamin from making use of Haas's point about the motif of forgetting in his own analyses, doing so emphatically, though in his own specific way.

the simultaneous hope and fear that it might encounter the halachic order and formula, the doctrine itself, en route."[157]

Benjamin uses this structure, this gesture of hesitant delay, altogether independent of the specifically Jewish contexts in order to illustrate what he believes has secured for Kafka's prose the distinction of being narrative (des Erzählerischen). By virtue of the fact that in this way the episodic becomes the center of Kafka's narrative art, his books are not novels but "stories pregnant with a moral to which they never give birth."[158] Benjamin sees even the theological contents reduced to this genuinely fragmentary structure of Kafka's prose. Hence, merciful grace for him consists of the fact that the law never declares itself, and atonement amounts to merely pointing to guilt—a guilt, to be sure, that takes shape only in forgetting.[159]

In the essay of 1934, more even than in his radio address, Benjamin is intent on translating the structures he had uncovered in his theological explication into profane contexts. Hence, he decodes the deformed world that Kafka's works describe as a premythical age. Seeking a description of it, he returns to the category of fated ambiguity[160] that he had developed in the essays about Elective Affinities and "Fate and Character." Being without tangible orders and hierarchies, this primal world appears as a creaturely world from which redemption is imaginable only after the pattern of the fairy tale. Seen from this perspective, Kafka's hands turn the mythic tales of the Greeks into "fairy tales for dialecticians,"[161] the fairy tale being the traditional way of telling about victory even over the powers of myth, which after all was not the redemption it had pretended to be. What in Kafka's works guarantees the presence of this, in Benjamin's sense, epic connection, is the significance of gesture in his writings. The dissolution of "events into their gestural components" that can be observed in Kafka's last novel, Amerika, in the description of the "Nature Theater of Oklahoma," merely illustrates "that Kafka's entire work constitutes a code of gestures which surely had no definite symbolic meaning for the author from the outset; rather, the author tried to derive such a meaning from them in ever-changing contexts and experimental groupings."[162]

In the radio address and again here it is the gesture of quoting, the mien of pointing toward the doctrine without the doctrine itself existing, that for Benjamin manifests the particular nature of Kafka's "parabolic" prose. And this doctrine's concern is the question of how life is (and is to be) organized, a question that has become impenetrable to the poet. In Jewish tradition the Haggadah, in its relationship to the Hallachah, that is, to the legal system of Judaism with its basis in religious statutes, has kept this question alive.[163] The same fundamental fact of an episodically fragmented relationship to the missing doctrine is given a variation in the figure of forgetting, which Benjamin recognizes as another, if not as the central, gesture in Kafka's work. For him, forgetting also expresses an existential experience of modernity:

> The invention of motion pictures and the phonograph came in an age of maximum alienation of human beings from one another, of unpredictably mediated relationships which have become their only ones. Experiments have proved that people do not recognize their own gait on film or their own voice on a phonograph. The situation of the subject in such experiments is Kafka's situation.[164]

In Benjamin's view, Kafka was convinced that hope of salvation was to be gained solely from a turn toward what has been forgotten—an assurance Kafka had found not in existential theology but in folk tradition, German as well as Jewish. In 1938, in the letter in which Benjamin outlined the basic ideas of the book he was planning to write, he holds fast to the reflections expressed in the two earlier works. But now he explicates them in close proximity to the categories he had developed in the intervening "Storyteller" essay. Kafka's poetic oeuvre, he says, is dominated by two poles, by the experience of the mystical tradition on the one hand, and by that of modern metropolitan man on the other. What is in a precise sense *"folly"* in Kafka "is that this, the most recent of experiential worlds, was conveyed to him precisely by the mystical tradition."[165] Kafka's appeal to the forces of this tradition, though, follows upon the realization that modern reality "can scarcely be experienced any longer by an *individual.*"[166]

The point of Benjamin's interpretation is that in view of this turn back toward tradition he emphatically understands Kafka as a failed writer. Speaking of Kafka's failure, however, is not intended as an evaluation but rather as a description of his work. Kafka's writings represent "tradition falling ill," to which he reacted by sacrificing truth "for the sake of clinging to transmissibility, to its haggadic element."[167] What is left of tradition is gesture, in Benjamin's understanding the very essence of narrative. Only in the figure of interruption, which Benjamin—herein following Brecht—understands as the principle of narrative, can the individual maintain the connection with tradition, and only in accordance with this same principle of interruption can the collective hope of using the new forms of narration in order to establish contact with tradition in the sense of its productive continuation.

Even though this letter is certainly not to be read as Benjamin's final word on Kafka, it does between the lines give an answer to Scholem's didactic poem[168] that explicitly puts the poet back into a Jewish theological context. Adorno also, who read the Kafka essay in its unabbreviated manuscript version (as did Scholem), made theological questions a central issue of his response. Characteristically enough, he also deemed it necessary to turn the image of an "inverse theology," which Adorno finds formulated in Benjamin's essay and into which he "would gladly see our thoughts dissolve,"[169] into an emphatic denunciation of Brecht.

Already in an earlier letter Adorno had with reference to the *Arcades* expressed his hope that Benjamin, in resuming work on this project, would work out their originally theological content, "without qualms, that is, concerning any objections stemming from that Brechtian atheism which we should perhaps one day attempt to salvage as a kind of inverse theology, but which we should certainly not duplicate!"[170] In this vein he criticizes Benjamin's Kafka essay for "the adoption of categories drawn from epic theatre" as "alien to [its] material," and explicitly insists that "the very form of Kafka's art . . . stands in the most extreme antithesis to the form of theatrical art in so far as it is [that of the] novel."[171] In the letter he wrote in response, Benjamin completely avoids touching on theological questions and diplomatically concedes that a more detailed clarification is needed with respect to the question of the form of Kafka's novels. This can, however, be arrived at only in a roundabout way. By contrast, Adorno's point about his own "insufficient grasp of the archaic"[172] and hence about the problem of primal history—a point Benjamin had picked up—turned out to be a topic that was to occupy him intensively during his work on the *Arcades*.

CHAPTER SIX

# Primal History of Modernity, 1931–40

## 1. Berlin Childhood around 1900

At the beginning of September 1932, Benjamin reported in a letter to Scholem that he had "begun a small series of vignettes, half of which are now finished, called 'Berliner Kindheit um 1900'—a portrayal of my earliest memories."[1] Perhaps more than any other factor, the biographical circumstances under which these recollections were written down appear to give *Berlin Childhood* a special place in Benjamin's work. A few years earlier, under the influence of his failed attempt to escape the politically and economically oppressive situation in Germany, Benjamin had made the decision to end his life. Obvious as it may seem that this decision suggests his reason for wanting to leave a record of autobiographical recollections, the text itself and the history of its genesis do not support this conjecture. "Recollections, even when they are expansive, do not always amount to an autobiography. And this thing certainly isn't one," Benjamin had already insisted in "Berlin Chronicle," from which *Berlin Childhood* emerged after incisive revisions. As the preface of the final version indicates, this applies all the more to the later text. To the extent, as he wrote there, that the "biographical features . . . altogether recede in the present undertaking,"[2] they join the more theoretically oriented texts from the same time as very revealing companion pieces. And *Berlin Childhood* vice versa illustrates how little the great theoretical projects can be separated from the experiences of the one who had ventured to formulate them under the politically and personally most trying conditions of exile.

Looking back on what he had written at the time of his exile in Paris, *Berlin Childhood* represents for Benjamin the experience that blasts the boundaries of what is merely autobiographical. In 1932, as he was trying, at first more intuitively than rationally, to come to terms with the fact that his exile was close at hand—that was the time, he wrote, when he started to write down his chronicle. Using an image he would later also employ in the preface, he compares his work on this text to a "kind of inoculation . . . that was meant to make me immune to the homesickness for the city in which I had spent my childhood."[3] As does *Berlin Childhood*, so also does the conception of the Paris *Arcades* go back to the time before his exile. When in the spring of 1935 the Institute for Social Research requested an outline of this project, Benjamin marked the new phase into which his work on this project had entered by giving it a new title: "Paris, Capital of the Nineteenth Century."[4] This draft and *Berlin Childhood*, sharing a focus on the nineteenth century, share not only a historical but also a theoretical interest: the primal history (*Urgeschichte*) of Modernity. As Benjamin emphasizes with respect to the exposé, however, the two texts pursue this interest in different ways:

> This of all books must not draw on forms such as those offered by 'Berliner Kindheit' at any point and to any extent whatsoever: . . . In it, the primal history of the nineteenth century, which is mirrored in the gaze of the child playing upon its threshold, assumes an entirely different guise from the signs it inscribes upon the map of history.[5]

*Berlin Childhood* could enter into this constellation not least because of the protracted and complicated history of its genesis. In October 1931, Benjamin had signed a contract with *Die Literarische Welt* to contribute a piece called "Berlin Chronicle."[6] He had apparently not started the actual writing of this "series of glosses on everything that from day to day seemed noteworthy to me in Berlin" and to be presented in a "loosely subjective form,"[7] until shortly before the agreed-upon deadline of February 1932, but instead continued his work during his sojourn on Ibiza and in Italy during the second half of 1932. "Berlin Chronicle," published posthumously in 1970 in a textual arrangement determined by the editor, provides the original material for *Berlin Childhood*. This version did not, however, absorb more than about two-fifths of the older text, moreover with a wording that had undergone fundamental changes. A "tiny book" by this title, from which a total of twelve pieces would be printed the following spring in *Frankfurter Zeitung*, is mentioned for the first time in November and again in December 1932.[8] During his exile Benjamin made various, unsuccessful, attempts to have his book published. In the meantime, he expanded the manuscript that in 1933, when it contained thirty pieces, he considered completed; he also changed the sequence of the sections. In view of the fact that Benjamin himself emphasized that the "individual parts belong together,"[9] the manuscript version of 1938, which was not discovered until 1981 and which contains revisions that were incorporated at this last stage of the work process, assumes a special importance. It is the author's own "final version." Beside this version, printed in the supplemental volume of *Gesammelte Schriften*,[10] and one that goes back to an earlier and more extensive manuscript,[11] there exists yet another, even earlier manuscript of *Berlin Childhood*. It is housed at Gießen University Library—and hence is referred to as "Gießener Fassung"— and was published as a separate book in 2000.

Benjamin did not want to call his recollections an autobiography because they do not have to do "with time, with sequence" nor with "what makes up the continuous flow of life." Rather, he is "talking of a space, of moments and discontinuities." In recollections that the text preserves in the form they have "at the moment of commemoration,"[12] the time of childhood fuses with the space of the city in which Benjamin had spent it at the end of the nineteenth century. It had been his purpose, he explains in the preface to the "final version," to "get hold of the *images* in which the experience of the big city is precipitated in a child of the bourgeoisie."[13]

But the episodic form of *Berlin Childhood* does not only derive from, as Benjamin emphasizes, the topographical structure of memory. In "Berlin Chronicle" he expressly makes it his task also to use the images of memory in order to give an account of the medium "in which alone such images take shape, assuming a transparency in which, however mistily, the contours of what is to come are delineated like mountain peaks. The present in which the writer lives is this medium."[14] Most closely connected with the image of the city that he has conjured up, this present and presence of the writer are noticeable everywhere in *Berlin Childhood*. As the grown-up becomes aware of the childhood he had spent in the last years of the nineteenth century, so the present becomes aware of its prehistory in the past century. Its relation to the present is an unrenounceable component of the archaeology of the most recent past, which Benjamin pursues not in *Berlin Childhood* alone. He gives to memory that specific space-time structure that he explicates in a "thought figure" from "Berlin Chronicle,"[15] titled "Ausgraben und Erinnern" (Excavating and Remembering).[16]

Memory, he writes there, is not an instrument for exploring things past but it is the venue, or medium, of this exploration. As in an archaeological excavation, it is no less important to identify the locale and exact place of the finds in today's ground than it is to inventory them. As precisely as the image explicates the idea, so insightfully does it combine Benjamin's use of conceptual language with his theory of epic narration, which obviously is not to be reduced to a theory of storytelling: "When it is epic and rhapsodic in the strictest sense, true remembrance must also render an image of the one who remembers, just like a good archaeological report must not only identify the strata from which its finds have been taken but must above all identify those other layers which had to be dug through first."[17] In *Berlin Childhood*, the present time of the writer marks both the historical and the subjective fixed point of remembrance. The quite considerable difficulty to which Benjamin seeks to find a theoretical answer in the outline of the *Passages* consists of transferring this approach to a collective historical subject that attempts to decode the enigmatic images of what is past on the map of history.

In the preface to the "final version" of *Berlin Childhood*, a potential temptation to wax nostalgic is opposed by the "insights into the . . . necessary social irretrievability of the past."[18] Even the images through which childhood takes shape in memory Benjamin would like to see removed from the barriers of the contingent biographical, because he considers it possible that a fate expressly theirs is held in reserve for them. As a childhood spent in the country encounters a store of forms that have been stamped by a feeling for nature and that are there for remembrance to use, so perhaps are the images of his "metropolitan childhood capable, at their core, of pre-forming later historical experience."[19]

In his poems Charles Baudelaire had created a visual image of metropolitan Paris, and in his poetics he had conceptualized Modernity. In the footsteps of Baudelaire and the Surrealists, Benjamin saw the metropolis become the privileged image space for an experience of Modernism. Already Baudelaire had sought to give shape to Modernity via an imagery that is the opposite of antiquity, and from Aragon's *Paysan de Paris* (1926), Benjamin was able to take the program of a modern mythology. As a critical successor of the Surrealists, the flâneur Franz Hessel, who appears in *Berlin Childhood* as the nameless "Berlin peasant" (*Bauer von Berlin*),[20] had taught him to see his hometown of Berlin as a landscape also.

As a man whose abode is the streets, the flâneur guards the knowledge of dwelling. To experience the city in this way as a space for living (*Wohnraum*) means for Benjamin that not only people and animals but "above all things can inhabit a place."[21] Such images, monuments belonging to a culture of dwelling from the previous century, the flâneur encounters in the ancient decorations of the residences of Berlin's old Westend district, which looks even older insofar as architectural Modernism at the beginning of the twentieth century had in the person of Adolf Loos declared its hostility to anything ornamental. As Benjamin insists, it is not a reverend gaze clinging to museum pieces that discovers the antiquity of the 'Alte Westen': "Only a man in whom modernity has already announced its presence, however quietly, can cast such an original and 'early' glance at what has only just become old."[22]

It is this glance with which Benjamin examines the city of his childhood, not by accident turning his attention first to the caryatid-decorated loggias. According to an idea he did heed in the "final version," the text with this title, "Loggias," would introduce the series of memory images of *Berlin Childhood*.[23] Located at the rear side of the grand-bourgeois rented house, the loggias open out toward the courtyards and backyards, the domain of the personnel and the living quarters of the less prosperous. They designate a threshold not only sociologically but also topographically: "They mark the outer limit of the Berliner's lodging. This is where Berlin—the city god itself—begins."[24] In this way the loggias' "uninhabitability" not only become a symbol of a changing culture of lodging but also a structure of solace for the one memorializing them from a place of exile, "one who himself no longer has a proper abode."[25]

In his deliberations concerning the sequence of the memory images, this piece, in which Benjamin saw a "kind of self-portrait," is given preference in the "final version" over that "photographic self-portrait in 'Die Mummerehlen.'"[26] In the "final version" Benjamin did, however, erase the passage in which he describes the photographic countenance of the boy who looks with ever greater alienation at the observer the more the person portrayed fuses with the things that surround him in the studio.[27] Observing the childhood photograph repeats an experience that had been just as natural to the child as it had become strange to the adult. The child had the gift of resembling things, furniture, and clothes while he was at play, the gift of disguising himself inside them. This is the ability to which the title of the piece refers—"sich zu vermummen." In reality it is a productive linguistic misunderstanding that onomatopoetically transformed the 'Muhme Rehlen' (Auntie Rehlen) of a nursery rhyme that was incomprehensible to the child, into a sprite: the Mummerehlen. *Berlin Childhood* is full of these frequently linguistic misunderstandings and distortions. For example, the unknown word "Kupferstich" (copperplate print) turned into

"Kopf-verstich" (head-stickout),[28] the Berlin suburb of Steglitz becomes a "Stieglitz" (goldfinch),[29] the "gnä(dige) Frau," as which the maid addressed his mother, magically turned into a "Näh-Frau," (seamstress;)[30] and the "Markthalle" (market hall), where the child went in the company of his mother, by the same distorting logic was changed into a "Mark-Thalle." As these misunderstandings opened a world of its own to the child's imagination, so they open to the adult's remembrance the access to the world of the child.

In "Die Mummerehlen" Benjamin attributes this experience to the "gift of perceiving similarities" which is "nothing but a weak remnant of the old compulsion to become similar and to behave mimetically."[31] The gift of perceiving similarities is discussed in a theoretical text that is extant in two divergent versions as "Doctrine of the Similar"[32] and as "On the Mimetic Faculty." Remarks in a letter of February 28, 1933, to Scholem provide evidence that the earlier text, which Benjamin calls "a new theory of language— encompassing four small, handwritten pages" had been "formulated while I was doing research for the first piece of Berliner Kindheit."[33]

The center of both texts is "the concept of a nonsensuous similarity,"[34] which Benjamin attributes to a "mimetic faculty,"[35] an ability to produce similarities that have both a phylogenetic and an ontogenetic history. Hence, mimetic behavior in children's games to this day reveals itself by the fact that a child pretends to be not only a merchant but also a windmill or a train. Phylogenetically, Benjamin gives the example of the horoscope, calling it a relic of prehistoric man's faculty for perceiving "natural correspondences."[36] The center of this linguistic theory revolves around the idea that this primal anthropological faculty has not by any means been lost, but has undergone change in the course of history. If one proceeds from the assumption that, "at the dawn of humanity, reading from stars, entrails, and coincidences . . . was reading per se," then "one might well assume that this mimetic gift, which was earlier the basis for clairvoyance, very gradually found its way into language and writing in the course of a development over thousands of years, thus creating for itself in language and writing the most perfect archive of non-sensuous similarity."[37]

These reflections establish a link with the earlier essay on language and its theory of the magic of language. The originally mimetic character of language, its, "if you will, magical aspect," Benjamin writes in "Doctrine of the Similar," can "appear at all only in connection with something alien as its basis."[38] The nexus between the two aspects of language is being established by a mode of time. Epistemologically, the faculty of perceiving similarities

depends on the tempo or the quickness of reading, on a critical moment
"in which similarities flash by fleetingly out of the stream of things only in
order to sink down once more."[39]

When Benjamin, in the later version of his text, in "On the Mimetic
Faculty," sees the hypostatized development of the mimetic faculty and of
its transformation into language and writing culminate in a liquidation of
magic,[40] it is hardly justified to consider this a fundamental change of his
position. Just as Benjamin is concerned in the early essay on language, so
also in this version of his linguistic theory he is interested in a noninstrumental concept of language and hence most of all in an epistemological
problem whose context calls for the discussion of theological or magical
conceptions of language as topics of a theory and not as the theoretician's
confessions.

It is not then fortuitous that the memory images of *Berlin Childhood*
gave Benjamin occasion for these theoretical reflections. These images
should be understood less as part of a theory of language than in the context of a historical epistemology, specifically as a way of applying such an
epistemology. The text itself gives a decisive hint in this direction. It is to
be found in the story of the "Little Hunchback," the concluding section in
all versions of *Berlin Childhood*. Benjamin had introduced him in the Kafka
essay as a person of disfigurement and forgetting. This little man appears to
the child as the embodiment of the child's own misfortune and oblivious-
ness to everything around him. To the adult this hunchback represents all
the things that have receded into oblivion. In this final piece of *Berlin Childhood*, Benjamin imagines "that this 'whole life' which is said to be flashing
before the eyes of those who are dying is composed of such images as the
little man has of us all. They flit by like those pages of the tightly bound
little books that were once the predecessors of our cinematographs."[41]

To decode one's own childhood in these images presupposes, however,
that one reads at a certain speed, which the theory of mimetic faculty had
made a condition for the perception of similarities. The fact that Benjamin
compares the memory images of *Berlin Childhood* to the way in which the
images in a motion-picture theater unreel emphasizes once more the, in a
strict sense, epic and rhapsodic form he has given his book of recollections.
If the childhood images thus become the exemplary case of a philosophy
of history, then the insight that Benjamin had formulated in the Kafka essay concerning the little hunchback is also true for them: "What has been
forgotten," he had noted there, "is never something purely individual" but
"mingles with what has been forgotten of a previous ('prehistoric') world."[42]
In this sense the images of the childhood Benjamin had spent in Berlin

around the turn of the century mirror their primal history, which is the nineteenth century.

## 2. Parisian Arcades

In the *Arcades* Benjamin is "essentially concerned with the 'primal history of the nineteenth century,'" as he emphasized in a letter to Adorno that accompanied the exposé (sent to him at the end of May 1935) of a venture that had occupied Benjamin with interruptions since the middle of the 1920s.[43] In this extensive communication he reviews the stages in the development of a project in which Adorno had from early on taken such an intensive part that occasionally he spoke of the *Arcades* as "our destined contribution to *prima philosophia*."[44] Adorno saw the intent of the work—which he strongly emphasized is philosophical—as endangered by the interest the Institute for Social Research began showing when at Benjamin's instigation it asked to be sent an outline of the project. Under these circumstances, their mutual project of a "*prima philosophia* in your own particular sense" now seemed to be sacrificed in favor of a "historical-sociological investigation"[45] of the kind that alone would be acceptable to the Institute and its journal. Adorno also implored Benjamin not to give up the themes and motifs the latter had included from earlier works and whose conclusive treatment he had again and again reserved for the *Arcades:* "The primal history of the nineteenth century; the thesis of the ever-same; of the newest as the most ancient; the gambler; the theme of plushness—all of this belongs in the domain of philosophical theory."[46] By emphasizing that the *Arcades* are connected with some of Benjamin's earlier works—Adorno expressly mentioned the Surrealism essay and "The Little History of Photography"—the claim of the work as outlined by these analyses seemed to him to be exposed to a further danger. He would consider it "a real misfortune," Adorno wrote, "if Brecht were to acquire any influence upon this work."[47]

In his reply, Benjamin assured him that the exposé was indeed that of the "great philosophical work," although this formulation "does not exactly strike me as the most appropriate." But in any case, "the decisive question concerning the historical image" will be "treated in all its range for the first time here," an issue of which Benjamin expects that his work has "actually reached solid ground through its Marxist discussion."[48] As he is looking back on the beginnings of the *Arcades*, Benjamin also counters Adorno's misgivings. His first sketches, he says, go back to the years when he read Aragon's *Paysan de Paris*, which had made his heart beat with excitement. (It is probably also at this time that he translated excerpts from the book, which were published in 1928.)[49] To his friendship with Franz Hessel, Benjamin continues, the project owes "the subtitle 'A Dialectical Fairy-Tale'—which no longer passes muster," suggesting the "rhapsodic character of the presentation as he then conceived it." This Romantic form had been overtaken as a result of the "seminal" conversation with Asja Lacis, Horkheimer, Adorno, and Adorno's wife in the fall of 1929. "Then followed the decisive encounter with Brecht, and with it the culmination of every aporia connected with this work. . . . The significant experience that I was able to gain for my work from this recent period—and it is by no means insubstantial—could not properly take shape before the limits of that significance had become indubitably clear to me, and all 'directives' from that quarter as well had thereby become quite superfluous."[50] On the contrary, as a consequence of thus delimiting external influences, Benjamin sees in his exposé above all the emergence of epistemological analogies to his book on Baroque drama. He considers them

> a particularly striking confirmation of that general process of fusion that has led the entire conceptual mass of this material, originally motivated as it was by metaphysical concerns, toward a final shape in which the world of dialectical images is immune to all objections that can be raised by metaphysics.[51]

In point of fact, Benjamin's earliest notes on the *Arcades* go back to a journal article that he had planned together with Hessel, and which then developed into a plan to write a more extensive essay. An essay titled "Parisian Arcades. A Dialectical Fairy Tale" is mentioned at the end of January 1928 in a letter to Scholem, where it is called a "work of a few weeks" that would conclude the productive cycle of *One-Way Street*. This comment applies first of all to the external form of the planned work [i.e., the *Arcades*], about which he occasionally says that in the event of its successful completion, *One-Way Street* would "only in this work display the form it was intended to have."[52] Like the book of aphorisms, the *Arcades* project moves even more into Surrealism's intellectual field of gravitation. While Benjamin calls this proximity "understandable and well-founded," he is nevertheless aware that "an all too ostentatious proximity to the *mouvement surréaliste* might become disastrous" for him. Instead of staying within the boundaries of the original framework, this project "will take possession of the *inheritance* of surrealism . . . with all the authority of a philosophical Fortinbras."[53]

How one would have to imagine this balancing act is a question to which the "Surrealism" essay gives a first answer. Benjamin calls it "a screen placed in front of the *Paris Arcades*" that for the time being keeps secret what goes on behind it. But he is prepared nonetheless to reveal in this letter that the issue here, as in *One-Way Street*, is "to attain the most extreme concreteness for an era, as it there manifested itself in children's games, a building, or a real-life situation."[54] One of the prominent topics that manifest this concreteness is fashion. To describe and fathom fashion philosophically defines Benjamin's efforts as motivated by his epistemological interest to find out "what this natural and totally irrational measure of the historical process is really all about."[55]

Benjamin had neither given up his theoretical purpose nor the central motifs and subjects when, at the beginning of 1930 and apparently under the impression of conversations with Adorno and Horkheimer, he drew up a preliminary summary of his work, which had meanwhile developed into the plan for a book. But the project did not develop past this summary until he resumed working on it at the beginning of 1934. It had become obvious to him, he explained to Scholem in a letter written in French, that the study of Hegel and *Das Kapital* was necessary in order to give both the material and the metaphysics a sufficiently solid foundation within the frame of the intended work. He considered it inevitable, he wrote, that this book, no less than the book on Baroque drama, could not do without an epistemology— and this time it would have to be above all an epistemology of history ("cette fois, surtout sur la théorie de la connaisance de l'histoire.")[56] There is no evidence either in the exposé or in the extant notes that a debate with Hegel, much less one with Heidegger, which most probably Adorno may have suggested to him as unavoidable for this perspective, ever took place—this being further evidence of how successfully Benjamin managed if not to guard his work against foreign influences then at least to subordinate them to his own interests.

A number of notes and rough drafts have been preserved from this phase of his work on the *Arcades*. While they do not reveal an overall outline, they do assemble a number of central motifs and theoretical reflections connecting them to the exposé of 1935. The two detailed sketches,[57] for example, each proceed from a description of the arcades that provide the titles for the original project. In historical retrospect they present themselves to the observer as "the matrix from which the image of 'Modernity' was cast," as the mirror "in which the century, self-complacently, reflected its very newest past."[58] Their charm results from the "ambiguity of space"[59] because all of a sudden the roofed streets change into an interior space, and they impart this ambiguity to the streets of Paris. Conversely, this makes the streets appear to be "the abode of the collective," and the arcade turns into the salon.[60] While the bourgeoisie of the Second Empire attempts to ward off this experience by banishing it into the interior space of the salon, for the flâneur who roves through it as if in a dream, the city transforms itself into a landscape. The city's glamour, however, turns out to be the reverse side of destructive energies which in the course of the century again and again push to the surface explosively:

> In the social order, Paris is a counter-image of what Mount Vesuvius is in the geographical order. A menacing, dangerous massif, an ever active June of revolution. But the way the slopes of Vesuvius have become paradisiacal fruit gardens thanks to the layers of lava covering them, thus from the lava of revolution blooms art, the festal life, fashion as nowhere else.[61]

It appears that Benjamin had wanted to confront this inside view of the century from a perspective that leads out of a spacetime (*Zeitraum*) that had become a dreamtime (*Zeit-traum*).[62] In this conception it is Surrealism that marks this vanishing point. Its father, according to Benjamin, was Dada, "but its mother was an arcade"—the "Passage de l'Opéra," that is—in which, as described by Aragon in *Paysan de Paris*, there was a café that served the Surrealists as a meeting place until the arcade was demolished to make room for Boulevard Haussman.[63] But already in his early sketches Benjamin also emphasizes "that the direction this work will take sets it off from Aragon: While Aragon remains fixed in the realm of dreams, Benjamin's purpose here is to find the constellation of awakening."[64] The basic orientation of this critical adoption of Surrealism is anticipated in the Surrealism essay of 1929. It serves as a point of connection for fragments that credit the Surrealists with being the first to have picked up out of the narcotic historicism and the passion for masks of the nineteenth century that signal of true historical existence that was coming through to the present time from the previous century. It is the task of Benjamin's own undertaking to "decipher this signal." The "revolutionary materialist basis of Surrealism," which his essay had laid open, is "sufficient warrant for the fact that the economic basis of the century had been given supreme expression."[65]

Already in his early notes, his theory of awakening (which originated in this context) is being expanded to become an epistemology of history that

Benjamin at the same time seeks to connect to his political philosophy. The dialectical structure of awakening becomes the model both for historical cognition and for political praxis. As dream images do not become fixed before awakening, so it is only from the present that the past can become known. In this sense Benjamin speaks of the "Copernican turn in historical perception." Whereas until now one considered what is past as the fixed point and saw the present as intent on groping its way toward cognizing this solid fixedness, the issue now is to reverse this relation and first of all to fix-ate things past from the vantage of the present. In this way "politics is given primacy over history. Hence the historical 'facts' turn into something that has just now happened to us: to ascertain them is the task of memory."[66] It is in this "act of political remembrance"[67] that Benjamin's material history of the nineteenth century as given representative shape in the arcades was meant to come to its end.

It is to be assumed that these fundamental premises provided the basis for the conversations in the fall of 1929 that led Benjamin to realize that a revision of the project's foundations was necessary, thus bringing about its temporary suspension. Before Benjamin started writing the exposé at the request of the Institute, Adorno became the tireless advocate for this pro-ject, whose realization under the conditions of exile Benjamin himself saw receding into an ever farther distance.

But it is to Scholem rather than Adorno that Benjamin made his first re-port concerning the new stage that his work had reached in May 1935 when the exposé was finished. The essay was now to grow into a book to be titled *Paris, Capital of the Nineteenth Century* (whose French title Benjamin se-cretly preferred over its German one). In even greater detail than in his sub-sequent letter to Adorno, he moved it into the orbit of his book on Baroque drama: as the unraveling of the traditional concept of tragic drama (*Trauer-spiel*) was his concern there, so it would now be that of the "fetish character of commodities." Beside the necessity of giving the book its own theory of knowledge, Benjamin hints at a further analogy: "just as the Baroque book dealt with the seventeenth century from the perspective of Germany, this book will unravel the nineteenth century from France's perspective."[68]

The exposé accounts for this historical interest by enlisting the aid of a peculiar historical experience. As the prehistory of one's own present, the past century, which had claimed the concept of Modernity for itself so em-phatically, does not move at all closer to this present time. Rather, it retreats into an infinite, prehistoric distance. The sense of time that characterizes this experience of remoteness is suggested by the way fashions change. Not only does every generation experience the fashion that has just elapsed, so

Benjamin notes, as "the most radical antiaphrodisiac imaginable."[69] But it is even more telling that the spectacle of fashion illustrates a fundamental dialectic of history because the newest thing in fashion will set the tone "only where it emerges in the medium of the oldest, the longest past, the most ingrained."[70] It is this experience that Benjamin explicates further in the exposé. In its endeavor "to distance itself from all that is antiquated— which means, however, from the most recent past"—any present time is being referred back to the primal past (*das Urvergangene*).

> In the dream in which every epoch entertains images of its successor, the latter appears wedded to elements of primal history (*Urgeschichte*)— that is, to elements of a classless society. And the experiences of such a society—as stored in the unconscious of the collective—engender, through interpenetration with what is new, the utopia that has left its trace in a thousand configurations of life, from enduring edifices to passing fashions.[71]

The focus of the book was to be the representation of these "phantasmagorias," as and how they are taking shape in the womb of capitalist, commodities-producing society (which defines the way the bourgeoisie established itself in the France of the nineteenth century), as outlined in the six sections of the exposé.

In the exposé, Paris, capital of the nineteenth century, reveals itself first of all through its architecture, paradigmatically represented by the arcades. With respect to the technology of their construction, they owe their existence to the use of glass and iron. These artificial building materials inaugurate the dominance of the constructive principle in architecture, as the engineer is poised to take over the traditional territory of the architect. But instead of adjusting their manner of building to the functional nature of iron, the master builders make every effort to hide the new construction material behind facades that imitate ancient motifs. The Empire saw in this new technology "a contribution to the revival of architecture in the classical Greek sense,"[72] thereby subjecting even architecture to the laws of fashion.

The same mental mechanism Benjamin discovered in the utopian designs of the social theoretician and socialist Charles Fourier (1772–1837), whose name the first section of the exposé places next to the arcades ("Fourier, or the Arcades"). Fourier, he writes, saw in the arcades "the architectural canon of the phalanstery."[73] In his utopia, in which he attunes man's passions to each other like the parts of a large machine in order to produce from this "machinery made of human beings" his land of Cockaigne, the arcades function as abodes. The *phalanstère* is imagined "as a city of arcades."[74] In this way, Fourier has combined the visionary perception of technology as the quintessence of Modernity by resorting to a primeval (*urgeschichtlich*) wish symbol, the land of milk and honey.

All its sympathy for Fourier notwithstanding, the exposé joins in the critique that Marx had leveled against utopian socialism in the *Communist Manifesto* (1848) and other writings. It is only in the present age, Benjamin writes, that the "social prerequisites"[75] for a significant increase in the use of glass as a building material are prevalent. Even in Scheerbart's *Glasarchitektur* (1914), he says, glass still appears in the context of utopia. To be sure, the idea that building materials are at present applied architecturally according to specific social prerequisites is left here without further explication. But Benjamin indicates nonetheless that the orientation of the work toward the present, previously connected to the concept of awakening, has not been invalidated at this new juncture of the work process.

This is confirmed by the final paragraph, in which Benjamin picks up Balzac's phrase about "the ruins of the bourgeoisie," which in his opinion the Surrealists had been the first to expose for what they are. The "development of the forces of production," according to his analysis of the image, demolished "the wish symbols of the previous century, even before the monuments representing them had collapsed." As a consequence of this development, with which the individual sections of the exposé deal in an exemplary way, the forms of construction had, in the course of the nineteenth century, emancipated themselves from art.[76]

The subversion of architecture by the engineer can be observed at the arcades, the subject of the first section. A further consequential facet of the confrontation between art and technology is treated in the section on "Daguerre, or the Panoramas." As photography demonstrates its superiority over painting in the representation of nature, so the imagination begins to leave the domain of art in advertising and creates for itself a fantasy world in fashion and in the world's exhibitions. The phantasmagoria of the pleasure industry, which Benjamin in the third section sees as the inspiration for the art of the caricaturist Grandville (1803–47), is given a companion piece in the fourth section on the intérieur, into which the private individual retreats as a collector and where, by decorating his dwelling place in the style of *art nouveau*, he creates his private universe. Even poetry is not safe from this general development. It is being challenged by the *feuilleton*, to which provocation Baudelaire answers with his theory of '*nouveauté*' as the supreme value of lyric verse. Hence, he makes the phantasmagoria of

Modernity the subject of his poetry, using images in which the modern metropolis is suffused with those of decay and ruin.

The driving force behind the developments Benjamin observed is the capitalistic interest in commercial exploitation. All these products, he summarizes, "are on the point of entering the market as commodities."[77] In the intermediate stage, in which they still appear to the observer in the nineteenth century, they unfold their potential as dream elements. But for the time being, this development encountered its fiery beacon signal in the Commune, the short-lived revolutionary government established in Paris on March 18, 1871. This first workers' uprising ended in its bloody suppression, to be sure; but it put an end to two phantasmagorias: in the street battles and in the burning of Paris in which the uprising culminated, the petrified phantasmagoria of the city as the quintessence of culture went up in flames. At the same time, the Commune did away with the phantasmagoria that it is "the task of the proletarian revolution to complete the work of 1789 hand in hand with the bourgeoisie."[78]

With this two-sided Janus, or to put it differently, in this half-baked, disfigured shape, the material world of the nineteenth century presents itself to the observer who looks back at it from the vantage of the twentieth. It is the task of this viewer's era to utilize the residue of this dream world at the time of his awakening. The organ of historical awakening is dialectical thinking: "With the destabilizing of the market economy, we begin to recognize the monuments of the bourgeoisie as ruins even before they have crumbled."[79]

In March 1939, Horkheimer requested a translation of the exposé for a potential sponsor of the project, which offered Benjamin the opportunity to revise his outline. This new (French) version[80] limits itself for the most part to a straight transposition but does make a few changes. For example, the section on photography, possibly in view of the "Work of Art" essay, has been omitted. Instead, Benjamin introduced this version with reflections that, in following the final section of the old exposé, provide an outline that is centered on the phantasmagoria of cultural history.[81] The decisive new factor is the integration of a text in which Benjamin focuses the culmination of the century's phantasmagorias, one that "clandestinely includes the severest criticism of the rest of them."[82] This text is a cosmological speculation that the revolutionary and conspirator Auguste Blanqui (1805–81) wrote while a prisoner of the counterrevolution during the Commune, *L'éternité par les astres* (1872, Eternity via the Stars).

Benjamin considered that here Blanqui, ten years before Nietzsche's *Zarathustra*, opposes the ideology of progress with his vision of the eternal return of the same—a vision based on the latest discoveries of the natural sciences—which is "a fundamental example of the primal history of the nineteenth century."[83] He refers to Blanqui's resigned vision as evidence for the contention that the century had been incapable

> of responding to the new technological possibilities with a new social order. . . . Hence, the deceitful mediations of the old and the new prevailed, which were the pattern of the century's phantasmagorias. The world ruled by these phantasmagorias is—to use a key word Baudelaire had found for it—*modernité* (*die Moderne*).[84]

When Benjamin has the visual imagination (*Bildphantasie*) of Modernity encounter society as it resorts to primal history, it is quite obvious that this idea relied on support from Johann Jakob Bachofen (1815–87), an anthropologist and mythologist whose writings he had become familiar with as early as the mid-1920s.

Shortly before writing the exposé of the *Arcades*, Benjamin had tried in vain to publish an essay (written in French), in which he had wanted to introduce the Swiss scholar to readers in France.[85] Benjamin knew the extensive introduction to the Bachofen edition (1926) prepared by its compiler, Alfred Baeumler (soon an outspoken Nazi ideologue), and he had studied Friedrich Engels's *The Origin of the Family, Private Property and the State* (1884), in which Bachofen is given the role of a witness for the construction of a communistic society at the dawn of history. Within the forcefield of both a Fascist and Communist usurpation of the scholar, Benjamin's concept of *Urgeschichte* and, even more so, his assumption that the experiences of primal history are deposited "in the unconscious of the collective,"[86] retains its iridescent ambiguity. Together with the central epistemological concept of his project, the concept of the dialectical image, it occupies the center of the epistolary discussion with Adorno that ensued after the latter's receipt of the exposé.

Adorno's central objection stated that in the exposé Benjamin has constructed "the relationship between the oldest and the newest . . . in terms of a utopian reference to the 'classless society.' "[87] In this way, however, the archaic "becomes a complementary addition," instead of being the 'new' itself. The exposé, by not presenting here a dialectical mediation, is pursuing a "mythologizing and archaistic tendency."[88] Adorno later summarized his critique by stating that "primal history *in* the nineteenth century is taking the place of primal history *of* the nineteenth century."[89] That is to say, if the archaic has been produced historically and hence "is dialectical in character and not 'pre-historical' (prähistorisch),"[90] then one could say (in abbreviating Adorno's argument) that the archaic as much as the utopian bears the stigma of false consciousness where the utopian resorts to archaic images. The resultant universal dynamic of self-deception, however, cannot be breached immanently. Adorno's alternative to Benjamin's attempt at defining the dialectical image as immanent, as a collective content of consciousness, expressly refers to the theological concept of Hell.

The discussion mentioned here briefly anticipates two pieces of writing that grew out of the context of the *Arcades* although each in its own way can claim an independent existence. In the *Arcades Project*, which has come down to us as an extensive collection of notes and excerpts found among Benjamin's posthumous papers, the files indexed as "J" and "N" assume a special status not only as to their quantity. From "Konvolut J," devoted to Baudelaire, the plan for a book (also extant only in fragmentary form) about the poet emerged. "Konvolut N," dealing with "Matters epistemological, Theory of progress," provides the basis for the theses "On the Concept of History."

## 3. Charles Baudelaire:
## A Lyric Poet in the Era of High Capitalism

When Benjamin turned to a study of Baudelaire barely two years after submitting the *Arcades* exposé, he did so more in response to a predicament than as the pursuit of a conclusive decision. With the completion of the Fuchs essay in spring 1937, there seemed to be no further obstacles to his starting work on the *Arcades*. In full agreement with Adorno's critique of the exposé and with his explicit support, Benjamin considered it his priority to work out the methodological and epistemological foundation of the book, that is, "the engagement between the dialectical and the archaic image."[91] This would have meant above all a critical debate with the theories of Ludwig Klages (1872–1956) and Carl Gustav Jung (1875–1961). This debate did not, however, come about. Instead, Horkheimer gave preference to the alternative that Benjamin proposed and supported the idea that the Baudelaire chapter should be started first. It was scheduled to be published as an independent essay in *Zeitschrift für Sozialforschung.*

But in spite of this arrangement, Benjamin seems to have been occupied until the summer with preliminary studies of the topic he and Adorno favored. As late as June 1937 he reported to Scholem that he was studying Jung in order "to safeguard certain foundations of the *Paris Arcades* methodologically by waging an onslaught on [Jung's] doctrines, especially those concerning archaic images and the collective unconscious." This, Benjamin continues, "would have a more openly political" importance apart "from its internal methodological" one: his study of Jung's volume of essays had taught him that their "auxiliary services to National Socialism have been in the works for some time."[92] This context of the political processes of his own immediate present cannot be overlooked in any of the works Benjamin started in exile and especially not in those that relate to the *Arcades.*

It is no less obvious, however, that this connection to the present resulted directly from Benjamin's historical interest, which defines the subject and method of what he wrote. Already in the exposé he had placed his studies of the world of Baudelaire's poetic imagery in a context defined by the dialectics of antiquity and Modernity, of primal history and Modernity, from which, he said, they were drawing their relevant inspiration. He saw in *nouveauté*, the overarching concept of Baudelaire's poetics, the origin of that semblance (*Schein*) that is produced by the collective unconscious; it is "the quintessence of false consciousness." This semblance of the new is reflected "like one mirror in another, in the semblance of the ever recurrent."[93] It is an aspect Benjamin found confirmed in Blanqui's *L'éternité par les astres*, which he referred to in a letter to Horkheimer on January 6, 1938. "In its theme of the 'eternal return,'" Blanqui's "piece has the most remarkable relationship to Nietzsche [and] a more obscure and profound relationship to Baudelaire, whom it almost literally echoes in some splendid passages. I will make the effort to bring this latter relationship to light."[94] Three months later he sketched the intent of the planned work in a letter to Scholem once more from the perspective of the present: He wanted

> to show how Baudelaire is embedded in the nineteenth century, and the vision of this must be seen as fresh and also bring about as difficult to define an attraction as that of a stone that has been lodged in the soil of a forest for decades, and whose imprint—after we have laboriously rolled it away from its place—lies before us with pristine distinctness.[95]

This image he used again verbatim in his letter of April 16, 1938, in which he gave Horkheimer a first detailed outline of the work. Insofar as it had originally been planned to be the central section of the *Arcades*, "the most important motifs" of the book converge here, so that "Baudelaire" shows the tendency of developing "into a miniature of the *Arcades*,"[96] On the basis of manuscripts discovered at the Bibliothèque nationale in

Paris as late as 1981, it is possible to reconstruct the various stages in the manuscript's genesis and to trace Benjamin's way of working. These reveal the extent to which he did indeed use the various *Konvolute* of materials assembled for the *Arcades* for the reorganization and writing of this text. They can also explain the status of fragments Benjamin himself titled "Zentralpark."[97] These fragments should be understood both as preliminary formulations of central reflections and as notes that specify reminders to himself about motifs and materials taken from the documentary collection of the *Arcades* files for use in the Baudelaire project. Accordingly, they assume an intermediary position between the *Arcades* and the notes specifically prepared for "Baudelaire."[98] A comparable textual genesis can also be observed with respect to the survey of the work Benjamin had forwarded to Horkheimer. This survey is extant as an early outline[99] and as a fully written out conspectus that should be considered as indicating the stage immediately preceding the letter. From this it can be ascertained that the extensive essay was to be divided into three parts.

As Benjamin explains in his letter to Horkheimer,[100] the first part is titled "Idea and Image." It will analyze the decisive significance of allegory for Baudelaire's *Fleurs du mal* and reconstruct the foundations of Baudelaire's allegorical inclinations.

"Antiquity and Modernity," the second part, will develop the central structural element of allegorical perception: "the fade-in/fade-out effect" of antiquity and Modernity that underpins the lyric and prose *Tableaux parisiens*. Into this poetic transposition of Paris, the crowd as the flâneur encounters it everywhere on his strolls through the city, intrudes in a decisive way. To capture the image of the city presenting itself in this manner, in other words, "the task of giving form to Modernity"—this had been Baudelaire's objective, and it was one he defined as heroic.

Section 3, "The New and the Ever Recurrent," treats "the commodity as the fulfillment of Baudelaire's allegorical vision." It turns out "that what is new, which explodes the experience of the ever recurrent under whose spell the poet was placed by spleen, is nothing other than the halo of the commodity."[101]

Two excursuses are to be added: one to prove the relevance of this conception for *Jugendstil* (art nouveau), the other to show to what extent the prostitute is to be seen as the commodity in which the allegorical perception is most perfectly realized and in this very realization turns into diffuseness. Baudelaire's unique importance, according to Benjamin's summary, "consists in having been the first, and the most unswerving, to have apprehended . . . the productive energy of the individual alienated from himself,"[102] doing so in a twofold way: fully acknowledging it and intensifying it through reification. While the first part presents the poet Baudelaire in monographic isolation, the second confronts him with contemporaries like Edgar Allan Poe (1809–49), Charles Méryon (1821–68), and Victor Hugo (1802–85). The final, third section, by virtue of the idée fixe of the new and the ever recurrent, places him into a historical configuration where he is joined by Blanqui and Nietzsche.

At that time Benjamin was still thinking of the project in the form of an essay. But at the beginning of August, when it had become predictable that its extent would far exceed the customary length assigned to such a piece, he suggested to Horkheimer to publish the individual sections of the work separately. This applied especially to the second part, which, as he reminded Horkheimer with a view toward the outline he had sent him, deals with two subjects: Baudelaire's "conception of Modernity in its relationship to antiquity" and "the first appearance of the metropolitan crowd in recent literature."[103] A few weeks later, the projected essay on Baudelaire, which originally was expected to take shape as an *Arcades* chapter to be written as the project's immediate priority, had grown into a separate book-length project.

For this book, to be titled *Charles Baudelaire—a Lyric Poet in the Era of High Capitalism*, the three-part outline of mid-April remained valid for the time being. Mindful of his obligation toward the Institute and its journal, Benjamin promised—as he had suggested to Horkheiner before—to work on finishing the second part of the whole manuscript first. This part would have the provisional title of "the Second Empire in Baudelaire's poetry" and be "completely independent."[104]

This part of the book, again subdivided into three parts, he mailed to Horkheimer on September 28, 1938, for publication in *Zeitschrift für Sozialforschung*, explaining to him once more and in detail the genesis of the complete project and the specific place within its frame taken up by the part now finished. He considered it especially necessary to emphasize "that the philosophical bases of the *whole* book [i.e., the planned book on Baudelaire] cannot be grasped on the basis of the completed second section, and were not meant to be grasped on this basis." This was, he argued, a consequence of the book's structure. "Within this structure, the first part—Baudelaire as allegorist—poses the question; the third part presents the resolution. The second provides the requisite data for this resolution." Generally speaking, the function of this second part is that of an antithesis. It formulated the critique of Baudelaire by *clarifying* the limits of his accomplishment. The interpretation of his achievement is reserved for the final, third part, in which also "the basic theme of the old 'Arcades' project" will come into its own: the new and the ever recurrent as the foundation of "the concept of *nouveauté*, which goes to the core of Baudelaire's creativity."[105]

Benjamin's remark that the planned study of Baudelaire would be, "if it were to succeed," a "very precise model of the *Arcades* project,"[106] emphasizes how closely it is related to the *Arcades* in terms of its content. Conversely, his comment also points out the fact that, methodologically and compositionally, the *Baudelaire* book furnishes the paradigm for the project out of whose context it arose. As for the structure of the book, he refers to a paradigm of his own making: he would like "the dialectical rigor" of this piece to be in no way inferior to that practiced in his "work on the *Elective Affinities*."[107] The great significance Benjamin accorded questions concerning the organization of his material and of its presentation, is borne out forcefully by the manuscripts discovered in Paris. This applies to his work on *Baudelaire* and hence also to the *Arcades,* even though one may not be prepared without reservation to accept the farther-reaching conclusions of their first commentators, Michael Espagne and Michael Werner. But it is no coincidence that Benjamin's insistent reference to the book's composition plays a decisive role in his response to Adorno's momentous critique of the text Benjamin had submitted in the fall of 1938.

After an enormous expense of energy in a "race against the war," eye to eye with the Sudeten Crisis and the Munich Agreement, the extensive essay Benjamin had "finally wrapped up just in time before the end of the world" was never published during his lifetime.[108] Even in its present printed form, "The Paris of the Second Empire in Baudelaire"[109] is incomplete. Two sections—according to Benjamin approximately six pages—are missing[110] in the first part of the essay which forms the middle part of a book that was planned to be tripartite, the essay in turn consisting of three parts: "The Bohème," "The Flâneur," and "Modernity." In keeping with the original arrangement, overarching theoretical reflections largely recede into the background throughout the text in favor of a detailed presentation of socio-historical data and of the interpretation of particular poems.

A socio-historical finding starts the discussion. Benjamin claims that the gesture of revolt and conspiracy has been inscribed into the formal structure of Baudelaire's poetry and into the argumentative structure of his theoretical writings even more than into the themes of particular poems. Their jumpiness, contradictoriness, and ironic impenetrability as well as the mystery mongering of allegory have imbued Baudelaire's production with conspiratorial features that suggest the poet's close proximity to the professional subversives. Their ambience in the Paris of the Second Empire had been that of the bohème. Their leader was thought to be Blanqui. The fact that Baudelaire made the quotidian world of the metropolis and that of social outsiders the subject of his poetry, and that at times he saw himself as a social poet is, in fact, as much part of his self-understanding as his commitment to *l'art pour l'art*. Benjamin interprets the reluctant acceptance of this contradiction as Baudelaire's attempt to make full use of the latitude that, in view of the crisis of lyric poetry, was available to him as he is trying to position himself on the literary market as a lyric poet. With the emergence of the feuilleton, which created a totally new market for belles-lettres, the literature business had undergone a revolution. It is against this background that Benjamin sees Baudelaire's contours: He was aware of "the true situation of a man of letters: he goes to the marketplace as a flâneur, supposedly to take a look at it, but in reality in search of a buyer."[111]

This introduces the keyword that is at the center of part 2 and there allows Benjamin *en passant* to comment that "flânerie could hardly have assumed the importance it did without the arcades."[112] On the street, which becomes his abode, the flâneur encounters the crowd of people whose ubiquitous presence is the decisive factor in shaping the experience of the modern metropolis. Benjamin recognizes physiologies, a literary genre that enjoyed great popularity during the first half of the century,[113] as the illusory attempt to confront this disquieting experience with a heightened knowledge of human nature. The menacing aspect of the metropolitan crowd, by contrast, is taken care of in the detective story, Baudelaire himself significantly contributing to its dissemination in France through his translations of Poe. The constitutive elements of the crime story—the victim, the scene of the crime, and the masses—can be identified in the poems of the *Fleurs du mal* as *disiecta membra*. What is missing, however, is the constructive element of the analytical mind, with which Baudelaire had dispensed in favor of a destructive impulse that, methodologically, benefits allogoresis and lends his poems a sadistic aspect.[114] On closer examination, then, the mask of idleness hides the intensified attentiveness of the observer as which the flâneur moves among the crowd. Prepared at any moment for a discovery, he develops a form of reacting that has adjusted to the speed of the metropolis. Baudelaire's sonnet "A une passante" [To a Passer-by] is a memorial to this shocklike experience.

The anonymous hero of Poe's short story "The Man of the Crowd," whom Baudelaire saw as a flâneur, and Hugo's transfiguration of the mass into the crowd of clients and *citoyens* served Benjamin as contrasting foils for a closer description of the image of the metropolis that takes shape in *Fleurs du mal*. Baudelaire, to be sure, let the spectacle of the crowd act on him with the appreciative attitude of the flâneur. But its deepest fascination for him lay in the fact "that, even as it intoxicated him, it did not blind him to the horrible social reality."[115] In the end, not even the poet was able to see "through the social semblance (*Schein*) which is crystallized in the crowd . . . . Whereas Hugo placed himself in the crowd as a *citoyen*, Baudelaire separated himself from the crowd as a hero."[116]

According to Benjamin's central thesis in the third, and final, part of his essay, it is the example of the hero by which Baudelaire had designed the image of the artist. Benjamin also states that Baudelaire had found a valid expression for the poet's activity in the metaphor of the fencer. Nonetheless, it is a specifically modern experience that is taking shape in the image of the ancient slave-fighter, the gladiator. The sure knowledge that "it takes a heroic constitution to live modernity" makes the "hero the true subject of *modernité*."[117] Those who live the social degradation of the modern metropolis, the proletarians, the ragpickers, and the apaches, personify for Baudelaire the varieties of that heroism whose features quite frequently intersect with those of the poet. In accordance with this self-understanding, a "task" has been imposed on the poet that is comparable to the "labors" of Hercules: it is nothing less than "to give shape to modernity."[118]

While Benjamin attributed minor significance to Baudelaire's theoretical utterances, he found the law governing his lyric oeuvre expressed programmatically in the imagery of his poems, first and foremost in the poem "Le cygne." It is an allegorical poem for good reason, he says, because as in the etchings of Charles Méryon, for whom Baudelaire felt an elective affinity, the interpretation of Modernity and antiquity in his poetry also takes place in the form of an allegory. In the end, the ever new shapes the hero takes on in this poetry illustrate the fact that no place has been set aside for him in Modernity. Modernity consigns him to eternal idleness and lets him take on his final embodiment in the figure of the dandy. In view of Baudelaire's failed attempt to give Modernity an ancient face, the linguistic gesture of the poems gains all the greater expressive force: "Baudelaire conspires with language itself."[119] By extracting, in the manner of a *coup de main*, allegories from the city's everyday language, his technique shows itself to be that of the putsch. The essay's conclusion, in returning to Blanqui, redeems its initial thesis, according to which Baudelaire's physiognomy is being revealed through the similarity he shares with the political type of the professional conspirator.[120] The "differences between them are superficial compared to their similarities: their obstinacy and their impatience, the power of their indignation and their hatred—as well as their impotence." In this sense Benjamin's summary reads: "Blanqui's action was the sister of Baudelaire's dream."[121]

The decision not to publish the essay in *Zeitschrift für Sozialforschung* as written was in very large measure a consequence of the detailed critique Adorno expressed in his letter to Benjamin of November 10, 1938. He makes no secret of his disappointment about what he had read. His central objection was that the essay assembles all the most important motifs of the *Arcades "without* theoretical interpretation."[122] This avoidance of theory, he writes, in the final analysis also diminishes the presentation of the empirical material. As he had done before in his response to the *Arcades* exposé, Adorno objected that the primal history *of* the nineteenth century had been substituted by a description of primal history *in* the nineteenth century: in other words, phantasmagoria is being presented not as "an objective historico-philosophical category" but rather as "a 'vision' on the part of social characters."[123] In this way, Benjamin's essay "switch[es] into the wide-eyed presentation of mere facts. If one wanted to put it rather drastically, one could say that your study is located at the crossroads of magic and positivism."[124] Adorno blames this dearth of theoretical mediation once again on "anthropological materialism," on the basis of which Benjamin's attempt to pay tributes to Marxism out of solidarity with the Institute[125] had by necessity to fail. Since this most important of works falls short of representing Benjamin appropriately, Adorno "earnestly entreats" him to "forgo publication of the present version and to write that other version."[126]

Even though he emphasized that this request does not express a decision by the editors, for Benjamin this letter "came as quite a blow,"[127] as he wrote on December 12, 1938, and was tantamount to a rejection. In his reply, Benjamin justifies the lack of theory that Adorno had criticized, first by pointing to the place the essay is to take up in the overall construction of the book. With his reproach concerning "wide-eyed presentation of mere facts" Adorno, he says, is characterizing "the proper philological attitude."[128] Referring to his own critique of *Elective Affinities*, he reminds him that the critique of the philological attitude is the initial incentive that provokes the philological effort itself. To use the terminology developed in the earlier essay, criticism "demands the exposure of the material content in which the truth content can be historically deciphered."[129]

By insistently pointing to its "construction," Benjamin obviously calls attention to the superficial fact that this text is a chapter in a longer piece of work. More important, however, his reference to the "construction" of the material content involves the problem of its appropriate historical presentation. What appears to be closed facticity attached to philological representation "dissolves precisely to the degree in which the object is construed from a historical perspective. The base lines of this construction," Benjamin continues, "converge in our own historical experience."[130] For this reason he also emphatically objects to Adorno's insinuated accusation of paying tribute to Marxism out of solidarity with the Institute. Neither mere solidarity with the Institute nor simple loyalty to dialectical materialism but rather "solidarity with the experiences which we have all shared during the last fifteen years" and hence his own innermost productive interests had motivated his refusal "to continue pursuing an esoteric intellectual path."[131]

Even though in a letter to Scholem he calls the objection raised against his manuscript "*raisonnable* in part," Benjamin uses the same occasion to lament, as he had done in his reply to Adorno's critique, the isolation in which he lives and which creates an "abnormal dependence on the reception [his] work encounters."[132] This could no doubt have been remedied by the publication of the essay, which Adorno's intervention had prevented.

Concerning the further destiny of his manuscript, Benjamin proposed to subject its middle chapter—the section about the flâneur, which, he emphasized, is an integrating part of the planned book—to a thorough revision for its separate publication. As the central issue of this new and altogether independent essay, the "critique of the concept of the masses, a phenomenon highlighted by the modern metropolis,"[133] is to be emphasized. In Benjamin's view it is Hugo who, more than anyone else, had "anticipated" the contemporary experience of the masses. The way this is to be understood is clarified by the remark that immediately follows that demagoguery had been an element of his genius,[134] a remark that is echoed by Adorno's observation on the occasion of Barcelona's surrender to Franco's troops in January 1939. In the capital of Catalonia was repeated what had happened the year before in Vienna: "The masses who now cheered the fascist conquerors were the very same who had cheered the opponents of the fascists only the day before."[135]

For the revision of this text Benjamin did not lose sight of its place in the overall design of the planned book. But this shift to a new direction also set in motion the whole mass of ideas to which the book owed its genesis. With this in mind, he wrote in a letter barely two months before the completion of his manuscript, which he sent to Horkheimer at the beginning of September 1939: "The new version of the flâneur chapter—for that is all I am working on—will seek to integrate decisive motifs from the Reproduction essay and the Storyteller, combined with some from the Arcades." And he continued: " Never before have I been so certain of the point at which all my reflections, even from the most different perspectives, converge (and it now seems to me that they have always done so.)"[136]

In "On Some Motifs in Baudelaire,"[137] Benjamin does indeed bring to the foreground a theme that had occupied him most seriously already in his earliest works and, in part connected to these, in his writings of the exile period: the structure of experience and the way it had been changing since the nineteenth century. As he wrote in a summary of the essay, Baudelaire's poetry gives expression to an experience whose origin is "existence in the midst of masses. Hence, it is one specific to the metropolis."[138] The concept of this experience is the opposite of the philosophical concept of experience that the philosopher Henri Bergson (1851–1941) developed in his theory of memory and on which Proust based his *Recherche*. While Proust's novel represents the impressive attempt to recreate in a synthetic way an experience that has been irretrievably lost in the information age, by contrast, the lyric poet Baudelaire counts on readers whose experience has been determined "by the standardized, denatured existence of the civilized masses."[139] The concept of *mémoire involontaire* signals, however, that Proust had been forced to limit his experiment—which is tantamount to the attempt "to restore the figure of the storyteller to the current generation"[140]—to the private realm and, as for the rest, to leave its success to chance. [141]

By contrast, Freud's reflections on the correlation between memory and consciousness in *Beyond the Pleasure Principle* (1920) provide the conceptual set of instruments that help Benjamin to describe the structure of the specifically modern experience. According to Freud, only what has not been experienced consciously can become part of memory (and thus of *mémoire involontaire* in Proust's sense). It is the function of consciousness to serve as a protective screen against stimuli, to keep the organism from absorbing the traumatic effect of shocks to which the inhabitant of the metropolis is constantly exposed. One would therefore expect a poetry that like Baudelaire's is grounded in an experience for which "the exposure to shock has become the rule" would "have a large measure of consciousness."[142] Impressions that are being worked through in a state of consciousness do not, according to this reflection, enter into long experience (*Erfahrung*) but, strictly speaking, fulfill the concept of isolated experience (*Erlebnis*).

The experience of shock, he writes, did not imprint itself on Baudelaire's creativity as the subject for a realistic description but as a "hidden figure."[143] With this in mind, Benjamin can go back to the analyses in the first essay that were concerned with the experience of the crowd but not without pointing out the connection between the reflex-determined behavior that is being practiced in the encounter with the metropolitan masses, and technology which "has subjected the human sensorium to a complex kind of training." Nowadays it is in film that "perception conditioned by shock (*chockförmige Wahrnehmung*)" makes itself felt as a formal principle. "What determines the rhythm of production on a conveyor belt is the same thing that underlies the rhythm of reception in a film."[144]

The perspective of the present makes it possible to arrive at a more detailed description of Baudelaire's historical circumstances and to define more closely the structure of the historical experience, and he considered it to be the poet's task to give shape to it. The *Fleurs du mal* are not solely familiar with *spleen*, which is their testimony to the reality of time as experienced by one who has been cheated out of accumulating experiences that endure. In Benjamin's understanding of the word "spleen"—the fashionable term the French Romantics borrowed from English for the experience of "weariness"—means "melancholy," the emotional state of those who live in the modern metropolis. In the sonnet "Correspondances," *spleen* is directly contrasted with an experience of time that has found an abode in *idéal*, the beautiful in art. Consequently, *Spleen et idéal* is the title of the cycle of poems that opens *Fleurs du mal*. The experience of *idéal* is turned toward something irretrievably lost, the remembrance of a fulfilled time before all historical time. It has retained cultic elements. "Only by appropriating these elements was Baudelaire able to fathom the full meaning of the breakdown which he, as a modern man, was witnessing."[145]

The experience described here as irretrievably lost and embedded in a collective continuity of tradition is none other than the experience of the aura, and Baudelaire becomes for Benjamin the most prominent witness of its decay in Modernity. In the *Fleurs du mal,* the last work of lyric poetry with a European resonance, the awareness of how problematic lyric poetry has become is part of the irreversible insight of a poet who so strongly claimed the distinction of Modernity for his poetry. According to Benjamin, it is this "experience"—that is, "the shattering of the aura in the shock experience"—"to which Baudelaire has given the weight of long experience (*Erfahrung*)."[146]

Before this text—together with the Jochmann introduction—was published as "On Some Motifs in Baudelaire" at the beginning of 1940 in a double issue of *Zeitschrift für Sozialforschung*, Benjamin was taken by surprise when war broke out in September 1939 and he was temporarily interned. It was not before the middle of November that he was able to return to Paris, whence in a letter to Scholem he expressed his hope that he may now be in a position to finish *Baudelaire*. Other than that, he continued, nobody here has any doubt "that Hitler is doomed."[147] Both hopeful expectations were to prove fallacious.

## 4. The Concept of History

"Every line we succeed in publishing today—no matter how uncertain the future to which we entrust it—is a victory wrenched from the powers of darkness."[148] The two essays that just then had appeared in *Zeitschrift für Sozialforschung*—to which Benjamin was calling Scholem's attention with these words—were to be the last of his major works to be published during his lifetime. Writing to his friend in Jerusalem (who had very recently returned from a lecture tour in the United States) at the beginning of January 1940, he also mentioned his plan to focus seriously on learning English. On May 26, 1939, the Gestapo had informed the German Embassy in Paris that Benjamin's citizenship had been revoked, which confirmed his realization that he had lost the prospect of establishing a sphere of activities in France. Even before the outbreak of war it seemed to him "an essential security measure to transfer all moveable goods—be they intellectual or material—to America as quickly as possible."[149] But the question is, he wrote to Gretel Adorno on March 20, 1939, "whether *I will still reach America*."[150]

Benjamin had no illusions about the fate in store for him in Europe. In a letter of June 4, 1939, to writer and art historian Stephan Lackner (1910–2000), he reported a story coming out of Vienna that would have found its appropriate chronicler in Karl Kraus:

> Gas has been turned off there in Jewish households at least for the time being. It has become too costly for the gas companies to supply Jewish customers. They were using too large a volume. And since this was done for the purpose of suicide, in many cases the bill would afterward remain unpaid.[151]

In the same letter he asked Lackner to inquire in the United States about his chances for selling his Klee drawing *Angelus Novus*. He seemed at first to have considered paying for his sojourn in America at least in part with the proceeds from this sale. But in the course of the dramatically intensifying events of that year, it turned out that the picture was the only piece of property he could fall back on in order to finance a passage to the New

World. His attempt, however, to liquidate his material heritage of Surrealism failed as much as his trying to cash in its intellectual patrimony.

On February 22, 1940, a little over two months before the German troops started their attack on France, Benjamin reported to Horkheimer in a letter written in French that he had finished writing a series of theses on the concept of history. The theses in question, he wrote, on the one hand connect to the reflections developed in the first chapter of the Fuchs essay. On the other, they serve as the theoretical armature of the second Baudelaire essay. They represent, he continued, a first attempt at formulating an aspect of history, an attempt that would bring about an irreparable rupture between our mode of interpretation and the remainders of positivism that, as Benjamin was convinced, still delineates those ways of understanding history that are closest and most familiar to us. The unfinished character of the theses militates against their being made public at this time. Even so he is letting Horkheimer know about them so as to inform him that the historical studies to which the latter knows him to be devoted have not kept him from another obligation: to be as intensely preoccupied as his friends in America with the theoretical problems with which the international situation is unavoidably confronting all of them.[152]

The connection of the theses with the continuation of the Baudelaire studies as well as their reference to the present political situation is also maintained in another letter, in which Benjamin speaks of them as a piece recently completed. Moreover, his letter to Gretel Adorno—datable to "late April/early May 1940"—puts the theses titled "On the Concept of History" by Benjamin himself in a typescript version into the larger context of his entire oeuvre. "The war and the constellation that brought it about," Benjamin writes, "led me to take down a few thoughts that I can say that I have kept with me, indeed kept from myself, for nigh on twenty years." In particular, he draws his addressee's attention "to the 17th reflection," calling it "the one that should make apparent the hidden, yet conclusive connection between these observations" and his previous works "by offering concise information about the method of the latter." As much as the character of these reflections is an experimental one, they do not, as to their method, "serve the sole purpose of paving the way for a sequel to the 'Baudelaire.'" Rather, they make him suspect "that the problem of remembering (and of forgetting), which appears in them on another level," will continue to occupy him for a long time. The warning he includes at the end of the paragraph that announces that he is mailing her the manuscript proved to be all too farsighted: "I need hardly tell you that nothing could be further from my mind than the thought of publishing these notes (let alone in the form I am sending them to you). It would be a perfect recipe for enthusiastic misunderstandings."[153]

Scholem, who read Benjamin's historico-philosophical theses as signaling his "awakening from the shock of the Hitler-Stalin Pact,"[154] saw their historical context in terms that surely are too narrow. It is true that the German-Soviet Nonaggression Pact of August 23, 1939, directly contributed to creating a foreign-policy constellation that made possible the German attack on Poland and hence the outbreak of the Second World War. But Benjamin most likely had a different constellation in mind. For example, in a letter of June 1939 he wrote of a deep disarray among the anti-Fascists, "which has been one of the causes and, to an even higher degree, one of the consequences of the defeat."[155] Two months later he makes an even more explicit reference in a letter to his son to "plagues which Hitler as well as the Social Democrats and Communists who were attendant at his birth had inflicted on the world."[156] And finally, his remark of December 1939 about the "*optimisme béat de nos leaders de gauche* (complacent optimism of our leaders on the left)" who have provoked his fierce hostility, establishes the direct connection with the tenth thesis, which is a polemic against the mindlessly "stubborn faith in progress" of those politicians "in whom the opponents of Fascism had placed their hopes."[157]

Benjamin found in the historical and political context of the Weimar era the immediate cause for the revision of the traditional concept of history, the subject of the theses. The theoretical and conceptual foundation, however, on which he carries this revision out has long been laid down in his writings. According to Adorno, the theses summarize "the epistemo-theoretical reflections, the development of which has accompanied those of the *Arcades* exposé."[158] It seems to make little sense to play this connection off against what Benjamin himself emphasized as the affiliation of the theses with the *Baudelaire,* which in turn had grown out of the context of the *Arcades.* It is instructive, however, that Adorno also placed the fragment he titled "Theologisch-politisches Fragment" close to the time of the *Arcades.*[159] Even though there is some reason to date the fragment considerably earlier, as do Scholem and the editors of *Gesammelte Schriften,* and to see it as one of the fragments from the purview of the important work on politics planned at the beginning of the 1920s, its thematic proximity to the theses "On the Concept of History" is nonetheless beyond question.

Benjamin's remark that he had kept the ideas to which the theses give expression with him, indeed had kept them from himself, for close to twenty years, should be taken altogether at face value. The reason for this

is the fact that the relevant philological findings are not limited to showing
the extent of borrowings from the Fuchs essay that can be found in various theses. Thesis 17, for example, in which, as Benjamin wrote to Gretel
Adorno, the connection of the "Theses" with his previous works in terms of
its methodology would have to be recognizable, quotes verbatim a passage
from the introductory chapter of the earlier work. Already there Benjamin
had countered the historiography of historicism, which has no theoretical
armature, with the constructive principle that underpins materialistic historiography. The idea, however, according to which the constructive principle blasts the epoch out of the homogeneous course of history in such a
way that the entire course of history is "preserved and sublated . . . *in* the
era,"[160] goes back to his study on the German *Trauerspiel*. As Benjamin
explained in a footnote in the Fuchs essay, his reflection complies with the
dialectical logic of origin. And origin is the central epistemological concept
of Benjamin's book on the Baroque, whose proximity to the *Arcades* he
emphasized more than once.

Under the overarching concept of origin the two pieces are connected
by a concept of history that is directed toward the present. In this vein a
work note relating to the *Arcades* reads: "The book on the Baroque exposed
the seventeenth century to the light of the present day. Here, something
analogous must be done for the nineteenth century, but with greater dis-
tinctness."[161] The consequence of this methodological premise contains
the "Copernican revolution in historical perception," which no longer sees
'what has been' as a fixed point but looks at it from the vantage point of
the present.[162] In this way, history becomes, as thesis 14 says, "the subject
of a construction whose site is not homogeneous, empty time, but time
saturated by now-time (*Jetztzeit*)."[163] Insofar as Benjamin understood this
revision of the traditional view of history as a collective process as early
as in the *Arcades*, he considered it tantamount to a displacement of the
historical interest in the past by a political interest.

It is not only the sway that the primacy of politics exerts over these reflections that moved them close to his early political philosophy. As he had
done in his early writings, in the *Arcades* Benjamin approximates politics
to a tension-filled closeness to theology. A late note, for example, datable
to 1937 through its reference to a remark Horkheimer had made in a letter dated March 16, states that in remembrance (*Eingedenken*) we have an
experience that forbids us "to conceive of history as fundamentally atheo-
logical." At the same time Benjamin is convinced that we must not try "to
write it with immediately theological concepts."[164] With these and similar-
sounding reflections the notes collected in files "J" and "N " outline the

thematic horizon of the "Theologisch-politische Fragment." It is to this fragment no less than to the relevant convolutes of notes for the *Arcades* project that the theses "On the Concept of History" are directly connected. Together with this thematic horizon, however, Adorno's thought figure of the definitive negation, which the fragment had used to outline the relationship of theology and politics, remains relevant for the theses.

In the figure of the chess-playing automaton (in thesis 1), Benjamin had found a succinct image to illustrate this relationship. The automaton was a puppet wearing Turkish attire and sitting before a chessboard placed on a spacious table. It had been presented in public for the first time in 1770 at the court of Maria Theresa by its constructor Wolfgang von Kempelen. After Kempelen's death it passed into the hands of the inventor Johann Nepomuk Maelzel, who made the Turk famous through numerous performances in Europe and the United States. Benjamin probably knew of the automaton from Poe's story of 1836, "Maelzel's Chess-Player," whose revelation of the supposed automaton's enigma, though not quite accurate in some details, he follows in thesis I.[165] Instead of an intricate mechanism, a hunchbacked dwarf hidden inside the apparatus turns out to be the secret of its success. According to an introductory comment that was omitted from the final text, the chess match illustrates "the controversy over the true concept of history."[166] The perpetual winner, both variants of this thesis continue, is to be the puppet called 'historical materialism,'" which can easily be the equal of anyone "if it enlists the services of theology, which today, as we know, is small and ugly and has to keep out of sight anyway."[167]

The bogey of progress that, as Social Democracy assumes, will lead the proletariat to victory more or less automatically is unmasked in theses 8–11. Already in the Fuchs essay Benjamin had held a sadly dilapidated concept of automatic functioning responsible for an attitude of this kind, which is a mixture of determinism and hefty optimism. This notion of mechanistic, or "self-acting," progress, he wrote, had its heyday in the eighteenth century: philosophically in Kant, in spontaneity, and "in technology, in the form of automated machines."[168] This is the connecting point with the theses. The ideology of progress—progress imagined as "self-acting" (*selbsttätig*) insofar as it is guaranteed by technological development—quite appropriately harks back to the supposed chess-playing automaton. Benjamin is convinced, however, that historical materialism can be victorious only if it bids farewell to this ideology. But historical materialism, whose position the theses affirm, can neither be identified with its actual historical emanations, nor is theology which it is meant to enlist in its service to be taken *à la lettre*.

The theological concept of redemption, around which thesis 2 circles, is given a profane interpretation there. The center of this thesis is taken up by "the image of happiness we cherish," which is also the central concept of Benjamin's political philosophy. His thought that "the idea of happiness is indissolubly bound up with the idea of redemption"[169] is beholden to the philosopher Hermann Lotze (1817–81), whose three-volume book *Mikrokos-mus. Ideen zur Naturgeschichte und Geschichte der Menschheit (Microcosmus; An Essay concerning Man and His Relation to the World*, 1885)—its subtitle is *Versuch einer Anthropologie*—he had excerpted at some length for the *Arcades*.[170] But he did not adopt Lotze's religious approach to history. In other words, in the context of the thesis the idea of redemption as well as that of "a *weak* messianic power" with which every generation has been endowed and "on which the past has a claim,"[171] does remain under the spell of history. Exactly such an immanently historical and hence profane reading of theological categories is also at issue in a note of the *Arcades*. The idea of a "preserving and bringing back of all things" Benjamin had encountered in Lotze as the consequence of a religious view of history.[172] By contrast, in Benjamin's note he speaks of a "historical apocatastasis," a restoration of all things, by whose logic the entire past is to be brought into the present.[173]

Benjamin's concern in the theses is not with the messianic restoration of all things at the end of times but with the immanently historical, topically political redemption of the unsettled claims of the past, of the victims and of the defeats suffered by past generations. Even if we can imagine happiness to apply only to our own lifetime, our omissions and failures nonetheless make us think beyond this kind of boundary. On account of this experience we feel solidarity with past generations. It is against the background of this consideration that the pursuit of happiness of which thesis 2 speaks, limited as it is to the present, becomes a category of that perspective on history that has undergone the Copernican turn.

As is Benjamin's early political philosophy, so also are the theses based on an inverse reading of Nietzsche's *On the Advantages and Disadvantages of History for Life* (1874). This implies a renunciation of the antiquarian interest in history, which for Benjamin is as important as his demand to grant politics primacy over history. Hence, Marx joins Nietzsche as an equal in the theses, complementing an anthropological materialism with a historical one. Nietzsche's insight that we need history, "but our need for it differs from that of the jaded idlers in the garden of knowledge,"[174] is the motto that introduces thesis 12. The subject that puts this insight to the test is, according to the first sentence of the thesis, "the fighting, oppressed class itself. Marx presents it as the last enslaved class—the avenger that completes the task of liberation in the name of generations of the downtrodden."[175] But conversely, this constellation also subjects the Marxian theory of revolution to a correction. Against Marx's statement that the revolutions are "the locomotives of world history," Benjamin raises his reservation in a paralipomenon to the theses: "But perhaps it is quite otherwise. Perhaps revolutions are an attempt by passengers on this train—namely, the human race—to activate the emergency brake."[176]

Benjamin's critique of the concept of progress, which he carries out on this theoretical foundation, is given expression in thesis 9 through the figure of the *Angelus Novus* and hence as an allegoresis of Klee's drawing that has fascinated scholarship ever since. The Angel of History whom Benjamin sees personified in the drawing is not a figure of salvation or redemption. Rather, he is a messenger who announces the true concept of history. As early as in the Kraus essay, Benjamin had introduced this angel as one announcing a new humanism, a "humanism that proves itself by destruction."[177] This idea has undergone a variation in a fragment from the context of the work on *Baudelaire*. This aphorism claims that the concept of progress must be grounded in the idea of catastrophe: "That things are 'status quo' *is* the catastrophe. Hence [catastrophe] is not something that may happen at any time, but what in each case is given."[178] Thesis 12 credits the Angel of History with this insight: "Where a chain of events appears before *us, he* sees one single catastrophe."[179] The incompatibility of these two perspectives culminates in the way they perceive the concept of progress. What *we* call progress represents *our* perception of history, that is, our distortion of the true concept of history. Once more the theological perspective serves to facilitate a revision of outdated notions.

This is easy to see insofar as already the preceding thesis had arrived at a changed view of history by uncovering the dialectics of exception and rule. The catastrophe of Fascism which faith in progress had considered impossible, comes as no surprise to those for whom the course of history until now had meant not progress but continuous suppression. A concept of history that accords with this insight would make us see "that it is our task to bring about a real state of emergency."[180] Its context suggests strongly that this formulation is to be read as a reply to the definition of sovereignty that Carl Schmitt had placed at the beginning of his *Politische Theologie* (1922/1934).[181] Also in view of this controversy it is of paramount importance that the theses avert their attention from theological speculation and return to profane history, which for Benjamin means a history that is subject to the primacy of the political.

Before Benjamin—in theses 8 through 11—brings about the break with the traditional concept of progress, he engages—in theses 5 through 7—in a polemical debate with historicism. It is a discussion, however, that seems not quite so compellingly necessary as would appear at first sight. For historicism's view of history—an approach Benjamin found to be most cogently represented by Ranke and Lotze—is based on the rejection of the concept of progress. With his well-known dictum according to which "every epoch is immediate to God," Leopold von Ranke (1795–1886), celebrated as the father of modern German historiography, opposed the speculative view of history as progress, which he had encountered in the tradition of idealism from Lessing through Kant to Hegel. Benjamin quotes Ranke's dictum approvingly in a note in order to put it to the service of a representation of history whose task it would be "to blast open the continuum of time."[182] And this may suggest that Benjamin, not only in their mutual opposition to the concept of progress, stands in closer proximity to historicism than he himself thought.[183]

On careful consideration, even the concept of universal history, which thesis 18 sees as the approach in which "historicism rightly culminates" and from which Benjamin resolutely delimits materialistic historiography, proves to be ambivalent. According to a note that relates to the theses, not every universal history has to be reactionary; only a universal history without a constructive principle is that. In the same breath Benjamin places his own, materialistic construction of history, his monadological principle, next to "salvation-history" as the example it emulates.[184]

This is also the direction in which thesis 3 points, crediting the chronicle narration of history with taking into account the truth "that nothing that has ever happened should be regarded as lost to history."[185] In the final analysis, the model for the chronicle is salvation-history. Apparently Benjamin's critique of historicism is not the least intent on revealing the latent theological implications inherent in this view of history. Whereas these implications manifest themselves quite openly in Lotze, they are hidden beneath aesthetic categories in Ranke. Recognizing the past "as it had really been," as Ranke's aphorism that introduces thesis 6 has it, calls for entering the past with an empathetic attitude and with an inclination to relive it.

In contrast to this stance of aesthetic contemplation, Benjamin insists on articulating the past historically. And whereas the aesthetic attitude of universal history is in danger of failing to apprehend history, Benjamin derives an inner-historical point from the genuine theological concept of universal history by insisting that "only redeemed mankind is fully in possession of its past." That is to say: the subject of the theses is not the redemption of mankind but the need to grasp history the way it would have to be imagined at any of its moments in accordance with the idea of redemption. A fragment from the context of the theses states that "whoever wishes to know what the situation of a 'redeemed humanity' might actually be, what conditions are required for the development of such a situation, and when this development can be expected to occur, poses questions to which there are no answers. He might just as well seek to know the color of ultraviolet rays."[186] Instead, Benjamin would like to recognize in the discontinuous structure of history, such as it appears to a person for whom any day could be his last day (and the day of his Last Judgment), "a revolutionary chance in the fight for the suppressed past."[187] The central categories of the theses "On the Concept of History" nowhere deny their theological origin. But at the same time, this theological context throughout brings about their transformation into anthropological-materialistic concepts, and for Benjamin this means political ones.

The theses are emphatically thought to be Benjamin's legacy not only on the basis of their place in the context of his writings, but more even in view of the historical circumstances under which they were written. Barely a month after he had sent them to Gretel Adorno—in a preliminary form, as he was careful to point out—he had to flee from Paris following France's capitulation on June 21, 1940. Before his flight he had just enough time to hand a portion of his manuscripts over to Georges Bataille, who hid them in the Bibliothèque nationale. For himself he was soon no longer able to see a way out. On September 25, 1940, he left a note with his companions whom he had joined in an attempt to escape to freedom. In it he wrote: "In a hopeless situation I have no other choice but to finish it. In a small village by the Pyrenees where nobody knows me my life comes to its end."[188]

## CHAPTER SEVEN

# Posthumous Influence and Stages of Reception

## 1. Record of Extant Material and Editions

"On the Concept of History" was the first of Benjamin's texts to be published posthumously. The work appeared in 1942 in a hectographed volume, *Walter Benjamin zum Gedächtnis* (In Memory of Walter Benjamin), edited as a special issue of *Zeitschrift für Sozialforschung* by the Institute for Social Research. (The journal itself had ceased publication the year before.) Beside Benjamin's text and a bibliographical note on his writings, the brochure contained three essays, two by Horkheimer and one by Adorno.

Benjamin's oeuvre remained largely unknown until the 1950s, as did this commemorative volume. It seemed at that time that even his hope for an "apocryphal influence,"[1] which he had mentioned occasionally and to which he had accustomed himself, was to prove overly optimistic. Indeed, his works and he as their author were not really known during his lifetime, even during the heyday of his journalistic presence in leading newspapers and journals of the Weimar Republic. Various reasons have been given to explain this fact: the thematic heterogeneity of his works and their scattered publication, their linguistic and intellectual complexity, and, not least, the fact that contemporary readers had no way of recognizing how closely his works are interconnected.[2] It can be said pointedly that while Benjamin was printed, he remained unread.

Difficult external circumstances notwithstanding, the public record of his writings is considerable. After all, later editors could rely on a considerable amount of published material: the important essays and articles, the works written for radio, and finally, the critiques and reviews. What is true of the pieces he published in newspapers and journals applies also to his books and especially to his two academic monographs.

His dissertation, "The Concept of Criticism in German Romanticism," as well as his *Habilitation* thesis, "Origin of German Tragic Drama," exerted their influence only in the context of his posthumous fame, however. Also *One-Way Street* (1928), which had appeared in the very recently founded Rowohlt Verlag, did not elicit the public attention its author had desired. Only two further monographs appeared during his lifetime. Given the increased difficulties of writing in exile, Benjamin was hardly in a position to anticipate a large readership for his annotated anthology of letters, *Deutsche Menschen* (German Men and Women), which he had published under a pseudonym in Switzerland in 1936. His contract, dated September 20, 1936, stipulated an edition of 2,000 copies. On March 12, 1938, the historian and journalist Karl Otto Thieme (1902–63) mentioned in a letter to Benjamin that only two hundred copies had been sold.[3] A special status must be granted the translations of *Tableaux parisiens* (introduced by the essay "The Task of the Translator"), which had been printed in 1923 in a small edition of five hundred copies. Ten years later, the elaborately designed, slender volumes of the first edition were still available from the publisher. Finally, Benjamin qua translator of Proust was denied enduring success. The enterprise of a German Proust edition, though started under favorable auspices, was canceled by the publisher soon after the appearance of the first two volumes of the *Recherche,* which Benjamin had translated together with Franz Hessel.

Even before his exile, Benjamin himself had started to build the foundation for what he hoped would be at least the apocryphal influence of his work by sending unpublished material especially to Scholem. "It always pleases me to hear of the care you bestow upon the collection of my writings," he wrote in a letter of April 4, 1937, to his friend in Jerusalem. "Troubling premonitions tell me that perhaps only our combined archives could present an exhaustive collection of them." But as conscientious as he was in administering his part of the archive, Benjamin continued, he "most likely did lose several pieces through [my] hasty departure from Berlin, and the unsettled existence of the early years of emigration. To be sure, only a handful of my own works have been lost—as opposed to, at least for now, a relatively complete collection of comments published on them."[4]

Although it is obvious that he had entrusted other friends with some of his writings, that part of his literary estate that he kept himself remained, other than Scholem's collection in Jerusalem, the most important one by far. Before his flight from Paris in June 1940, Benjamin managed to deposit a section of his materials at the Bibliothèque nationale in Paris, doing so with the help of Georges Bataille (1897–1962), who was then one of its librarians. From there Benjamin's sister Dora transferred two suitcases with manuscripts to Martin Domke (1892–1980), an attorney, who, following his emigration to the United States, handed them over to Adorno in June 1941, thereby fulfilling Benjamin's testamentary disposition. This part of the estate returned to Germany with Adorno in 1949 and, after the latter's death in 1969, was incorporated into the Theodor W. Adorno Archive in Frankfurt am Main as a separate Benjamin Archive.

But as it turned out, only a part of what Benjamin had left at the Bibliothèque nationale had been recovered back then. In 1981, for example, Giorgio Agamben discovered there further materials relating to the *Baudelaire* and the *Arcades,* which until then had been considered lost. They were added to the collection in Frankfurt in 1997.

The fate of the writings and documents Benjamin had left behind in his Paris apartment is more complicated. Some of them were taken out of occupied Paris to the United States in roundabout ways and also were sent to Adorno. Others, confiscated by the German authorities and first taken to Berlin, were seized as spoils of war by the Red Army and taken to a special archive in Moscow. There is no reliable information on the details of this removal.[5] Pursuant to a return agreement between the Soviet Union and the German Democratic Republic (GDR), these materials were handed over to the Central State Archive of the GDR in 1957. Fifteen years later they were transferred to the Academy of the Arts of the GDR. Thus the archival care and publication of Benjamin's literary estate for a time became a part of German postwar history. It was to take a good number of years before Scholem, in 1966, was given permission to examine those of his letters to Benjamin that were being kept at Potsdam, and to select at the end of the 1970s the ones to be included in the edition of his correspondence with Benjamin.[6] After the fall of the Wall, the GDR material was incorporated into the Benjamin Archive in Frankfurt. But as it turned out, the former Special Archive in Moscow had apparently not filed its complete contents. In 2004, for example, a small amount of previously unknown materials were discovered there.

Thanks to an initiative of the Hamburg *Stiftung zur Förderung von Wissenschaft und Kultur* (Trust in Support of Science and Culture), which after the death of Adorno and his wife Gretel became the sole proprietor of their estate, the materials collected in Frankfurt were transferred to the newly established Walter Benjamin Archive at the Academy of the Arts in Berlin in 2004. Ever since, the originals of Benjamin's writings, now united in one place, and copies of the materials in Jerusalem, Moscow, and Gießen have been accessible in his native city. Documents from private collections relating to Benjamin, such as the Rang Estate (acquired in 2005), are also available at the same location.

The posthumous publication of Benjamin's writings was based on the corpus of manuscripts held in safekeeping by Scholem and Adorno. The latter, whom Benjamin himself had designated the administrator of his intellectual heritage, tried tenaciously, though at first with only modest success, to make his friend's work accessible again to the public. Ten years after Benjamin's death, *Berlin Childhood around 1900* appeared in 1950 as one of the first books of the newly founded Suhrkamp Verlag. But after the sluggish sale of the childhood book, Adorno's plan for a multivolume edition of Benjamin's writings found only lukewarm support from Suhrkamp.[7] In addition, quarrels about the format of the publication, especially about the necessity of a scholarly apparatus, delayed the appearance of an edition of selected works that would reflect Adorno's suggestions. It was not until the publication of *Schriften* (1955; Writings), in the end reduced to two volumes and edited by Theodor W. and Gretel Adorno in cooperation with Friedrich Podszus, that the interested public had access to a first survey of Benjamin's work.

In the 1960s, this edition was replaced by the *Ausgewählte Werke* (Selected Works) in two volumes: *Illuminationen* (1961) and *Angelus Novus* (1966). Beyond that, the numerous editions of individual works that Suhrkamp Verlag brought out parallel to the selected works volume testify to a growing interest in Benjamin. Likewise, reprints of the books published during Benjamin's lifetime as well as editions of the Baudelaire studies (1963) and of the essay on *Elective Affinities* (1964) became available. This first editorial phase ended in 1966 with the *Briefe* (Letters), edited by Adorno together with Scholem.

By now Benjamin was no longer an unknown quantity even to the non-academic public. Some of his books, for example, *Das Kunstwerk im Zeitalter seiner technischen Reproduzierbarkeit* and the *Berliner Kindheit um Neunzehnhundert*, published as separate volumes in the edition suhrkamp and Bibliothek Suhrkamp series, respectively, had sold a considerable number of copies. Consequently, starting in 1967, plans were made for a multivolume edition of the kind Adorno had envisioned.

It took all of five years, however, before the first volume of *Gesammelte Schriften* (Collected Writings) was to appear in 1972—thirty-two years after Benjamin's death. And it was more than a quarter century later, in 1999, that this edition was completed, when the final volume of *Supplementa* with Benjamin's translations appeared. The *Gesammelte Schriften*, seven volumes, all but volume 3 in two or three parts and with supplements, though hardly undisputed, continue to provide the obligatory textual basis for any scholarly work on Benjamin. Since 1988, this edition (without the documentary material) has been available also in a twelve-volume paperback edition, and is supplemented by the six volumes of *Gesammelte Briefe* (1995–2000; Collected Letters).

The concentration, since 2004, of Benjamin's entire literary estate in the Archive in Berlin provides the necessary precondition for a new critical and complete edition of his writings, which will gradually replace the *Gesammelte Schriften*. This new publishing venture, *Walter Benjamin: Werke und Nachlaß; Kritische Gesamtausgabe*, is being prepared on behalf of the aforementioned Hamburg *Stiftung* by Christoph Gödde and Henri Lonitz in cooperation with the Archive. Each of the individual volumes—an anticipated total of twenty-one, published by Suhrkamp Verlag and to be completed by 2015—will be edited by a reputable Benjamin expert. The first volume to appear (spring of 2008) was his dissertation, followed by *Deutsche Menschen* (fall of 2008).

In contrast to those of *Gesammelte Schriften*, the editors of *Werke und Nachlaß* will have access to Benjamin's literary estate to the extent that it is known and assembled in the Archive. This advantage makes possible not only a greater degree of completeness but also a clearly arranged presentation of the material in an edition that seeks to do justice "to the particular factors that characterize the circumstances under which [Benjamin's] writings originated and were preserved for posterity, including the fragmentary books as well as the notes and similar papers."[8] Since this type of material can hardly ever be dated precisely, and since some phases extended over longer periods, the editors have decided against a chronological edition of all separate texts. Instead, they opted in favor of a "cautiously chronological sequence in which all books printed during Benjamin's lifetime will again be published in one volume each, a practice that will also be respected in those volumes that collect writings on the basis of editorial decisions."[9] This proviso applies, for example, to the early philosophical and aesthetic notes as well as to numerous other texts and fragments that Benjamin had not himself prepared for publication. Each volume brings together all versions, notes, sketches, and preliminary drafts pertaining to any specific text. It is also supplemented by an extensive apparatus that informs about the history of the respective work's origin and of its publication, makes additional sources such as unpublished letters available, and documents contemporary reviews. For the first time, this edition will present Benjamin's notebooks and tablets integrally, and include the Convolutes of notes for his late works, that is, preliminary formulations in connection with the

Baudelaire essays and the *Arcades* in facsimile with diplomatic transcriptions. Since the new edition has not progressed beyond its very early stages, it is premature to judge whether it can truly fulfill what is required of a critical and complete edition.

Beginning in the 1960s and aided by Benjamin's posthumous fame, his most important works were soon translated into French, Italian, Spanish—and English. In a letter dated March 18, 1934, from his Parisian exile written to Adorno, who was then living in Oxford, Benjamin had mused that "London is still the gateway to the world. And if one can also get by in English, then there are probably much greater openings there than for someone in Paris, however familiar he may be with the place."[10] Benjamin himself, it turned out, would not have the opportunity to put this to the test. Whereas the roads of his homeland in exile proved to be dead-end streets, Michael W. Jennings, the general editor of his *Selected Writings*, has posthumously opened a gateway to an incalculable readership in the English-speaking world. *Selected Writings*, published between 1996 and 2003 in four volumes by Harvard University Press, are now also available in a five-volume paperback edition. On more than 2,000 pages, Jennings and coeditors Marcus Bullock, Howard Eiland, and Gary Smith present Benjamin's texts in translations that will remain the mandatory English versions for the foreseeable future. They are based on the *Gesammelte Schriften* but follow a chronological sequence determined by a particular title's date of origin. This decision has caused a large number of inconsistencies, which the principles of selection chosen by the German editors both of *Gesammelte Schriften* and *Werke und Nachlaß* tried to avoid. The U.S. edition contains short explanatory endnotes to the texts and, at the end of each volume, a chronology with information on the biography of the works and an index of personal names. There is no critical apparatus.

Jennings's edition makes considerable use of existing translations from older publications such as *Illuminations* (1968) and *Reflections* (1978). Aside from numerous shorter texts and fragments, the dissertation, the *Elective Affinities* essay, the *Berlin Childhood*, the collection of letters titled *Deutsche Menschen*, the Fuchs essay, and the different versions of the "Work of Art" essay have now been made available in English for the first time. An annotated collection of texts by Benjamin on topics related to "Work of Art" has recently been edited, also by Michael W. Jennings, as *The Work of Art in the Age of Its Technological Reproducibility, and Other Writings on Media* (2008). These texts have been culled from *Selected Writings*; some of them appear in a modified translation. Missing from *Selected Writings* are the *Moscow Diary* (1986) and the *Arcades* (1999), both of which are available in separate editions from the same publisher. What weighs more heavily, though, is the fact that an Anglo-American postlude has now been appended to the German academic *Trauerspiel* surrounding Benjamin's book on Baroque drama. Nowhere in *Selected Writings* does one find the text of Benjamin's most important monograph, or a note that an English translation, with the problematical title of *The Origin of German Tragic Drama*, has been obtainable since 1977.

Under the impression of the continuing, and increasingly international, interest in Benjamin and in view of his great affinity for French culture and its language, of which his exile in Paris is only one, though especially indicative expression, a decision has been made in France to publish a complete edition of his works. A French translation, to be published by Fayard and supervised by Gérard Raulet, will closely follow after the individual volumes of *Werke und Nachlaß*. The first volume, Benjamin's dissertation, is scheduled to be available as early as 2009.

## 2. Reception

The first phase in the reception of Benjamin's work was substantially influenced by Scholem and Adorno. Scholem presented his analysis from a Jewish theological perspective and with the undeniable authority of his intimate knowledge of Benjamin's person and work. Along with numerous essays, the evidence of this privileged position is, above all, Scholem's 1975 memoir, an inestimable testimony even for those who do not accept his interpretive approach.[11] With Adorno it was less personal closeness than their mutual philosophical interest, asserted with the proficiency of the intellectual companion and partner in discussions, that defined the focal points of Adorno's analysis and gave them considerable weight. Beyond that, as the designated administrator of Benjamin's literary estate and as the editor of the early selected texts, he was instrumental *nolens volens* in guiding Benjamin's postwar reception merely by his choice of what to publish. Adorno's most important essays on Benjamin, among them many afterwords and introductions to the collections he supervised, have been gathered in *Über Walter Benjamin* (1970).

When this volume appeared, Adorno's authority had for some time lost its unquestioned acceptance. Instead, Benjamin's discovery by the Student Movement of the late 1960s and an emphatic interest in his particular reading of Marxism pushed another aspect of his multifaceted work to the foreground. The immediate cause of the debate about Benjamin during the late 1960s, in part conducted acrimoniously and involving a wide array of journalistic voices, was the publication of the two-volume edition of his correspondence in 1966. The letters, chronicling Benjamin's material destitution during his exile and his dependence on the Institute for Social Research, seemed to justify the accusation that his work was being edited tendentiously and in general was being subjected to biased manipulations. Further evidence in support of this reproach were the abridgements and the selection of specific letters to be included in a volume for which Adorno and Scholem shared editorial responsibility.[12] But it was no coincidence that this controversy in many ways followed in the tracks already laid out during Benjamin's lifetime by Adorno and Brecht and by the controversial influences they imprinted on his work, Adorno in particular being confronted by an eloquent opponent and advocate of the analytic approach he had rejected. This antagonist was Hannah Arendt, who in 1968 published a widely discussed essay in the monthly journal *Merkur* (and in Harry Zohn's translation in *The New Yorker* and as her introduction to *Illuminations*, 1968; also in her collection *Men in Dark Times*, 1969). When the Student Movement rediscovered Benjamin, its contemporary political interests had inadvertently been overtaken and shaped by the theoretical and political debates of the 1920s and 1930s.

With the publication of *Gesammelte Schriften*, Benjamin's reception had irrevocably entered its academic phase and had itself become a subject of scholarly research. These facts apply also to the controversy surrounding his work and person during the first stage of his reception. Benjamin's writings had become material for the kind of investigation that no longer presupposed their claim to contemporary relevance without reservation. Instead, his works were examined in the context of the specific circumstances under which they were written, and their relevance for the present was at best discussed critically. That is the way Siegfried Unseld, director of Suhrkamp Verlag, intended the title of the commemorative volume *Zur Aktualität Walter Benjamins* (1972; The Contemporary Relevance of Walter Benjamin) to be understood. It is a book Unseld edited on the occasion of Benjamin's eightieth birthday to serve as a companion piece to *Gesammelte Schriften*, the first volumes of which were just then being published. The most important contribution to this critical revaluation was the essay by Jürgen Habermas titled "Bewußtmachende oder rettende Kritik" (Consciousness-Raising or Rescuing Critique), which presented a historically relativizing refutation of Benjamin's presumably messianic Marxism.[13]

The academic-philological reception of Benjamin, searching for a more differentiated image of him and hence calling for a more critical approach,[14] registered its unease with limiting scholarly attention primarily to topically political interests. The rapidly growing number of dissertations and *Habilitation* theses, conference papers and essay collections, and not least research essays, illustrate emphatically that soon there no longer existed an alternative to Benjamin's academic treatment, for which *Gesammelte Schriften* provided the indispensable precondition, one, however, which in turn was ever more frequently subjected to philological criticism.

The large variety of interpretive approaches, further differentiated also by its international character, nonetheless can be grouped into a number of dominant trends.[15] There is a political-sociological, if not neo-Marxist, trend that extends debates from Benjamin's own time and takes its principal cues from his reflections on the position of the intelligentsia and from theorems central to Marxism, such as the concept of revolution.[16] In tense proximity to this approach, a Jewish theological interpretive tradition, decisively inspired by Scholem, has established itself. Its principal attention is directed toward messianic undertones in Benjamin's concept of revolution and, frequently in a productive continuation of Scholem's works on Jewish mysticism, toward specifically Jewish aspects of his thinking.[17]

The theoretical premises of deconstructivism in general and specifically Jacques Derrida's and Paul de Man's interpretations of Benjamin have elicited a notable response especially in the United States. In accordance with Derrida's theory of deconstruction and guided by the widespread attention accorded Paul de Man's essay "Conclusions: Walter Benjamin's 'The Task of the Translator'" (1986), the discussion of his theory of language and of translation became a central concern. Propelled by Derrida's controversial reading of "Critique of Violence," his theory of law (*des Rechts*) and of sovereignty emerged as a second focal point in the deconstructivist reception of Benjamin. Derrida had presented his interpretation, which aroused significant interest beyond the circle of his adherents, in two lectures that were first published in the *Cardozo Law Review* (1990) and reprinted in a volume of essays edited by Drucilla Cornell and others as *Deconstruction and the Possibility of Justice* (1992). Also Giorgio Agamben's work derived decisive cues from Benjamin's short but rich essay of 1921, which he developed further in a theoretical discussion of his own concerning the concepts of life and sovereignty.[18]

In view of Benjamin's numerous works dealing with issues of literary history and theory, it is not surprising that literary scholarship has taken him up. Both his dissertation and his rejected *Habilitation* thesis on the *Trauerspiel* of the Baroque era—the latter at first received only hesitantly by professional Germanists[19]—by now enjoy the status of scholarly classics. The same can be said of his Kafka studies, even if they cannot easily be connected with established approaches and always reveal as much about their author as they say about their subject. More narrowly focused discussions of literary theory have profited especially from Benjamin's theory of allegory, as developed in his book on Baroque drama,[20] and from his reflections on the history of reception[21] that are scattered across his entire oeuvre.

Whenever literary scholarship has reexamined its theoretical foundations critically in recent years, more often than not it has referred to Benjamin and has discovered him as a precursor of newly relevant orientations. This is true above all for media theory and, closely related to its concerns, for what in Germany is called *Kulturwissenschaft*, a discipline that should not simply be equated with Anglo-American "cultural studies." The academic discussion in Germany, which is gaining increasing influence also in the United States, is developing a scholarly approach to culture from the perspective of literary studies. It is less concerned with the cultures of minorities than with expanding the compass of literary analysis beyond the written and printed text. This approach can lay claim to a wide tradition that extends from Herder, Nietzsche, and Freud to Simmel, Aby Warburg, and Benjamin. Benjamin's *Trauerspiel* book, his Baudelaire studies, and not least the unfinished project of the *Arcades*, have attained paradigmatic importance for research interests of this kind.[22] His writings on the theory of narration (in *One-Way Street*, the "Storyteller" essay, the "Work of Art" theses) are of fundamental importance to the theory of media studies.[23] Likewise, the recent "iconic turn" in the humanities has a precursor in Benjamin, who both in his reflections on linguistic images (*Sprachbilder*) and through his interest in the visual arts offered its practitioners a variety of key concepts.[24]

Conversely, poets and artists working in the visual media have preserved the memory of Benjamin the person and his gesture of meditative absorption in thought images—among which the *Angelus Novus*, inspired by Paul Klee's watercolor painting, is surely the most widely known. Their testimonials have been collected in a slender volume titled *Glückloser Engel* (1992; Luckless Angel). In a different way, two other nonacademic documents testify to Benjamin's entrance into the memory of the "general reader": *Introducing Walter Benjamin* was published in 1998 in the well-known Totem Books series, and the year before Jay Parini published his novel *Benjamin's Crossing* (1997) about Benjamin's attempted flight across the Pyrenees and his last days in Portbou.

In looking back on what is by now half a century of reception history, it can be stated that Benjamin's work continues to invite controversial analyses. Hence, the suspicion cannot be dismissed that it is quite possibly this

# CHRONOLOGY

1892  15 July    Walter (Benedix Schönflies) Benjamin born, the oldest of three children of Emil Benjamin (1856–1926) and his wife, Pauline (née Schoenflies; 1869–1930); brother Georg (1895–1942) and sister Dora (1901–1946)

1902–12   attends Kaiser Friedrich Schule in Berlin-Charlottenburg

1905–6    attends *Landerziehungsheim* Haubinda, a country boarding school, in Thuringia; intellectual friendship with Gustav Wyneken (1875–1964), a teacher there

1912    graduates from Kaiser Friedrich *Gymnasium* in Berlin

1912–15   studies philosophy in Freiburg (Breisgau) and Berlin; intense commitment to *Freie Studentenschaft* (Free Students' Association) in Freiburg; friendship with Christoph Friedrich Heinle (1894–1914)

1914    president of *Freie Studentenschaft* in Berlin; meets Dora Sophie Pollak, née Kellner (1890–1974); outbreak of First World War; suicide of C. F. Heinle and Friederike (Rika) Seligson (1891–1914)

1915    makes acquaintance of Gerhard (Gershom) Scholem (1897–1982)

1915–17   continues his studies in Munich; breaks with Wyneken (March 1915) and withdraws from *Freie Studentenschaft*

1917    marries Dora Pollak

1917–19   studies at the University of Bern (Switzerland)

1918    son Stefan Rafael (1918–1972) born; makes acquaintance of Ernst Bloch (1885–1977)

1919    obtains doctoral degree "summa cum laude" in Bern; dissertation "The Concept of Criticism in German Romanticism"

1920    returns to Berlin; meets Florens Christian Rang (1864–1924)

1921–22   plan for a journal, *Angelus Novus*, fails; writes essay titled "Goethe's *Elective Affinities*"

1923    sojourn in Frankfurt am Main; agreement on a topic for his *Habilitation* thesis; makes acquaintance of Theodor Wiesengrund Adorno (1903–1969) and Siegfried Kracauer (1889–1966); Scholem emigrates to Palestine

1924    begins correspondence with Hugo von Hofmannsthal (1874–1929); his essay on *Elective Affinities* appears in *Neue Deutsche Beiträge*; studies primary sources for his second thesis in Berlin; writes his study of the German Baroque *Trauer-spiel* on Capri (May through October); meets Asja Lacis (1891–1979)

1925    withdraws petition for *Habilitation* in October; first articles for *Frankfurter Zeitung*; starts contributing to *Literarische Welt*

1926 March–October    sojourn in Paris; Proust translation together with Franz Hessel (1880–1941)

1926–1927 December/January    trip to Moscow

1927    Benjamin's first radio broadcast; second sojourn in Paris; plans an essay on the Parisian arcades; drug experiments under medical supervision

1928    *One-Way Street* and *Origin of German Tragic Drama* published by Rowohlt Verlag; plans a trip to Palestine

1929    regular broadcasts for Southwest German Radio and Berlin's *Funkstunde* (Radio Hour), arranged by Ernst Schoen (1894–1960); "Surrealism" essay published; meets Bertolt Brecht (1898–1956)

1930    Walter and Dora Benjamin divorce; plans for a journal, *Krisis und Kritik*; contract with Rowohlt for a volume of essays

1931    publishes Kraus essay and "Little History of Photography"; radio lecture on Kafka's *Building the Great Wall of China*

1932 April–June    first sojourn on Ibiza; works on *Berlin Chronicle*; contemplates suicide; writes his last will

1933 March    leaves Berlin for Paris: exile; April–September on Ibiza; malaria infection

1934    "The Present Social Situation of the French Writer," his first contribution to *Zeitschrift für Sozialforschung*; *Jüdische Rundschau* publishes his Kafka essay; his first stay with Brecht in Skovsbostrand (Denmark)

1935    exposé of the *Arcades Project*

1936    publishes the "Work of Art" and "Storyteller" essays; his collection of letters, *Deutsche Menschen*, published in Switzerland under a nom de plume, Detlef Holz

1937    "Eduard Fuchs, Collector and Historian" appears in *Zeitschrift für Sozialforschung*

1938 July–October    last stay with Brecht; completes "The Paris of the Second Empire in Baudelaire"

1939    revocation of his German citizenship (May); internment in a camp near Nevers at outbreak of war; returns to Paris early in November; completes "On Some Motifs in Baudelaire"

1940    writes "On the Concept of History"; in June flees to Lourdes with his sister; in September attempts to reach Portugal, setting out from Marseille; flight on foot across the Pyrenees, where Walter Benjamin, on September 26, takes his life in the Spanish border town of Port Bou

# NOTES

## CHAPTER ONE

1. Walter Benjamin, "Experience and Poverty," in *Selected Writings*, general editor, Michael W. Jennings, 4 vols. (Cambridge, MA: Harvard University Press, Belknap Press, 1996–2003), 2: 732.

2. Samuel Lublinski, *Die Bilanz der Moderne*, ed. Gotthart Wunberg (Tübingen: Niemeyer, 1974), 409.

3. Walter Benjamin, *Gesammelte Schriften*, 7 vols. and suppl., ed. Theodor W. Adorno, Gershom Scholem, and Rolf Tiedemann (Frankfurt am Main: Suhrkamp, 1972–1999), 2: 1.9.

4. Benjamin, "A Berlin Chronicle," *Selected Writings*, 2: 596.

5. Ibid., 2: 613.

6. Benjamin, *Selected Writings*, 4: 343.

7. Benjamin, *Selected Writings*, 4: 63.

8. Benjamin, *Gesammelte Schriften*, 5.1: 50.

9. Benjamin, *Selected Writings*, 3: 404.

10. Benjamin, "A Berlin Chronicle," *Selected Writings*, 2: 600.

11. Ibid., 2: 599.

12. Detlev Schöttker, *Konstruktiver Fragmentarismus. Form und Rezeption der Schriften Walter Benjamins* (Frankfurt am Main: Suhrkamp, 1999), 187.

13. Walter Benjamin, *Gesammelte Briefe*, 6 vol., ed. Theodor W. Adorno Archiv (Frankfurt am Main: Suhrkamp, 1995–2000), 3: 477 f.

14. Benjamin, *Gesammelte Briefe*, 4: 130.

15. Benjamin, *Gesammelte Briefe*, 3: 268.

16. Benjamin, "A Berlin Chronicle," 2: 599.

17. See Benjamin, *Selected Writings*, 3: 346 f.

18. See Benjamin, *Selected Writings*, 3: 391.

19. Benjamin, *Selected Writings*, 3: 387.

20. Benjamin, *Selected Writings*, 3: 349.

21. Benjamin, "A Berlin Chronicle," 2: 603.

22. Benjamin, *Selected Writings*, 1: 3–5.

23. Benjamin, "On the Concept of History," *Selected Writings*, 4: 389–411.

24. Benjamin, "Experience and Poverty," *Selected Writings*, 2: 732.

25. Ibid, 2: 733.

26. Benjamin, *Gesammelte Schriften*, 2.3: 902.

27. Walter Benjamin, *The Correspondence of Walter Benjamin, 1910–1940*, ed. Gershom Scholem and Theodor W. Adorno, trans. Manfred R. Jacobson and Evelyn Jacobson Chicago: University of Chicago Press, 1994), 486.

28. Benjamin, *Correspondence of Walter Benjamin*, 489.

29. Benjamin, "Introductory Remarks for a Series for *L'Humanité*," *Selected Writings*, 2: 20.

30. Benjamin, "Curriculum Vitae (III)," *Selected Writings*, 2: 77.

31. Benjamin, "A Berlin Chronicle," *Selected Writings*, 2: 618 f.

32. Benjamin, *Correspondence of Walter Benjamin*, 75.

33. Benjamin, *Correspondence of Walter Benjamin*, 72.

34. Benjamin, "Curriculum Vitae (III)," *Selected Writings*, 2: 77.

35. Benjamin, *Gesammelte Briefe*, 2: 331 f.

36. Gershom Scholem, *Walter Benjamin: The Story of a Friendship*, trans. Harry Zohn (Philadelphia: Jewish Publication Society of America, 1981), 119.

37. Benjamin, *Correspondence of Walter Benjamin*, 322.

38. Benjamin, *Correspondence of Walter Benjamin*, 359.

39. Benjamin, *Correspondence of Walter Benjamin*, 276.

40. Heinrich Kaulen, "Walter Benjamin und Asja Lacis: Eine biographische Konstellation und ihre Folgen," *Deutsche Vierteljahrsschrift für Literaturwissenschaft und Geistesgeschichte* 69, no. 1 (March 1995): 92–122.

41. Benjamin, *Gesammelte Briefe*, 3: 530.

42. Benjamin, *Correspondence of Walter Benjamin*, 385.

43. Benjamin, *Correspondence of Walter Benjamin*, 396.

44. Benjamin, "Hashish in Marseille," in *Selected Writings*, 2: 673–679.

45. Jürgen Habermas, "Walter Benjamin: Consciousness-Raising or Rescuing Critique" (1972), in Jürgen Habermas, *Philosophical-Political Profiles* (Cambridge, MA: MIT Press, 1983), 129–163, quotation on 130.

46. Peter Gay, *The Outsider as Insider* (New York: Harper & Row, 1970), 46–69.

47. Gershom Scholem, *Walter Benjamin: The Story of a Friendship*, trans. Harry Zohn (Philadelphia: Jewish Publication Society of America, 1981).

48. Benjamin, *Correspondence of Walter Benjamin*, 364.

49. Benjamin, *Correspondence of Walter Benjamin*, 262.

50. Benjamin, *Correspondence of Walter Benjamin*, 252.

51. Benjamin, *Gesammelte Briefe*, 3: 307.

52. Benjamin, *Gesammelte Schriften*, 4.2: 791 f.

53. Benjamin, *Correspondence of Walter Benjamin*, 257.

54. Erdmut Wizisla, *Benjamin und Brecht. Die Geschichte einer Freundschaft* (Frankfurt am Main: Suhrkamp, 2004), 55–89.

55. Gershom Scholem, *Walter Benjamin und sein Engel. Vierzehn Aufsätze und kleine Beiträge*, ed. Rolf Tiedemann (Frankfurt am Main: Suhrkamp, 1983), 26.

56. Benjamin, *Correspondence of Walter Benjamin*, 368.

57. Siegfried Kracauer, "On the Writings of Walter Benjamin" (1928), in idem, *The Mass Ornament*, ed. and trans. Thomas Y. Levin (Cambridge, MA: Harvard University Press, 1995), 259–264.

58. Benjamin, *Gesammelte Briefe*, 3: 146.

59. *Theodor W. Adorno and Walter Benjamin: The Complete Correspondence, 1928–1940*, ed. Henri Lonitz, trans. Nicholas Walker (Cambridge: Polity Press; and Cambridge, MA: Belknap Press, 1999), 53.

60. Burkhardt Lindner, ed., *"Links hatte noch alles sich zu enträtseln . . .": Walter Benjamin im Kontext* (Frankfurt am Main: Syndikat, 1978), 7.

61. *Gretel Adorno and Walter Benjamin: Correspondence, 1930–1940*, ed. Henri Lonitz and Christoph Gödde, trans. Wieland Hoban (Cambridge: Polity Press, 2008), 105.


CHAPTER TWO

1. Benjamin, "The Life of Students," *Selected Writings*, 1: 37–47.

2. Benjamin, "The Life of Students," *Selected Writings*, 1: 37.

3. Ibid.

4. Benjamin, "The Life of Students," *Selected Writings*, 1: 38.

5. Benjamin, "On the Program of the Coming Philosophy," *Selected Writings*, 1: 100–110.

6. Benjamin, "Critique of Violence" (1921), in *Selected Writings*, 1: 236–252.

7. See Benjamin, letter dated April 15, 1914, in *Gesammelte Briefe*, 6 vols., ed. Theodor W. Adorno Archiv (Frankfurt am Main: Suhrkamp, 1995–2000),1: 226.

8. Walter Benjamin, *The Correspondence of Walter Benjamin, 1910–1940*, ed. Gershom Scholem and Theodor W. Adorno, trans. Manfred R. Jacobson and Evelyn Jacobson (Chicago: University of Chicago Press, 1994), 68.

9. Benjamin, *The Correspondence of Walter Benjamin, 1910–1940*, 74.

10. Benjamin, *The Correspondence of Walter Benjamin, 1910–1940*, 75.

11. Ibid., 75.

12. Benjamin, *The Correspondence of Walter Benjamin, 1910–1940*, 55.

13. Gary Smith, "'Das Jüdische versteht sich von selbst.' Walter Benjamins frühe Auseinandersetzung mit dem Judentum," *Deutsche Vierteljahrsschrift für Literaturwissenschaft und Geistesgeschichte* 65 (1991): 318–334.

14. Benjamin, *Gesammelte Briefe*, 1: 72.

15. Benjamin, *Gesammelte Briefe*, quotations on 1: 71, 1: 72, 1: 72, 1: 82.

16. Benjamin, *Gesammelte Briefe*, 1: 81.

17. Benjamin, *Gesammelte Briefe*, 1: 83.

18. Gay, *Weimar Culture*, 79.

19. Benjamin, *Gesammelte Briefe*, 1: 71.

20. Walter Benjamin, *Gesammelte Schriften*, 7 vols. and suppl., ed. Theodor W. Adorno, Gershom Scholem with Rolf Tiedemann (Frankfurt am Main: Suhrkamp, 1972–1999), 2.1: 32.

21. Immanuel Kant, *The Metaphysics of Morality*, trans. Mary Gregor (Cambridge: Cambridge University Press, 1991), 275.

22. Benjamin, *Gesammelte Schriften*, 2.1: 32.

23. Benjamin, *Gesammelte Schriften*, 2.1: 29.

24. *Simmel on Culture: Selected Writings*, ed. David Frisby and Mike Featherstone (London: Sage, 1997), 55–75, quotation on 72.

25. Max Weber, "Science as a Vocation," in Max Weber, *The Vocation Lectures*, ed. and with an intro. by David Owen and Tracy B. Strong, trans. Rodney Livingstone (Indianapolis: Hackett, 2004), 24.

26. Benjamin, "The Life of Students," *Selected Writings*, 1: 42.

27. Benjamin, "The Life of Students," *Selected Writings*, 1: 46.

28. Gustav Wyneken, "Schöpferische Erziehung," in *Das Ziel. Aufruf zu tätigem Geist*, ed. Kurt Hiller (Munich and Berlin: Georg Müller, 1916), 123.

29. Benjamin, "A Berlin Chronicle," *Selected Writings*, 2: 606.

30. "You must not flee into a metaphysic but actively sacrifice yourselves to the *evolving culture!*" Nietzsche, *Writings from the Early Notebooks*, trans. Ladislas Löb (Cambridge: Cambridge University Press, 2009), 137.

31. Benjamin, "The Life of Students," *Selected Writings*, 1: 38.

32. Friedrich Nietzsche, *The Nietzsche Reader*, ed. Keith Ansell Pearson and Duncan Large (Oxford, UK: Blackwell, 2006), 45.

33. Benjamin, "Curriculum Vitae (III)," *Selected Writings*, 2: 77.

34. Benjamin, "The Concept of Criticism in German Romanticism," *Selected Writings*, 1: 116–200.

35. Benjamin to Leo Löwenthal, letter dated July 1, 1934, in *Gesammelte Briefe*, 4: 445.

36. Benjamin, *Selected Writings*, 1: 80.

37. Ibid., 1: 79.

38. Novalis, *Werke, Tagebücher, Briefe*, ed. Hans-Joachim Mähl and Richard Samuel, 2 vols. (Munich: Hanser, 1978), 2: 421.

39. Benjamin, *Selected Writings*, 1: 19.

40. Ibid., 1: 21.

41. Hellingrath, Norbert von. "Pindarübertragungen von Hölderlin. Prolegomena zu einer Erstausgabe" (1910), in von Hellingrath, *Hölderlin-Vermächtnis. Forschungen und Vorträge* (Munich: Bruckmann, 1936), 65.

42. Heinrich Kaulen, "Rationale Exegese und nationale Mythologie. Die Hölderlin-Rezeption zwischen 1870 und 1945," *Zeitschrift für deutsche Philologie* 113 (1994): 554–577, see 563ff.

43. Friedrich von der Leyen, "Norbert von Hellingrath," *Hölderlin-Jahrbuch* 11 (1958–1960): 4.

44. Hellingrath, *Hölderlin-Vermächtnis*, 48.

45. Ibid., 22.

46. Theodor W. Adorno, *Notes to Literature*, trans. Shierry Weber Nicholsen (New York: Columbia University Press, 1991–1992), 2: 34.

47. Friedrich Nietzsche "On the Uses and Disadvantages of History for Life" (1874), in *Untimely Meditations*, trans. R. J. Hollingdale (Cambridge: Cambridge University Press, 1983), 12.

48. Benjamin, *Selected Writings*, 1: 20.

49. Ibid., 1: 18.

50. Ibid.

51. Georg Simmel, "Gesetzmäßigkeit im Kunstwerk" (1917–18), in Georg Simmel, *Gesamtausgabe*, vol. 13, *Aufsätze und Abhandlungen 1909–1918*, ed. Klaus Latzel (Frankfurt am Main: Suhrkamp, 2000), 382–94.

52. See Benjamin, "Curriculum Vitae (III)," *Selected Writings*, 2: 77.

53. Gershom Scholem, *Walter Benjamin: The Story of a Friendship*, trans. Harry Zohn (Philadelphia: Jewish Publication Society of America, 1981), 52–85.

54. Benjamin, *The Correspondence of Walter Benjamin, 1910–1940*, 57.

55. Klaus Christian Köhnke, *Entstehung und Aufstieg des Neukantianismus. Die deutsche Universitätsphilosophie zwischen Idealismus und Positivismus* (Frankfurt am Main: Suhrkamp, 1986), 293.

56. Hermann Cohen, *Kants Theorie der Erfahrung* [1871], 3rd ed. (1918; reprinted Hildesheim and New York: Olms), 1987.

57. Scholem, *Walter Benjamin*, 52–85.

58. Benjamin, *Gesammelte Schriften*, 3: 564.

59. Friedrich Albert Lange, *History of Materialism and Criticism of Its Present Importance*, trans. Ernest Chester Thomas, 3rd ed., 3 vols. (New York: Harcourt, Brace, 1925).

60. Herbert Schnädelbach, *Philosophie in Deutschland, 1831–1933* (Frankfurt am Main: Suhrkamp, 1994), 135.

61. Benjamin, *Gesammelte Schriften*, 3: 565.

62. Benjamin, "On the Program of the Coming Philosophy," *Selected Writings*, 1: 100.

63. Ibid.

64. Ibid., 1: 102.

65. Ibid., 1: 103.

66. Ibid., 1: 102.

67. Immanuel Kant, "Prolegomena to Any Future Metaphysics that Will be Able to Come Forward as a Science," in *The Cambridge Edition of the Works of Immanuel Kant: Theoretical Philosophy after 1781* (Cambridge: Cambridge University Press, 2002), 54.

68. Immanuel Kant, *Basic Writings of Kant*, ed. and with an intro. by Allen W. Wood (New York: Random House, 2001), 15.

69. Ibid., 17.

70. Ibid., 19.

71. Benjamin, *Selected Writings*, 1: 105.

72. Benjamin, "On the Program of the Coming Philosophy," *Selected Writings*, 1: 101.

73. Benjamin, *Selected Writings*, 1: 298.

74. Benjamin, "On the Program of the Coming Philosophy," *Selected Writings*, 1: 102.

75. Ibid.

76. Ibid., 1: 103.

77. Ibid., 1: 104.

78. Ibid.

79. Ibid., 1: 105.

80. Ibid., 1: 108.

81. Ibid.

82. Benjamin, *Gesammelte Schriften*, 6: 37.

83. Benjamin, *Selected Writings*, 3: 284.

84. Benjamin, *The Correspondence of Walter Benjamin, 1910–1940*, 97.

85. Benjamin, *The Correspondence of Walter Benjamin, 1910–1940*, 97 f.

86. Benjamin, *The Correspondence of Walter Benjamin, 1910–1940*, 94.

87. Benjamin, *Selected Writings*, 1: 269–271.

88. Benjamin, *Gesammelte Schriften*, 6: 19–26.

89. Benjamin, *The Correspondence of Walter Benjamin, 1910–1940*, 261.

90. Benjamin, *The Correspondence of Walter Benjamin, 1910–1940*, 414.

91. Benjamin, "Doctrine of the Similar" and "On the Mimetic Faculty," *Selected Writings*, 2: 694–698, 2: 720–722, respectively.

92. Benjamin, *The Correspondence of Walter Benjamin, 1910–1940*, 372.

93. Benjamin, *The Correspondence of Walter Benjamin, 1910–1940*, 229.

94. See Benjamin, *The Correspondence of Walter Benjamin, 1910–1940*, 68.

95. Benjamin, *The Correspondence of Walter Benjamin, 1910–1940*, 79.

96. Benjamin, *The Correspondence of Walter Benjamin, 1910–1940*, 80.

97. Benjamin, *Gesammelte Schriften*, 2.1: 49.

98. Benjamin, *The Correspondence of Walter Benjamin, 1910–1940*, 52.

99. Benjamin, *Gesammelte Schriften*, 2.1: 50.

100. Benjamin, *The Correspondence of Walter Benjamin, 1910–1940*, 81.

101. Benjamin, *Selected Writings*, 1: 292.

102. Gerhard Scholem, "Jüdische Jugendbewegung," *Der Jude. Eine Monatsschrift* 1, no. 2 (March 1917): 822–825.

103. Benjamin, *The Correspondence of Walter Benjamin, 1910–1940*, 108.

104. Benjamin, "On Language as Such and on the Language of Man," *Selected Writings*, 1: 64.

105. Ibid., 1: 67.

106. Winfried Menninghaus, *Walter Benjamins Theorie der Sprachmagie* (Frankfurt am Main: Suhrkamp, 1980), 22 ff.

107. Benjamin, *The Correspondence of Walter Benjamin, 1910–1940*, 67.

108. Hamann, *Briefwechsel, Sechster Band: 1785–1786*, ed. Arthur Henkel (Frankfurt am Main: Insel, 1975), 106.

109. Benjamin, "On Language as Such and on the Language of Man," *Selected Writings*, 1: 62.

110. Ibid., 1: 67.

111. Ibid., 1: 69.

112. Ibid.

113. Ibid., 1: 70.

114. Hamann, *Sämtliche Werke*, 3: 27.

115. Benjamin, "On Language as Such and on the Language of Man," *Selected Writings*, 1: 71.

116. Ibid., 1: 71.

117. Benjamin, "Doctrine of the Similar" *Selected Writings*, 2: 694–698.

118. Ibid., 2: 697.

119. Benjamin, *Selected Writings*, 1: 273.

120. Benjamin, *Selected Writings*, 1: 298.

121. Scholem, *Walter Benjamin*, 59.

122. Benjamin, *Selected Writings*, 1: 300.

123. Benjamin, "The Task of the Translator," *Selected Writings*, 1: 253–63.

124. Ibid., 1: 253.

125. Ibid., 1: 254.

126. Ibid.

127. Ibid., 1: 255.

128. Ibid., 1: 257.

129. Ibid., 1: 259.

130. Ibid., 1: 257.

131. *Gretel Adorno and Walter Benjamin: Correspondence, 1930–1940*, ed. Henri Lonitz and Christoph Gödde, trans. Wieland Hoban (Cambridge: Polity Press, 2008), 287.

CHAPTER THREE

1. Benjamin, *The Correspondence of Walter Benjamin, 1910–1940*, 119.

2. Uwe Steiner, "Von Bern nach Muri. Vier unveröffentlichte Briefe Walter Benjamins an Paul Häberlin im Kontext," *Deutsche Vierteljahrsschrift für Literaturwissenschaft und Geistesgeschichte* 75 (2001): 463–90.

3. See Benjamin, *The Correspondence of Walter Benjamin, 1910–1940*, 98.

4. Benjamin, *The Correspondence of Walter Benjamin, 1910–1940*, 119.

5. Karl Heinz Bohrer, *Die Kritik der Romantik. Der Verdacht der Philosophie gegen die literarische Moderne* (Frankfurt am Main: Suhrkamp, 1989), 276–83.

6. Klaus Peter, *Romantikforschung seit 1945* (Königstein/Ts: Athenäum, 1980), 8.

7. Wilhelm Windelband, *Geschichte*, vol. 2, *Von Kant bis Hegel und Herbart*, 6th ed. (Leipzig: Breitkopf & Härtel, 1919), 280.

8. Winfried Menninghaus, *Unendliche Verdopplung. Die frühromantische Grundlegung der Kunsttheorie im Begriff absoluter Selbstreflexion* (Frankfurt am Main: Suhrkamp, 1987), 230–54.

9. Benjamin, *The Correspondence of Walter Benjamin, 1910–1940*, 89.

10. See Benjamin, "The Concept of Criticism in German Romanticism," *Selected Writings*, 1: 185, note 3.

11. Benjamin, *The Correspondence of Walter Benjamin, 1910–1940*, 139.

12. Benjamin, "The Concept of Criticism in German Romanticism," *Selected Writings*, 1: 149.

13. Ibid., 1: 126.

14. Ibid., 1: 168.

15. Ibid., 1: 155.

16. Ibid., 1: 175.

17. Ibid., 1: 177.

18. Ibid., 1: 154.

19. Benjamin, *The Correspondence of Walter Benjamin, 1910–1940*, 113.

20. Benjamin, *The Correspondence of Walter Benjamin, 1910–1940*, 143.

21. Benjamin, "The Concept of Criticism in German Romanticism," *Selected Writings*, 1: 155.

22. Ibid., 1: 183.

23. Benjamin, *The Correspondence of Walter Benjamin, 1910–1940*, 141.

24. Benjamin, "The Concept of Criticism in German Romanticism," *Selected Writings*, 1: 116.

25. Benjamin, *Gesammelte Schriften*, 1.2: 707.

26. Benjamin, "The Concept of Criticism in German Romanticism," *Selected Writings*, 1: 116.

27. Ibid., 1: 179.

28. Ibid., 1: 199.

29. Ibid., 1: 181.

30. Benjamin, *The Correspondence of Walter Benjamin, 1910–1940*, 163.

31. Benjamin, *The Correspondence of Walter Benjamin, 1910–1940*, 198.

32. Benjamin, *Gesammelte Schriften*, 1.3: 835–37.

33. Benjamin, *Gesammelte Briefe*, 2: 218 f.

34. Benjamin, "Announcement of the Journal *Angelus Novus*" (1922), *Selected Writings*, 1: 293.

35. Ibid., 1: 294.

36. Ibid., 1: 293.

37. Benjamin, *The Correspondence of Walter Benjamin, 1910–1940*, 194.

38. Bernd Witte, *Walter Benjamin—Der Intellektuelle als Kritiker. Untersuchungen zu seinem Frühwerk* (Stuttgart: Metzler, 1976), 41.

39. Benjamin, "Curriculum Vitae (III)," *Selected Writings*, 2: 77.

40. Benjamin, "The Concept of Criticism in German Romanticism," *Selected Writings*, 1: 180.

41. Benjamin, *Selected Writings*, 1: 315.

42. Benjamin, *Selected Writings*, 1: 356.

43. Benjamin, *Selected Writings*, 1: 297.

44. Benjamin, *Selected Writings*, 1: 300.

45. Benjamin, *Selected Writings*, 1: 97–99.

46. Benjamin, *Selected Writings*, 1: 309.

47. See Benjamin, *Selected Writings*, 1: 327.

48. Benjamin, *Selected Writings*, 1: 323.

49. Benjamin, *Selected Writings*, 1: 314.

50. Benjamin, *Selected Writings*, 1: 73.

51. Benjamin, *Selected Writings*, 1: 334.

52. Benjamin, *Selected Writings*, 1: 334.

53. Benjamin, *Selected Writings*, 1: 334.

54. Benjamin, *Selected Writings*, 1: 351.

55. See Kant, *Critique of the Power of Judgment*, §10.

56. Benjamin, *Selected Writings*, 1: 351.

57. See Walter Benjamin, *Werke und Nachlaß. Kritische Gesamtausgabe,* vol. 3, *Der Begriff der Kunstkritik in der deutschen Romantik,* ed. Uwe Steiner (Frankfurt am Main: Suhrkamp, 2008), 338–63 and 92–94.

58. Benjamin, *The Correspondence of Walter Benjamin, 1910–1940,* 320.

59. *Gretel Adorno and Walter Benjamin: Correspondence,* 229.

60. Walter Benjamin, *Origin of German Tragic Drama,* trans. John Osborne (London: New Left Books, 1977), 54.

61. Benjamin, *Origin of German Tragic Drama,* 176.

62. Ibid., 54.

63. Ibid., 55.

64. Ibid., 56.

65. Ibid., 53.

66. Ibid., 44.

67. Ibid., 182.

68. Benjamin, "*Trauerspiel* and Tragedy, " "The Role of Language in *Trauerspiel* and Tragedy," *Selected Writings,* 1: 55–58, 1: 59–61.

69. Benjamin, *Selected Writings,* 1: 201–6.

70. Benjamin, *Selected Writings,* 1: 363–86.

71. Benjamin, *Gesammelte Briefe,* 2: 354.

72. Benjamin, *Gesammelte Briefe,* 3: 35.

73. Benjamin, *Gesammelte Schriften,* 6: 772 f.

74. Benjamin, *The Correspondence of Walter Benjamin, 1910–1940,* 276.

75. Benjamin, *Gesammelte Briefe,* 3: 73.

76. Benjamin, *Origin of German Tragic Drama,* 138–58.

77. Ibid., 27–48.

78. Benjamin, *Selected Writings,* 1: 269–71.

79. Benjamin, *The Correspondence of Walter Benjamin, 1910–1940,* 264.

80. Benjamin, *Gesammelte Briefe,* 4: 107.

81. Benjamin, *The Correspondence of Walter Benjamin, 1910–1940,* 372.

82. Benjamin, *Origin of German Tragic Drama,* 78.

83. Ibid., 81.

84. Ibid., 194.

85. Ibid., 79.

86. Benjamin, *Gesammelte Briefe,* 3: 558.

87. Benjamin, *Gesammelte Schriften,* 1.3: 947.

88. Benjamin, *Gesammelte Schriften,* 1.3: 915.

89. Benjamin, *Origin of German Tragic Drama,* 142.

90. Benjamin, "Curriculum Vitae (III)," *Selected Writings,* 2: 78.

91. Benjamin, *Selected Writings,* 1: 273.

92. Benjamin, *Origin of German Tragic Drama,* 47.

93. Ibid., 45 f.

94. Benjamin, *Gesammelte Schriften,* 1.3: 952.

95. Benjamin, *The Correspondence of Walter Benjamin, 1910–1940,* 224.

96. Benjamin, *Origin of German Tragic Drama,* 182.

97. Benjamin, *Gesammelte Schriften*, 1.3: 919.

98. Benjamin, *Gesammelte Schriften*, 1.3: 951.

99. Benjamin, *Origin of German Tragic Drama*, 54.

100. See Benjamin, *Selected Writings*, 4: 363.

101. Benjamin, *The Correspondence of Walter Benjamin, 1910–1940*, 257.

102. Ibid.

103. Benjamin, *The Correspondence of Walter Benjamin, 1910–1940*, 148.

104. Benjamin, *The Correspondence of Walter Benjamin, 1910–1940*, 158.

105. Benjamin, *Gesammelte Schriften*, 2.1: 203.

106. Salomo Friedlaender, "Der Antichrist und Ernst Bloch," *Das Ziel. Jahrbücher für geistige Politik* 4 (1920): 114.

107. Benjamin, *Selected Writings*, 3: 305 which has "secular."

108. Ibid.

109. Benjamin, *Selected Writings*, 4: 390.

110. Benjamin, *Selected Writings*, 3: 305.

111. Ibid., 3: 306.

112. Benjamin, *Gesammelte Schriften*, 6: 64–67, and "Outlines of the Psychophysical Problem," Benjamin, *Selected Writings*, 1: 393–401.

113. Uwe Steiner, "'The True Politician': Walter Benjamin's Concept of the Political," *New German Critique* 83 (2001): 43–88.

114. Benjamin, *Selected Writings*, 1: 236–52.

115. Benjamin, *Selected Writings*, 1: 288–91.

116. Benjamin, *Selected Writings*, 1: 289.

117. Friedrich Nietzsche, *On the Genealogy of Morality*, trans. Carol Dieth (Cambridge: Cambridge University Press, 2007), 39.

118. Weber, "Science as a Vocation," 22–24.

119. Benjamin, *Selected Writings*, 1: 395.

120. Benjamin, "Critique of Violence," *Selected Writings*, 1: 244.

121. Ibid., 1: 246.

122. Georges Sorel, *Reflections on Violence*, ed. Jeremy Jennings (Cambridge: Cambridge University Press, 1999), 118.

123. Benjamin, "Critique of Violence," *Selected Writings*, 1: 246.

124. Ibid., 1: 248.

125. Benjamin, *Selected Writings*, 1: 252.

126. Benjamin, *Selected Writings*, 1: 252.

127. Benjamin, *Selected Writings*, 1: 244.

128. Benjamin, *The Correspondence of Walter Benjamin, 1910–1940*, 151.

129. Benjamin, *Gesammelte Schriften*, 2.2: 619.

130. Benjamin, *Gesammelte Schriften*, 2.2: 631.

131. Benjamin, *Gesammelte Schriften*, 6: 148.

132. Benjamin, *Gesammelte Schriften*, 7.2: 880.

133. Benjamin, *Moscow Diary*, 82.

134. Benjamin, *Selected Writings*, 2: 733.

135. Benjamin, *Selected Writings*, 1: 487.

136. Benjamin, *The Correspondence of Walter Benjamin, 1910–1940*, 276.

137. Benjamin, *The Correspondence of Walter Benjamin, 1910–1940*, 248.

138. Benjamin, "Theories of German Fascism," *Selected Writings*, 2: 321.


CHAPTER FOUR

1. Benjamin, *The Correspondence of Walter Benjamin, 1910–1940*, 266.

2. Ibid., 267.

3. Ibid., 268.

4. Benjamin, *Gesammelte Schriften*, suppl. 1, 9–11.

5. Benjamin, "Gloss on Surrealism," *Selected Writings*, 2: 3–5.

6. Benjamin, *The Correspondence of Walter Benjamin, 1910–1940*, 257.

7. Benjamin, *Selected Writings*, 1: 444.

8. Louis Aragon, *Nightwalker*, trans. Frederick Brown (Englewood Cliffs: Prentice-Hall), 1970), 96.

9. Aragon, *Nightwalker*, 95.

10. Benjamin, "Dream Kitsch," *Selected Writings*, 2: 3.

11. Ibid., 2: 4.

12. Benjamin, *Selected Writings*, 1: 444.

13. Ibid., 1: 456.

14. Ibid.

15. Ibid., 1: 459.

16. Ibid., 1: 476.

17. Ibid., 1: 457.

18. Ibid., 1: 460.

19. Benjamin, *The Correspondence of Walter Benjamin, 1910–1940*, 258.

20. Scholem, *Walter Benjamin*, 143–156.

21. Benjamin, "Curriculum Vitae (III)," *Selected Writings*, 2: 78.

22. Benjamin, "One-Way Street," *Selected Writings*, 1: 470.

23. Benjamin, *Selected Writings*, 1: 487.

24. Benjamin, *The Correspondence of Walter Benjamin, 1910–1940*, 313.

25. Benjamin, "Moscow," *Selected Writings*, 2: 22.

26. Ibid.

27. Ibid., 2: 23.

28. Ibid., 2: 30.

29. See Benjamin, *Selected Writings*, 1: 419 f.

30. Benjamin, "The Return of the *Flâneur*," *Selected Writings*, 2: 264.

31. André Breton, "Manifesto of Surrealism" (1924), in *Manifestoes of Surrealism*, trans. Richard Seaver and Helen R. Lane (Ann Arbor: University of Michigan Press, 1969), 66.

32. Breton, "Manifesto of Surrealism," 18 f.

33. Benjamin, "Surrealism," *Selected Writings*, 2: 209.

34. Benjamin, *Gesammelte Schriften*, 6: 148.

35. Benjamin, "Surrealism," *Selected Writings*, 2: 207.

36. Benjamin, *Gesammelte Schriften*, 3: 113.

37. Benjamin, "Surrealism," *Selected Writings*, 2: 207.

38. Breton, "Manifesto of Surrealism," 26.

39. Benjamin, "Surrealism," *Selected Writings*, 2: 209.

40. Karl Marx, *Critique of Hegel's Philosophy of Right*, trans. Annette Jolin and Joseph O'Malley (Cambridge: Cambridge University Press, 1970), 131.

41. Benjamin, "Surrealism," *Selected Writings*, 2: 210.

42. Ibid., 2: 217.

43. Ibid., 2: 212.

44. Benjamin, *The Correspondence of Walter Benjamin, 1910–1940*, 372 f.

45. Benjamin, *Selected Writings*, 1: 456.

46. Benjamin, *Gesammelte Schriften*, 3: 301.

47. Benjamin, *Gesammelte Schriften*, 4.2: 925.

48. Ibid., 926.

49. Ibid., 925.

50. Benjamin, "Program for Literary Criticism," *Selected Writings*, 2: 291.

51. Benjamin, *Gesammelte Schriften*, 3: 87 f.

52. Benjamin, "Against a Masterpiece," *Selected Writings*, 2: 379.

53. Ibid., 2: 381.

54. Ibid., 2: 379.

55. Benjamin, "Literary History and the Study of Literature," *Selected Writings*, 2: 463.

56. Benjamin, *Gesammelte Schriften*, 3: 50.

57. Benjamin, "Literary History and the Study of Literature," *Selected Writings*, 2: 461.

58. Ibid.

59. Ibid., 2: 463.

60. Benjamin, *Gesammelte Schriften*, 3: 366.

61. See Benjamin, "Literary History and the Study of Literature," *Selected Writings*, 2: 463.

62. Benjamin, *Gesammelte Schriften*, 3: 51.

63. Ibid.

64. Benjamin, "The Rigorous Study of Art," *Selected Writings*, 2: 667.

65. Ibid., 2: 668.

66. Benjamin, *Gesammelte Schriften*, 3: 373.

67. See Benjamin, "Literary History and the Study of Literature," *Selected Writings*, 2: 464.

68. Ibid.

69. Ibid., 2: 462.

70. Benjamin, *Gesammelte Schriften*, 3: 277.

71. Benjamin, *The Correspondence of Walter Benjamin, 1910–1940*, 372.

72. Benjamin, *Gesammelte Schriften*, 3: 173.

73. Ibid., 175.

74. Benjamin, "Left-Wing Melancholy," *Selected Writings*, 2: 424.

75. Ibid.

76. Ibid., 2: 425.

77. Benjamin, *Gesammelte Schriften*, 3: 351.

78. Ibid.

79. Benjamin, *Gesammelte Schriften*, 3: 183.

80. Benjamin, "Left-Wing Melancholy," *Selected Writings*, 2: 426.

81. Benjamin, "An Outsider Makes His Mark," *Selected Writings*, 2: 309.

82. Siegfried Kracauer, *The Salaried Masses: Duty and Distraction in Weimar Germany*, trans. Quintin Hoare (London: Verso, 1998), 101.

83. Benjamin, "Review of Kracauer's *Die Angestellten*," *Selected Writings*, 2: 356.

84. Benjamin, "An Outsider Makes His Mark," *Selected Writings*, 2: 310.

85. Benjamin, "Theories of German Fascism," *Selected Writings*, 2: 312–321.

86. Ibid., 2: 314.

87. Ibid., 2: 312.

88. Ibid., 2: 319.

89. Ibid., 2: 320.

90. Ibid., 2: 321.

91. Benjamin, *The Correspondence of Walter Benjamin, 1910–1940*, 395.

92. Ibid.

93. Benjamin, "Task of the Translator," *Selected Writings*, 1: 253–263.

94. Benjamin, *The Correspondence of Walter Benjamin, 1910–1940*, 368.

95. Benjamin, *Gesammelte Briefe*, 4: 14.

96. Benjamin, *Gesammelte Schriften*, 6: 176.

97. Benjamin, *Gesammelte Schriften*, 3: 294 f.

98. Benjamin, "Gottfried Keller," *Selected Writings*, 2: 51–61.

99. Benjamin, *Gesammelte Briefe*, 4: 19.

100. Benjamin, "Program for Literary Criticism," *Selected Writings*, 2: 292.

101. Benjamin, "Curriculum Vitae (III)," *Selected Writings*, 2: 78.

102. Benjamin, *Gesammelte Schriften*, 6: 174.

103. Benjamin, *Selected Writings*, 1: 460.

104. Benjamin, "Program for Literary Criticism," *Selected Writings*, 2: 294.

105. Benjamin, "False Criticism," *Selected Writings*, 2: 408.

106. Benjamin, *Gesammelte Schriften*, 6: 172.

107. Benjamin, "The Task of the Critic," *Selected Writings*, 2: 548 f.

108. Benjamin, "Karl Kraus," *Selected Writings*, 2: 456.

109. Benjamin, *Selected Writings*, 2: 79.

110. Benjamin, *Selected Writings*, 2: 52.

111. Ibid., 2: 54.

112. Ibid., 2: 55.

113. Ibid., 2: 57.

114. Benjamin, *Selected Writings*, 2: 260.

115. Benjamin, *Selected Writings*, 2: 244.

116. Benjamin, *Selected Writings*, 2: 333.

117. Benjamin, *Selected Writings*, 2: 335.

118. Benjamin, *Gesammelte Schriften*, suppl. nos. 2–3.

119. Benjamin, "On the Image of Proust," *Selected Writings*, 2: 237–247.

120. Ibid., 2: 239.

121. Sigmund Freud, *The Standard Edition of the Complete Psychological Works*, vol. 4, *The Interpretation of Dreams* (1900; London: Hogarth Press, 1953), 320–326.

122. Benjamin, "On the Image of Proust," *Selected Writings*, 2: 240.

123. Marcel Proust, "About Baudelaire," in Proust, *Pleasures and Days, and Other Writings,* trans. Louise Varese, Gerard Hopkins, and Barbara Dupee (Garden City, NY: Doubleday, 1957), 252.

124. Benjamin, *The Correspondence of Walter Benjamin, 1910–1940,* 291.

125. Benjamin, *Selected Writings,* 4: 315.

126. Benjamin, *Selected Writings,* 4: 316.

127. Benjamin, *Selected Writings,* 2: 316.

128. Benjamin, *Selected Writings,* 2: 244.

129. Scholem, *Walter Benjamin,* 227–234.

130. Benjamin, *Gesammelte Schriften,* 2.3: 1093.

131. According to Benjamin, *Gesammelte Schriften,* 2.3: 1082.

132. Benjamin, "Karl Kraus," *Selected Writings,* 2: 454 f.

133. See Benjamin, *Selected Writings,* 2: 723–727.

134. Benjamin, "Karl Kraus," *Selected Writings,* 2: 456.

135. Ibid., 2: 455.

136. Benjamin, *Gesammelte Schriften,* 2.3: 1102.

137. Benjamin, "Karl Kraus," *Selected Writings,* 2: 456.

138. Ibid., 2: 438.

139. Ibid., 2: 442.

140. Ibid., 2: 435.

141. Ibid.

142. Benjamin, *Gesammelte Schriften,* 2.3: 1110.

143. Benjamin, *The Correspondence of Walter Benjamin, 1910–1940,* 277.

144. Benjamin, *Selected Writings,* 4: 251–283.

145. Benjamin, "Paul Valéry," *Selected Writings,* 2: 533.

146. Benjamin, "The Present Social Situation of the French Writer," *Selected Writings,* 2: 744–767.

147. Ibid., 2: 757.

148. Benjamin, "Bert Brecht," *Selected Writings,* 2: 367.

149. Benjamin, "The First Form of Criticism That Refuses to Judge," *Selected Writings,* 2: 374.

150. Benjamin, *Gesammelte Schriften,* 2.2: 524.

151. Ibid., 2.2: 524.

152. Ibid., 2.2: 527.

153. Ibid., 2.2: 523, 2.2: 534.

154. Ibid., 2.2: 530.

155. Ibid., 2.2: 531.

CHAPTER FIVE

1. Benjamin, *The Correspondence of Walter Benjamin, 1910–1940,* 381.

2. Benjamin, *Gesammelte Briefe,* 4: 91.

3. Benjamin, *Gesammelte Briefe,* 4: 149.

4. Benjamin, *Gesammelte Schriften,* 6: 220.

5. *The Correspondence of Walter Benjamin and Gershom Scholem, 1932–1940,* 21.

6. Max Horkheimer, "Vorwort" (to vol. 1 of *Zeitschrift für Sozialforschung*), in Max Horkheimer, *Gesammelte Schriften*, ed. Alfred Schmidt and Guntzelin Schmid Noerr (Frankfurt am Main: Fischer, 1985–1997), 36, 38.

7. *Gretel Adorno and Walter Benjamin: Correspondence*, 11.

8. Benjamin, "The Present Social Situation of the French Writer" (1934), *Selected Writings*, 2: 744–767.

9. *The Correspondence of Walter Benjamin and Gershom Scholem, 1932–1940*, 41.

10. *The Correspondence of Walter Benjamin and Gershom Scholem, 1932–1940*, 54.

11. *The Correspondence of Walter Benjamin and Gershom Scholem, 1932–1940*, 110.

12. Benjamin, "Surrealism," *Selected Writings*, 2: 213.

13. Benjamin, "The Present Social Situation of the French Writer," *Selected Writings*, 2: 745.

14. Ibid, 2: 754.

15. Ibid., 2: 755.

16. Ibid., 2: 756.

17. Ibid.

18. Benjamin, "Surrealism," *Selected Writings*, 2: 216, and "The Present Social Situation of the French Writer," *Selected Writings*, 2: 762.

19. Benjamin, "The Present Social Situation of the French Writer," *Selected Writings*, 2: 763.

20. Ibid.

21. Benjamin, *The Correspondence of Walter Benjamin, 1910–1940*, 438, and Benjamin, *Gesammelte Schriften*, 6: 181 f.

22. Chryssoula Kambas, *Walter Benjamin im Exil. Zum Verhältnis von Literaturpolitik und Ästhetik* (Tübingen: Niemeyer, 1983), 16–32.

23. *Theodor W. Adorno and Walter Benjamin: The Complete Correspondence, 1928–1940*, ed. Henri Lonitz, trans. Nicholas Walker (Cambridge: Harvard University Press, 1999), 49.

24. Benjamin, *The Correspondence of Walter Benjamin, 1910–1940*, 443.

25. Benjamin, *The Correspondence of Walter Benjamin, 1910–1940*, 440.

26. See Benjamin, *Selected Writings*, 2: 763.

27. Benjamin, "The Author as Producer," *Selected Writings*, 2: 769.

28. Ibid., 2: 770.

29. Ibid., 2: 771.

30. Ibid.

31. Ibid., 2: 772.

32. Ibid., 2: 778.

33. Ibid., 2: 779.

34. Benjamin, *Selected Writings*, 3: 107.

35. Quoted in Benjamin, *Gesammelte Schriften*, 2.3: 1319.

36. Ulrich Weitz, *Salonkultur und Proletariat. Eduard Fuchs—Sammler, Sittengeschichtler, Sozialist* (Stuttgart: Stöffler und Schütz, 1991), 413.

37. *Gretel Adorno and Walter Benjamin: Correspondence*, 166.

38. *Theodor W. Adorno and Walter Benjamin: Correspondence*, 169.

39. Benjamin, *Gesammelte Briefe*, 5: 463.

40. Benjamin, *Selected Writings*, 3: 263.

41. Benjamin, *Selected Writings*, 3: 260.

42. Benjamin, *Selected Writings*, 3: 267, and 4: 392.

43. Nietzsche *On the Genealogy of Morality*, 44 f.

44. Nietzsche, *The Nietzsche Reader*, 90.

45. Benjamin, *Selected Writings*, 3: 268.

46. Benjamin, *Selected Writings*, 4: 392.

47. Benjamin, *Selected Writings*, 3: 262.

48. Ibid.

49. Ibid.

50. Benjamin, *Selected Writings*, 3: 283.

51. Benjamin, *Gesammelte Briefe*, 5: 492.

52. Benjamin, *Selected Writings*, 4: 357.

53. Documented in Benjamin, *Gesammelte Schriften*, 2.3: 1397–1403.

54. Benjamin, *Gesammelte Briefe*, 5: 492.

55. Benjamin, *Gesammelte Briefe*, 5: 623.

56. Ibid.

57. Benjamin, "The Author as Producer," *Selected Writings*, 2: 768.

58. Ibid., 2: 777.

59. Benjamin, *Selected Writings*, 4: 361.

60. Ibid., 4: 362.

61. Ibid., 4: 363.

62. Benjamin, *Gesammelte Schriften*, 2.3: 1408.

63. Benjamin, *Selected Writings*, 4: 363.

64. Benjamin, *The Correspondence of Walter Benjamin, 1910–1940*, 509.

65. See Benjamin, *Selected Writings*, 3: 35 f.

66. Walter Benjamin, *The Arcades Project*, trans. Howard Eiland and Kevin McLaughlin (Cambridge, MA: Belknap Press, 1999), K 3, 3.

67. Benjamin, *The Arcades Project*, 394.

68. Benjamin, *Gesammelte Schriften*, suppl. no. 1, 8–11.

69. Benjamin, "Surrealism," *Selected Writings*, 2: 211.

70. Benjamin, *The Correspondence of Walter Benjamin, 1910–1940*, 528.

71. Ibid.

72. Benjamin, *Selected Writings*, 3: 127.

73. Benjamin, *Selected Writings*, 3: 310.

74. Benjamin, *Selected Writings*, 3: 120.

75. Benjamin, "Little History of Photography," *Selected Writings*, 2: 507.

76. Ibid., 2: 520.

77. Ibid., 2: 523.

78. Ibid., 2: 508.

79. Ibid., 2: 510 f.

80. Karl Bloßfeldt, "Urformen der Kunst" (1928), in *Urformen der Kunst / Art Forms in Nature / Formes originelles de l'art*, ed. Hans Christian Adam (Cologne and New York: Taschen, 1999), 69.

81. Benjamin, "News about Flowers," *Selected Writings*, 2: 155.

82. Benjamin, "Little History of Photography," *Selected Writings*, 2: 518.

83. Ibid., 2: 512.

84. Ibid., 2: 514.

85. Ibid., 2: 517.

86. Ibid., 2: 517.

87. Ibid., 2: 518.

88. Ibid., 2: 519.

89. Ibid., 2: 527.

90. Ibid., 2: 512.

91. Ibid., 2: 527.

92. Benjamin, *Selected Writings*, 3: 108.

93. Benjamin, *Selected Writings*, 3: 132.

94. Benjamin, *Selected Writings*, 3: 108.

95. Benjamin, *The Correspondence of Walter Benjamin, 1910–1940*, 509.

96. Rolf Wiggershaus, *Die Frankfurter Schule. Geschichte, theoretische Entwicklung, politische Bedeutung* (Munich and Vienna: Hanser, 1986), 154.

97. Benjamin, *Gesammelte Briefe*, 5: 184.

98. Benjamin, *Gesammelte Schriften*, 1.2: 709–739.

99. Benjamin, *Gesammelte Schriften*, 1.2: 471–508.

100. Benjamin, *Gesammelte Schriften*, 7.1: 350–384.

101. Benjamin, *Gesammelte Schriften*, 7.2: 681–682.

102. Benjamin, *Selected Writings*, 3: 106.

103. Benjamin, *Selected Writings*, 3: 107.

104. Benjamin, *Selected Writings*, 3: 109.

105. Benjamin, *Selected Writings*, 3: 116.

106. Benjamin, *Selected Writings*, 3: 117.

107. Benjamin, *Selected Writings*, 3: 113.

108. Benjamin, *Selected Writings*, 3: 104.

109. Benjamin, *Selected Writings*, 3: 118.

110. Benjamin, *Selected Writings*, 3: 120.

111. Benjamin, *Selected Writings*, 3: 121 f.

112. Nietzsche, *On the Genealogy of Morality*, 44 and 45.

113. Benjamin, *Selected Writings*, 3: 122.

114. *Theodor W. Adorno and Walter Benjamin: Correspondence*, 127–134.

115. Benjamin, "Experience and Poverty," *Selected Writings*, 2: 731 f.

116. Ibid., 2: 733.

117. Ibid., 2: 734.

118. Friedrich Nietzsche, *The Will to Power*, trans. Walter Kaufmann and R. J. Hollingdale (New York: Vintage Books), 479.

119. Benjamin, "Experience and Poverty," *Selected Writings*, 2: 735.

120. Ibid., 2: 732.

121. Benjamin, "Curriculum Vitae (III)," *Selected Writings*, 2: 78.

122. Benjamin, *The Correspondence of Walter Benjamin, 1910–1940*, 342.

123. Benjamin, "The Crisis of the Novel," *Selected Writings*, 2: 299.

124. Ibid., 2: 300.

125. Ibid., 2: 301.

126. Ibid., 2: 301.

127. Benjamin, *The Correspondence of Walter Benjamin, 1910–1940*, 525.

128. Benjamin, *Gesammelte Briefe*, 5: 606.

129. Ibid., 5: 606 f.

130. Bertolt Brecht, "The *Threepenny* Lawsuit. A Sociological Experiment," in *Brecht on Film and Radio*, trans. and ed. Marc Silberman (London: Methuen, 2000), 161.

131. Benjamin, *Selected Writings*, 3: 143.

132. Ibid., 3: 145 f.

133. Ibid., 3: 157.

134. Ibid.

135. Ibid.

136. Benjamin, *Selected Writings*, 3: 107.

137. Benjamin, *Selected Writings*, 3: 147.

138. Benjamin, *Gesammelte Schriften*, 2.3: 962.

139. Benjamin, *Gesammelte Schriften*, 2.3: 1282–1283.

140. Benjamin, *Gesammelte Schriften*, 3.3: 1282.

141. Benjamin, "Franz Kafka: *Beim Bau der Chinesischen Mauer*," *Selected Writings*, 2: 497.

142. Benjamin, *The Correspondence of Walter Benjamin, 1910–1940*, 279.

143. *The Correspondence of Walter Benjamin and Gershom Scholem, 1932–1940*, 220–226.

144. See Benjamin, *Selected Writings*, 3: 317–321.

145. Hartmut Binder, ed., *Kafka-Handbuch in zwei Bänden* (Stuttgart: Kröner, 1979), 2: 609.

146. Jürgen Born, ed., *Franz Kafka. Kritik und Rezeption, 1924–1928* (Frankfurt am Main: Fischer, 1983), 101.

147. Born, *Franz Kafka*, 141.

148. Ibid., 304.

149. Benjamin, "Franz Kafka," *Selected Writings*, 2: 803.

150. Benjamin, *Gesammelte Schriften*, 3: 277.

151. Benjamin, "Franz Kafka," *Selected Writings*, 2: 806.

152. *The Correspondence of Walter Benjamin and Gershom Scholem, 1932–1940*, 111.

153. Benjamin, *The Correspondence of Walter Benjamin, 1910–1940*, 442.

154. *The Correspondence of Walter Benjamin and Gershom Scholem, 1932–1940*, 128.

155. Benjamin, "Franz Kafka: *Beim Bau der Chinesischen Mauer*," *Selected Writings*, 2: 496.

156. Ibid.

157. Ibid.

158. Ibid., 2: 497.

159. Ibid., 2:498 f.

160. Benjamin, "Franz Kafka," *Selected Writings*, 2: 797.

161. Ibid., 2: 799.

162. Ibid., 2: 801.

163. Ibid., 2: 803.

164. Ibid., 2: 814.

165. Benjamin, *The Correspondence of Walter Benjamin, 1910–1940*, 564.

166. Ibid.

167. Ibid., 565.

168. *The Correspondence of Walter Benjamin and Gershom Scholem, 1932–1940*, 123–125.

169. *Theodor W. Adorno and Walter Benjamin: The Complete Correspondence, 1928–1940*, 67.

170. Ibid., 53.

171. Ibid., 70.

172. Ibid., 74.


CHAPTER SIX

1. *The Correspondence of Walter Benjamin and Gershom Scholem, 1932–1940*, 18.

2. Benjamin, *Selected Writings*, 3: 344.

3. Benjamin, *Gesammelte Briefe*, 5: 629.

4. Benjamin, *The Correspondence of Walter Benjamin, 1910–1940*, 482.

5. *Gretel Adorno and Walter Benjamin: Correspondence*, 155.

6. Benjamin, *Gesammelte Briefe*, 4:54 and 4: 58.

7. Benjamin, "A Berlin Chronicle," *Selected Writings*, 2: 603.

8. *Theodor W. Adorno and Walter Benjamin: Correspondence*, 19 and 21.

9. Benjamin, *Gesammelte Briefe*, 4: 395.

10. Benjamin, *Gesammelte Schriften*, 7.1: 385–432.

11. Benjamin, *Gesammelte Schriften*, 4.1: 253–304.

12. Benjamin, "A Berlin Chronicle," *Selected Writings*, 2: 612.

13. Benjamin, *Selected Writings*, 3: 344.

14. Benjamin, "A Berlin Chronicle," *Selected Writings*, 2: 599.

15. Ibid., 2: 611.

16. Benjamin, *Gesammelte Schriften*, 4.1: 400 f.

17. Benjamin, "A Berlin Chronicle," *Selected Writings*, 2: 611.

18. Benjamin, *Selected Writings*, 3: 344.

19. Ibid.

20. Benjamin, *Selected Writings*, 3: 352.

21. Benjamin, "The Return of *the Flâneur*," *Selected Writings*, 2: 264.

22. Ibid.

23. *Gretel Adorno and Walter Benjamin: Correspondence*, 48.

24. Benjamin, *Selected Writings*, 3: 346.

25. Ibid.

26. *Gretel Adorno and Walter Benjamin: Correspondence*, 48.

27. Benjamin, *Selected Writings*, 3: 390–92.

28. Ibid., 3: 390.

29. Ibid., 3: 358.

30. Ibid., 3: 381.

31. Ibid., 3: 374.

32. Benjamin, "Doctrine of the Similar," *Selected Writings*, 2: 694–98.

33. Benjamin, *The Correspondence of Walter Benjamin, 1910–1940*, 402.

34. Benjamin, "Doctrine of the Similar," *Selected Writings*, 2: 696.

35. Ibid., 2: 694.

36. Ibid., 2: 695.

37. Ibid., 2: 697.

38. Ibid.

39. Ibid., 2: 698.

40. Benjamin, "On the Mimetic Faculty," *Selected Writings*, 2: 722.

41. Benjamin, *Gesammelte Schriften*, 4.1: 304.

42. Benjamin, "Franz Kafka," *Selected Writings*, 2: 809 f.

43. *Theodor W. Adorno and Walter Benjamin, Correspondence*, 90.

44. Ibid., 53.

45. Ibid., 83.

46. Ibid., 84.

47. Ibid., 84.

48. Ibid., 88–90.

49. Benjamin, *Gesammelte Schriften*, suppl. no. 1, 16–33.

50. *Theodor W. Adorno and Walter Benjamin: Correspondence*, 89.

51. Ibid.

52. Benjamin, *Gesammelte Briefe*, 3: 342.

53. Benjamin, *The Correspondence of Walter Benjamin, 1910–1940*, 342.

54. Ibid., 348.

55. Benjamin, *The Correspondence of Walter Benjamin, 1910–1940*, 329.

56. Benjamin, *Gesammelte Briefe*, 3: 503.

57. Benjamin, *Gesammelte Schriften*, 5.2: 1041–43 and 5.2: 1044–59.

58. Ibid., 5.2: 1045.

59. Ibid., 5.2: 1050.

60. Ibid., 5.2: 1051–2.

61. Ibid., 5.2: 1056.

62. Benjamin, *The Arcades Project*, K1.4.

63. Benjamin, *Gesammelte Schriften*, 5.2: 1057.

64. Ibid., 5.2: 1014.

65. Benjamin, *The Arcades Project*, K1a.6.

66. Benjamin, *Gesammelte Schriften*, 5.2: 1057.

67. Ibid., 5.2: 1058.

68. Benjamin, *The Correspondence of Walter Benjamin, 1910–1940*, 482.

69. Benjamin, *The Arcades Project*, B1a.4.

70. Benjamin, *The Arcades Project*, B1a. 1.

71. Benjamin, *Selected Writings*, 3: 33 f.

72. Benjamin, *Selected Writings*, 3: 34.

73. Ibid., 3: 34.

74. Ibid., 33.

75. Ibid.

76. Benjamin, *Selected Writings*, 3: 43.

77. Ibid.

78. Ibid., 3: 44.

79. Ibid., 3: 44.

80. Benjamin, *Gesammelte Schriften*, 5.1: 60–77.

81. Ibid., 5.2: 1255 f.

82. Ibid., 5.2: 1256.

83. Benjamin, *The Arcades Project*, D10, 2.

84. Benjamin, *Gesammelte Schriften*, 5.2: 1257 f.

85. Benjamin, *Selected Writings*, 3: 11–24.

86. Benjamin, *Selected Writings*, 3: 34.

87. *Theodor W. Adorno and Walter Benjamin: Correspondence*, 106.

88. Ibid., 110.

89. Ibid., 282.

90. Ibid., 38.

91. Ibid., 192.

92. Benjamin, *The Correspondence of Walter Benjamin, 1910–1940*, 540.

93. Benjamin, *Selected Writings*, 3: 41.

94. Benjamin, *The Correspondence of Walter Benjamin, 1910–1940*, 549.

95. Benjamin, *The Correspondence of Walter Benjamin, 1910–1940*, 554.

96. Benjamin, *The Correspondence of Walter Benjamin, 1910–1940*, 556.

97. Benjamin, *Selected Writings*, 4: 160–99.

98. Michel Espagne and Michael Werner, "Vom Passagen-Projekt zum Baudelaire. Neue Handschriften zum Spätwerk Walter Benjamins," *Deutsche Vierteljahrsschrift für Literaturwissenschaft und Geistesgeschichte* 58 (1984): 593–657, see 624–27.

99. Benjamin, *Gesammelte Schriften*, 7.2: 739.

100. Benjamin, *The Correspondence of Walter Benjamin, 1910–1940*, 556–58.

101. Ibid., 557.

102. Ibid.

103. Benjamin, *Gesammelte Briefe*, 6: 150.

104. Ibid., 6: 159.

105. Benjamin, *The Correspondence of Walter Benjamin, 1910–1940*, 573 f.

106. Benjamin, *The Correspondence of Walter Benjamin, 1910–1940*, 567.

107. *Theodor W. Adorno and Walter Benjamin: Correspondence*, 247; *Gretel Adorno and Walter Benjamin: Correspondence*, 219.

108. *Theodor W. Adorno and Walter Benjamin: Correspondence*, 278.

109. Benjamin, *Selected Writings*, 4: 3–92.

110. Benjamin, *Gesammelte Schriften*, 1.3: 1193 f.

111. Benjamin, *Selected Writings*, 4: 17.

112. Ibid., 4: 19.

113. Ibid., 4: 18.

114. Ibid., 4: 23.

115. Ibid., 4: 34.

116. Ibid., 4: 39.

117. Ibid., 4: 44.

118. Ibid., 4: 49.

119. Ibid., 4: 61.

120. See ibid., 4: 63.

121. Ibid., 4: 63.

122. *Theodor W. Adorno and Walter Benjamin: Correspondence*, 281.

123. Ibid., 281.

124. Ibid., 283.

125. See Benjamin, *Selected Writings*, 4: 284.

126. *Theodor W. Adorno and Walter Benjamin: Correspondence*, 285.

127. Ibid., 289.

128. Ibid., 291.

129. Ibid., 292.

130. Ibid., 292.

131. Benjamin, *Selected Writings*, 4: 291.

132. Benjamin, *The Correspondence of Walter Benjamin, 1910–1940*, 593.

133. *Theodor W. Adorno and Walter Benjamin: Correspondence*, 293.

134. See ibid., 294.

135. Ibid., 304.

136. *Gretel Adorno and Walter Benjamin: Correspondence*, 262.

137. Benjamin, *Selected Writings*, 4: 313–55.

138. Benjamin, *Gesammelte Schriften*, 1.3: 1186.

139. Benjamin, *Selected Writings*, 4: 314.

140. Ibid., 4: 316.

141. Ibid.

142. Ibid., 4: 318.

143. Ibid., 4: 321.

144. Ibid., 4: 328.

145. Ibid., 4: 333.

146. Ibid., 4: 343.

147. *Correspondence of Walter Benjamin and Gershom Scholem*, 259.

148. Benjamin, *The Correspondence of Walter Benjamin, 1910–1940*, 623.

149. *Gretel Adorno and Walter Benjamin, Correspondence*, 254.

150. *Gretel Adorno and Walter Benjamin: Correspondence*, 251.

151. Benjamin, *Gesammelte Briefe*, 6: 288.

152. Benjamin, *Gesammelte Briefe*, 6: 400–1.

153. *Gretel Adorno and Walter Benjamin: Correspondence*, 286 f.

154. Gershom Scholem, *Walter Benjamin und sein Engel. Vierzehn Aufsätze und kleine Beiträge*, ed. Rolf Tiedemann (Frankfurt am Main: Suhrkamp, 1983), 64.

155. Benjamin, *Gesammelte Briefe*, 6: 304.

156. Benjamin, *Gesammelte Briefe*, 6: 319.

157. Benjamin, *Selected Writings*, 4: 393.

158. Theodor W. Adorno, *Über Walter Benjamin* (Frankfurt am Main: Suhrkamp, 1970), 26.

159. Ibid., 29.

160. Benjamin, *Selected Writings*, 4: 396.

161. Benjamin, *The Arcades Project*, N 1a.2.

162. Benjamin, *The Arcades Project*, K1.2

163. Benjamin, *Selected Writings*, 4: 395.

164. Benjamin, *The Arcades Project*, 8,1.

165. Tom Standage, *The Turk: The Life and Times of the Famous Eighteenth-Century Chess-Playing Machine* (New York: Walker, 2002), 176–221.

166. Benjamin, *Gesammelte Schriften*, 1.3: 1247.

167. Benjamin, *Selected Writings*, 4: 389.

168. Benjamin, *Selected Writings*, 3: 296, note 48.

169. Benjamin, *Selected Writings*, 4: 389.

170. Benjamin, *The Arcades Project*, N13.2–14a.5.

171. Benjamin, *Selected Writings*, 4: 390.

172. Hermann Lotze, *Mikrokosmus. Ideen zur Naturgeschichte und Geschichte der Menschheit. Versuch einer Anthropologie* (Leipzig: Hirzel, 1856–64), 3: 52.

173. Benjamin, *The Arcades Project*, N1a.3.

174. Benjamin, *Selected Writings*, 4: 394.

175. Ibid.

176. Benjamin, *Selected Writings*, 4: 402.

177. Benjamin, "Karl Kraus," *Selected Writings*, 2: 456.

178. Benjamin, *Selected Writings*, 4: 184 f.

179. Benjamin, *Selected Writings*, 4: 392.

180. Ibid.

181. Schmitt, *Politische Theologie*, 11.

182. Benjamin, *Gesammelte Schriften*, 1.3: 1244.

183. Heinz Dieter Kittsteiner, "Walter Benjamins Historismus," in *Passagen. Walter Benjamins Urgeschichte des XIX. Jahrhunderts*, ed. Norbert Bolz and Witte, Bernd (Munich: Fink, 1984), 163–97.

184. Benjamin, *Gesammelte Schriften*, 1.3: 1234.

185. Benjamin, *Selected Writings*, 4: 390.

186. Ibid., 4: 402.

187. Ibid., 4: 396.

188. Benjamin, Gesammelte Briefe, vi: 483.

## CHAPTER SEVEN

1. *Theodor W. Adorno and Walter Benjamin: Correspondence*, 35.

2. Detlev Schöttker, *Konstruktiver Fragmentarismus. Form und Rezeption der Schriften Walter Benjamins* (Frankfurt am Main: Suhrkamp, 1999), 19.

3. Walter Benjamin, *Werke und Nachlaß; Kritische Gesamtausgabe*, vol. 10, *Deutsche Menschen*, ed. Momme Brodersen (Frankfurt am Main: Suhrkamp, 2008), 402 and 441.

4. Benjamin, *The Correspondence of Walter Benjamin, 1910–1940*, 538 f.

5. See *Adressbuch*, 14.

6. See *The Correspondence of Walter Benjamin and Gershom Scholem,
1932–1940*, 3–5.

7. Rolf Tiedemann, *Die Abrechnung. Walter Benjamin und sein Verleger* (Hamburg:
Kellner, 1989), 9.

8. Benjamin, *Werke und Nachlaß*, 3: 383.

9. Ibid.

10. *Theodor W. Adorno and Walter Benjamin: Correspondence*, 34.

11. Scholem, *Walter Benjamin*, idem, *Walter Benjamin und sein Engel. Vierzehn
Aufsätze und kleine Beiträge*, ed. Rolf Tiedemann (Frankfurt am Main: Suhrkamp, 1983).

12. Detlev Schöttker, *Konstruktiver Fragmentarismus. Form und Rezeption der
Schriften Walter Benjamins* (Frankfurt am Main: Suhrkamp, 1999), 115f.

13. Habermas, "Walter Benjamin: Consciousness-Raising or Rescuing Critique,"
129–63.

14. Gerhard Kurz, "Benjamin. Kritischer gelesen," *Philosophische Rundschau* 23
(1976): 161–90.

15. See Burkhardt Lindner, *Benjamin-Handbuch. Leben, Werk, Wirkung*, with the
cooperation of Thomas Küpper and Timo Skandries (Stuttgart: Metzler, 2006), 17–58.

16. Wolfgang Fietkau, *Schwanengesang auf 1848. Ein Rendezvous am Louvre.
Baudelaire, Marx, Proudhon und Victor Hugo* (Reinbek: Rowohlt, 1987); on Heinz Dieter
Kittsteiner, see chapter 6, note 182; Kambas, *Walter Benjamin im Exil*; Susan Buck-
Morss, *The Dialectics of Seeing: Walter Benjamin and the Arcades Project* (Cambridge:
MIT Press, 1989).

17. Smith, "'Das Jüdische versteht sich von selbst'"; Michael Bröcker, *Die Grund-
losigkeit der Wahrheit. Zum Verständnis von Sprache, Geschichte und Theologie bei
Walter Benjamin* (Würzburg: Königshausen und Neumann, 1993); Stéphane Mosès, *Der
Engel der Geschichte: Franz Rosenzweig, Walter Benjamin, Gershom Scholem* (Frankfurt
am Main: Suhrkamp, 1994).

18. Giorgio Agamben, *Homo Sacer. Sovereignty and Bare Life* (Stanford: Stanford
University Press, 1998).

19. Hans-Jürgen Schings, Walter Benjamin, das barocke Trauerspiel und die Ba-
rockforschung," in *Daß eine Nation die andere verstehen möge. Festschrift für Marian
Szyrocki*, ed. Hans-Gert Roloff (Amsterdam: Rodopi 1988); Klaus Garber, *Rezeption und
Rettung. Drei Studien zu Walter Benjamin* (Tübingen: Niemeyer, 1987), 59–120.

20. Harald Steinhagen, "Zu Walter Benjamins Begriff der Allegorie," in *Formen und
Funktionen der Allegorie*, ed. Dirk Baecker (Stuttgart: Metzler, 1979), 666–85; Bettine
Menke, *Sprachfiguren: Name, Allegorie, Bild nach Benjamin* (Munich: Fink, 1991).

21. Klaus Garber, *Rezeption und Rettung. Drei Studien zu Walter Benjamin*. Tübingen: Niemeyer, 1987), 3–58; Heinrich Kaulen, *Rettung und Destruktion. Untersuchungen
zur Hermeneutik Walter Benjamins* (Tübingen: Niemeyer, 1987).

22. Hartmut Böhme, Peter Matussek, and Lothar Müller, *Orientierung Kulturwissenschaft. Was sie kann, was sie will* (Reinbek: Rowohlt, 2000), 179–202; Christian Emden,
*Walter Benjamins Archäologie der Moderne. Kulturwissenschaft um 1930* (Munich: Fink,
2006).

23. Norbert Bolz, *Theorie der neuen Medien* (Munich: Raben, 1990); Heiko Reisch,

*Das Archiv und die Erfahrung: Walter Benjamins Essays im medientheoretischen Kontext* (Würzburg: Köningshausen & Neumann, 1992).

24. Detlev Schöttker, ed., *Schrift, Bilder, Denken—Walter Benjamin und die Kunst der Gegenwart* (Frankfurt am Main: Suhrkamp, 2004); Heinz Brüggemann, *Walter Benjamin über Spiel, Farbe und Phantasie* (Würzburg: Königshausen & Neumann, 2007); Sigrid Weigel, *Walter Benjamin. Das Heilige, die Kreatur und die Bilder* (Frankfurt am Main: Fischer, 2008).

25. Norbert Bolz, "Walter Benjamins Ästhetik," in *Walter Benjamin, 1892–1940: Zum 100. Geburtstag*, ed. Uwe Steiner (Bern: Peter Lang, 1992), 11.

26. Benjamin, *Selected Writings*, 4: 402.

# SELECT BIBLIOGRAPHY

PRIMARY SOURCES

Adorno, Theodor W. *Notes to Literature*. Trans. Shierry Weber Nicholsen. 2 vols. New York: Columbia University Press, 1991–1992.

Agamben, Giorgio. *Homo Sacer. Sovereignty and Bare Life*. Stanford, CA: Stanford University Press, 1998.

Aragon, Louis. *Nightwalker (Le Paysan de Paris* [1926]). Trans. Frederick Brown. Englewood Cliffs, NJ: Prentice-Hall, 1970.

Bachofen, Johann Jakob. *Der Mythus von Orient und Occident. Eine Metaphysik der Alten Welt. Aus den Werken von J. J. Bachofen* [1926]. Ed. Manfred Schroeter. 2nd ed. Munich: Beck, 1956.

Ball, Hugo. *Critique of the German Intelligentsia* [1919]. Trans. Brian L. Harris. New York: Columbia University Press, 1993.

Benda, Julien. *The Betrayal of the Intellectuals* [1927]. Trans. Richard Aldington. Boston: Beacon Press, 1955.

Berl, Emmanuel. *Mort de la pensée bourgeoise*. Paris: Grasset, 1929.

Bloch, Ernst. *The Spirit of Utopia* [1918]. Trans. Anthony Nassar. Stanford, CA: Stanford University Press, 2000.

Bloßfeldt, Karl. "Urformen der Kunst" [1928]. In *Urformen der Kunst/Art Forms in Nature/Formes originelles de l'art*, ed. Hans Christian Adam, 66–195. Cologne and New York: Taschen, 1999.

Brecht, Bertolt. "The *Threepenny* Lawsuit. A Sociological Experiment." In *Brecht on Film and Radio*, trans. and ed. Marc Silberman, 147–199. London: Methuen, 2000.

Breton, André. *Nadja* [1928]. Trans. Richard Howard. New York: Grove Press, 1960.

———. "Manifesto of Surrealism" [1924]. In *Manifestoes of Surrealism*, trans. Richard Seaver and Helen R. Lane, 1–47. Ann Arbor: University of Michigan Press, 1969.

Buber, Martin. *On Judaism* [1911]. Ed. Nahum N. Glatzer. New York: Schocken, [1967].

Cohen, Hermann. *Kants Theorie der Erfahrung* [1871]. Hildesheim and New York: Olms, 1987.

———. *Religion of Reason out of the Sources of Judaism* [1919]. Trans. and with an intro. by Simon Kaplan. Atlanta: Scholars Press, 1995.

Freud, Sigmund. *The Standard Edition of the Complete Psychological Works.* Vol. 4, *The Interpretation of Dreams* [1900]. London: Hogarth Press, 1953.

Friedlaender, Salomo. "Der Antichrist und Ernst Bloch." *Das Ziel. Jahrbücher für geistige Politik* 4 (1920): 103–117.

———. *Schöpferische Indifferenz.* Munich: Georg Müller, 1918.

Gundolf, Friedrich. *Goethe* [1916; 12th ed., 1925]. Berlin: Bondi, 1925.

Haas, Willy. *Gestalten der Zeit.* Berlin: Kiepenheuer, 1930.

Häberlin, Paul. *Der Leib und die Seele.* Basel: Kober, 1923.

Hamann, Johann Georg. "*The Last Will and Testament of the Knight of the Rose-Cross*" [1772]. In Johann Georg Hamann, *Writings on Philosophy and Language,* trans. and ed. Kenneth Haynes. Cambridge: Cambridge University Press, 2007.

———. *Briefwechsel. Dritter Band, 1770–1777.* Ed. Walther Ziesemer and Arthur Henkel. Wiesbaden: Insel, 1957.

Hellingrath, Norbert von. *Pindarübertragungen von Hölderlin. Prolegomena zu einer Erstausgabe* [1910]. In Norbert von Hellingrath, *Hölderlin-Vermächtnis. Forschungen und Vorträge.* Munich: Bruckmann, 1936.

Horkheimer, Max. "Vorwort" [to vol. 1 of *Zeitschrift für Sozialforschung*]. In Max Horkheimer, *Gesammelte Schriften,* ed. Alfred Schmidt and Guntzelin Schmid Noerr, 3: 36–39. Frankfurt am Main: Fischer, 1985–1997.

Huch, Ricarda. *Blüthezeit der Romantik.* Leipzig: Haessel, 1899.

Jamme, Christoph, and Helmut Schneider, eds. *Mythologie der Vernunft. Hegels "ältestes Systemprogramm" des deutschen Idealismus.* Frankfurt am Main: Suhrkamp, 1984.

Kant, Immanuel. *Basic Writings of Kant.* Ed. and with an intro. by Allen W. Wood. New York: Modern Library, 2001.

———. "*Prolegomena to Any Future Metaphysics That Will be Able to Come Forward as a Science.*" In *The Cambridge Edition of the Works of Immanuel Kant: Theoretical Philosophy after 1781.* Cambridge: Cambridge University Press, 2002.

Korsch, Karl. *Karl Marx.* London: Chapman & Hall, 1938.

Kracauer, Siegfried. *The Salaried Masses: Duty and Distraction in Weimar Germany* [1930]. Trans. Quintin Hoare. London: Verso, 1998.

Loos, Adolf. "Ornament and Crime" [1908]. In Adolf Loos, *Ornament and Crime: Selected Essays,* selected and with an intro. by Adolf Opel, trans. Michael Mitchell. Riverside: Ariadne Press, 1998.

Lotze, Hermann. *Mikrokosmus. Ideen zur Naturgeschichte und Geschichte der Menschheit. Versuch einer Anthropologie.* 3 vols. Leipzig: Hirzel, 1856–1864.

———. *Microcosmus: An Essay concerning Man and His Relationship to the World.* Edinburgh: T. & T. Clark, 1885; and New York, NY: Scribner & Welford, 1887, 5th ed., 1899.

Lublinski, Samuel. *Die Bilanz der Moderne.* Edited by Gotthart Wunberg. Tübingen: Niemeyer, 1974.

Lukács, Georg. *Soul and Form. Essays.* Trans. Anna Bostock. Cambridge: MIT Press, 1974.

———. *The Theory of the Novel. A Historico-philosophical Essay on the Forms of Great Epic Literature* [1916]. Trans. Anna Bostock. Cambridge: MIT Press, 1974.

———. *History and Class Consciousness; Studies in Marxist Dialectics.* Trans. Rodney Livingstone. Cambridge: MIT Press, [1971].

Mannheim, Karl. *Ideology and Utopia: An Introduction to the Sociology of Knowledge* [1929]. Trans. Louis Wirth and Edward Shils. London: Routledge & Kegan Paul, 1948.

Marx, Karl. *Randglossen zum Programm der Deutschen Arbeiterpartei.* Mit einer ausführlichen Einleitung und sechs Anhängen herausgegeben von Karl Korsch. Berlin: Franke, 1922.

———. *Critique of Hegel's "Philosophy of Right."* Trans. Annette Jolin and Joseph O'Maley. London and New York: Cambridge University Press, 1970.

Marx, Karl, and Friedrich Engels. *The Communist Manifesto.* Ed. Frederic Bender. New York: Norton, 1988.

Naville, Pierre. *La révolution et les intellectuels. Que peuvent faire les surréalistes?* Paris: Gallimard, 1926.

Nietzsche, Friedrich. *The Will to Power.* Trans. Walter Kaufmann and R. J. Hollingdale. New York: Vintage Books, 1968.

———. *The Metaphysics of Morals.* Intro., trans., and notes by Mary Gregor. Cambridge: Cambridge University Press, 1991.

———. "On the Uses and Disadvantages of History for Life" [1874]. In *Untimely Meditations,* trans. R. J. Hollingdale. Cambridge: Cambridge University Press, 1983.

———. *The Nietzsche Reader.* Ed. Keith Ansell Pearson and Duncan Large. Oxford: Blackwell, 2006.

———. *On the Genealogy of Morality.* Trans. Carol Dieth. Cambridge: Cambridge University Press, 2007.

Novalis [Friedrich von Hardenberg]. *Werke, Tagebücher und Briefe.* Herausgegeben von Hans-Joachim Mähl und Richard Samuel. Munich: Hanser, 1978.

Proust, Marcel. "About Baudelaire." In Marcel Proust, *Pleasures and Days, and Other Writings,* trans. Louise Varese, Gerard Hopkins, and Barbara Dupee, 241–264. Garden City, NY: Doubleday, 1957.

Rang, Florens Christian. *Deutsche Bauhütte. Ein Wort an uns Deutsche über mögliche Gerechtigkeit gegen Belgien und Frankreich und zur Philosophie der Politik.* Sannerz and Leipzig: Arnold, 1924.

———. *Historische Psychologie des Karnevals* [1927–1928]. Herausgeggeben von Lorenz Jäger. Berlin: Brinkman & Bose, 1983.

Riegl, Alois. *Late Roman Art Industry.* Trans. Rolf Winkes. Rome: Giorgio Bretschneider Editore, 1985.

Rosenzweig, Franz. *The Star of Redemption.* Trans. Barbara E. Galli. Madison: University of Wisconsin Press, 2005.

Scheerbart, Paul. *Glass Architecture* [1914], trans. James Palmes. In *Glass Architecure by Paul Scheerbart and Alpine Architecture by Bruno Taut,* ed. with an intro. by Dennis Sharp, 31–74. New York and Washington: Praeger, 1972.

———. *Lesabéndio. Ein Asteroïdenroman* [1913]. Munich: Spangenberg, 1986.

Schmitt, Carl. *Politische Theologie. Vier Kapitel zur Lehre von der Souveränität* [1922]. Munich: Duncker & Humblot, 1934.

———. *Hamlet oder Hekuba. Der Einbruch der Zeit in das Spiel* [1956]. Stuttgart: Klett-Cotta, 1985.

Scholem, Gerhard. "Jüdische Jugendbewegung." *Der Jude. Eine Monatsschrift* 1, no. 2 (March 1917): 822–825.

————. "On Jonah and the Concept of Justice." *Critical Inquiry* 25 (1999): 353–361.

Simmel, Georg. *Goethe* [1911]. 4th ed. Leipzig: Klinkhardt & Biermann, 1921.

————. "Gesetzmäßigkeit im Kunstwerk [1917–1918]." In Georg Simmel, *Gesamtausgabe*, vol. 13, *Aufsätze und Abhandlungen 1909–1918*, ed. Klaus Latzel, 382–394. Frankfurt am Main: Suhrkamp, 2000.

Sorel, Georges. *Reflections on Violence* [1915]. Ed. Jeremy Jennings, trans. Thomas Ernest Hulme [with revisions by the editor]. Cambridge: Cambridge University Press, 1999.

Tumarkin, Anna. *Die romantische Weltanschauung*. Bern: Haupt, 1920.

Unger, Erich. *Gegen die Dichtung*. Leipzig: Meiner, 1925.

————. *Politik und Metaphysik* [1921]. Ed. Manfred Voigts. Würzburg: Königshausen & Neumann, 1989.

————. *Vom Expressionismus zum Mythos des Hebräertums. Schriften, 1909–193*. Ed. Manfred Voigts. Würzburg: Königshausen & Neumann, 1992.

Weber, Max. *The Protestant Ethic and the Spirit of Capitalism; with Other Writings on the Rise of the West*. Trans. and with an intro. by Stephen Kalberg. New York: Oxford University Press, 2009.

————. "Science as a Vocation." In Max Weber, *The Vocation Lectures*, ed. and with an intro. by David Owen and Tracy B. Strong, trans. Rodney Livingstone. Indianapolis: Hackett, 2004.

Windelband, Wilhelm. *A History of Philosophy; with Special Reference to the Formation and Development of Its Problems and Conceptions* [1878–1880]. 2nd rev. ed. New York and London: Macmillan & Co., 1919.

Wölfflin, Heinrich. *Principles of Art History; the Problem of the Development of Style in Later Art* [1915]. Trans. M. D. Hottinger. New York, NY: Dover, 1950.

Wyneken, Gustav. *Der Gedanke der Freien Schulgemeinde*. Jena: Diederichs, 1919.

————. *Wickersdorf*. Lauenburg: Saal, 1922.

## SECONDARY SOURCES

### Bibliographies

Markner, Reinhard, and Thomas Weber. *Literatur über Walter Benjamin. Kommentierte Bibliographie, 1983–1992*. Hamburg: Argument, 1993.

Markner, Reinhard, and Ludger Rehm. "Bibliographie zu Walter Benjamin (1993–1997)." In *Global benjamin. Internationaler Walter-Benjamin-Kongreß 1992*, ed. Klaus Garber and Ludger Rehm. Vol. 3, 1849–1916. Munich: Fink, 1999.

Brodersen, Momme. *Walter Benjamin: Eine kommentierte Bibliographie*. Morsum and Sylt: Cicero Presse, 1995.

### Biographial Writings, Documents, Introductions

Benjamin, Hilde. *Georg Benjamin: Eine Biographie*. Leipzig: Reclam, 1977.

Bolz, Norbert, and Willem van Reijen. *Walter Benjamin*. Trans. Laimdota Mazzarins. Atlantic Heights, NJ: Humanities Press, 1996.

Brodersen, Momme. *Walter Benjamin: A Biography*. Trans. Malcolm R. Green and Ingrida Ligers, ed. Martina Dervis. London: Verso, 1996.

Caygill, Howard, Alex Cole, and Andrzy Klimowski. *Introducing Walter Benjamin*. New York: Totem Books, 1998.

Eiland, Howard, and Michael Jennings. *The Author as Producer: A Life of Walter Benjamin*. Cambridge: Harvard University Press, 2007.

Ferris, David. *The Cambridge Introduction to Walter Benjamin*. Cambridge: Cambridge University Press, 2008.

Fittko, Lisa. *Escape through the Pyrenees*. Trans. David Koblick, 103–115. Evanston: Northwestern University Press, 1991.

Fuld, Werner. *Walter Benjamin. Zwischen den Stühlen. Eine Biographie*. Munich: Hanser, 1979.

*Die Kinderbuchsammlung Walter Benjamins. Ausstellung des Instituts für Jugendbuchforschung der Johann Wolfgang Goethe-Universität und der Stadt- und Universitätsbibliothek Frankfurt am Main*. 1987.

Lacis, Asja. *Revolutionär im Beruf. Berichte über proletarisches Theater, über Meyerhold, Brecht, Benjamin und Piscator*. Herausgegeben von Hildegard Brenner. Munich: Rogner & Bernhard; 2nd ed., 1976.

Leslie, Esther. *Walter Benjamin*. London: Reaktion Books, 2007.

Luhr, Geret, ed. *"Was noch begraben lag." Zu Walter Benjamins Exil. Briefe und Dokumente*. Berlin: Bostelmann & Siebenhaar, 2000.

Puttnies, Hans, and Gary Smith. *Benjaminiana. Eine biographische Recherche*. Giessen: Anabas, 1991.

Reijen, Willem van, and Herman van Doorn. *Aufenthalte und Passagen. Leben und Werk Walter Benjamins. Eine Chronik*. Frankfurt am Main: Suhrkamp, 2001.

Scheuermann, Ingrid. *Neue Dokumente zum Tode Walter Benjamins*. Herausgegeben vom Arbeitskreis selbständiger Kultur-Institute und von der Gemeinde Port Bou. Bonn, 1992.

Scheuermann, Ingrid, and Konrad, eds. *Für Walter Benjamin. Dokumente, Essays und ein Entwurf*. Frankfurt am Main: Suhrkamp, 1992.

Scholem, Gershom. *Walter Benjamin: The Story of a Friendship*. Trans. Harry Zohn. Philadelphia: Jewish Publication Society of America, 1981.

Tiedemann, Rolf, Christoph Gödde, and Henri Lonitz, eds. *Walter Benjamin, 1892–1940. Eine Ausstellung des Theodor W. Adorno Archivs Frankfurt am Main in Verbindung mit dem Deutschen Literaturarchiv Marbach am Neckar* (=Marbacher Magazin 15), 1990.

*Über Walter Benjamin*. Mit Beiträgen von Theodor W. Adorno, Ernst Bloch, Max Rychner, Gershom Scholem, Jean Selz, Hans Heinz Holz, und Ernst Fischer. Frankfurt am Main: Suhrkamp, 1968.

Witte, Bernd. *Walter Benjamin. An Intellectual Biography*. Trans. James Rolleston. Detroit: Wayne State University Press, 1991.

*Critical Studies*

Adorno, Theodor W. *Über Walter Benjamin*. Frankfurt am Main: Suhrkamp, 1970.

Arendt, Hannah. "Walter Benjamin, 1892–1940." In Hannah Arendt, *Men in Dark Times*, 153–206. New York: Harcourt, Brace & World, [1968].

Baecker, Dirk, ed. *Kapitalismus als Religion*. Berlin: Kadmos, 2003.

Benjamin, Andrew, and Peter Osborne, eds. *Walter Benjamin's Philosophy. Destruction and Experience*. Manchester: Clinamen Press, 2000.

Bolz, Norbert. *Auszug aus der entzauberten Welt. Philosophischer Extremismus zwischen den Weltkriegen*. Munich: Fink, 1989.

———. *Theorie der neuen Medien*. Munich: Raben, 1990.

Bolz, Norbert, ed. *Goethes Wahlverwandtschaften. Kritische Modelle und Diskursanalysen zum Mythos Literatur*. Hildesheim: Olms, 1981.

Bolz, Norbert, and Bernd Witte, eds. *Passagen. Walter Benjamins Urgeschichte des XIX. Jahrhunderts*. Munich: Fink, 1984.

Bredekamp, Horst. "From Walter Benjamin to Carl Schmitt, via Thomas Hobbes." *Critical Inquiry* 25 (1999): 247–266.

Brüggemann, Heinz. *Walter Benjamin über Spiel, Farbe und Phantasie*. Würzburg: Königshausen & Neumann, 2007.

Buck-Morss, Susan. *The Dialectics of Seeing: Walter Benjamin and the Arcades Project*. Cambridge: MIT Press, 1989.

Bulthaupt, Peter, ed. *Materialien zu Benjamins Thesen 'Über den Begriff der Geschichte'*. Frankfurt am Main: Suhrkamp 1975.

Caygill, Howard. *Walter Benjamin. The Colour of Experience*. London and New York: Routledge, 1998.

Cohen, Margaret. *Profane Illumination: Walter Benjamin and the Paris of Surrealist Revolution*. Berkeley: University of California Press, 1993.

De Man, Paul. "Conclusions. Walter Benjamin's 'The Task of the Translator.'" In Paul De Man, *The Resistance to Theory*, 73–105. Minneapolis: University of Minnesota Press, 1986.

Derrida, Jacques. "Force of Law: The 'Mystical Foundations of Authority.'" In *Deconstruction and the Possibility of Justice*, ed. Drucilla Cornell, Michael Rosenfeld, and David Gray Carlson, 3–67. New York and London: Routledge, 1992.

Deuber-Mankowsky, Astrid. *Der frühe Walter Benjamin und Hermann Cohen. Jüdische Werte, kritische Philosophie und vergängliche Erfahrung*. Berlin: Vorwerk, 1999.

Doderer, Klaus, ed. *Walter Benjamin und die Kinderliteratur. Aspekte der Kinderkultur in den zwanziger Jahren. Mit einem Katalog der Kinderbuchsammlung*. Weinheim and Munich: Juventa, 1988.

Emden, Christian. *Walter Benjamins Archäologie der Moderne. Kulturwissenschaft um 1930*. Munich: Fink, 2006.

Espagne, Michel, and Michael Werner. "Vom Passagen-Projekt zum Baudelaire. Neue Handschriften zum Spätwerk Walter Benjamins." *Deutsche Vierteljahrsschrift für Literaturwissenschaft und Geistesgeschichte* 58 (1984): 593–657.

Faber, Richard. *Sagen lassen sich die Menschen nichts, aber erzählen lassen sie sich alles. Über Grimm-Hebelsche Erzählkunst, Moral und Utopie in Benjaminscher Perspektive*. Würzburg: Königshausen und Neumann, 2002.

Ferris, David S., ed. *Walter Benjamin. Theoretical Questions*. Stanford: Stanford University Press, 1996.

————. *The Cambridge Companion to Walter Benjamin*. Cambridge: Cambridge University Press, 2004.

Figal, Günter. "Recht und Moral bei Kant, Cohen und Benjamin." *Zeitschrift für philosophische Forschung* 36 (1982): 361–377.

————. "Vom Sinn der Geschichte. Zur Erörterung der politischen Theologie bei Carl Schmitt und Walter Benjamin." In *Dialektischer Negativismus. Michael Theunissen zum 60. Geburtstag*, ed. Emil Angehrn, 252–269. Frankfurt am Main: Suhrkamp, 1992.

Fürnkäs, Josef. *Surrealismus als Erkenntnis. Walter Benjamin—Weimarer Einbahnstraße und Pariser Passagen*. Stuttgart: Metzler, 1988.

Gagnebin, Jeanne Marie. *Geschichte und Erzählung bei Walter Benjamin*. Würzburg: Königshausen und Neumann, 2001.

Garber, Klaus. *Rezeption und Rettung. Drei Studien zu Walter Benjamin*. Tübingen: Niemeyer, 1987.

————. *Zum Bilde Walter Benjamins. Studien, Porträts, Kritiken*. Munich: Fink, 1992.

Garber, Klaus, and Ludger Rehm, eds. *Global Benjamin. Internationaler Walter-Benjamin-Kongreß 1992*. 3 vols. Munich: Fink, 1999.

Geulen, Eva. *Das Ende der Kunst. Lesarten eines Gerüchts nach Hegel*, 88–116. Frankfurt am Main: Suhrkamp, 2002.

Geyer-Ryan, Helga. *Perception and Experience in Modernity. International Walter Benjamin Congress 1997*. Amsterdam and New York: Rodopi, 2002.

Gilloch, Graeme. *Walter Benjamin. Critical Constellations*. Cambridge: Polity Press, 2002.

Giuriato, Davide. *Mikrographien. Zu einer Poetologie des Schreibens in Walter Benjamins Kindheitserinnerungen (1932–1939)*. Munich: Fink, 2006.

Gnam, Andrea. *Die Bewältigung der Geschwindigkeit. Robert Musils Roman 'Der Mann ohne Eigenschaften' und Walter Benjamins Spätwerk*. Munich: Fink, 1999.

Goebel, Rolf. *Benjamin heute. Großstadtdiskurs, Postkolonialität und Flanerie zwischen den Kulturen*. Munich: Iudicium, 2001.

Habermas, Jürgen. "Walter Benjamin: Consciousness-Raising or Rescuing Critique" (1972). In Jürgen Habermas, *Philosophical-Political Profiles*. Cambridge: MIT Press, 1983.

Hanssen, Beatrice. *Walter Benjamin's Other History. Of Stones, Animals, Human Beings, and Angels* Berkeley: University of California Press, 1998.

Hanssen, Beatrice, and Andrew Benjamin, eds. *Walter Benjamin and Romanticism*. New York and London: Continuum, 2002.

Hansen, Miriam Bratu. "Benjamin and Cinema: Not a One-Way Street." *Critical Inquiry* 25 (1999): 306–343.

Hart Nibbrig, Christiaan L., ed. *Übersetzen: Walter Benjamin*. Frankfurt am Main: Suhrkamp, 2001.

Haverkamp, Anselm, ed. *Gewalt und Gerechtigkeit. Derrida—Benjamin*. Frankfurt am Main: Suhrkamp, 1994.

Heil, Susanne. *Gefährliche Beziehungen. Walter Benjamin und Carl Schmitt*. Stuttgart and Weimar: Metzler, 1996.

Honold, Alexander. *Der Leser Walter Benjamin. Bruchstücke einer deutschen Litera-turgeschichte.* Berlin: Vorwerk, 2000.

Isenberg, Noah. "The Work of Walter Benjamin in the Age of Information." *New German Critique* 83 (2001): 119–150.

Jäger, Lorenz and Thomas Regehly, eds. *Was nie geschrieben wurde lesen. Frankfurter Benjamin Vorträge.* Bielefeld: Aisthesis, 1992.

Jennings, Michael W. *Dialectical Images, Walter Benjamin's Theory of Literary Criti-cism.* Ithaca: Cornell University Press, 1987.

Kaiser, Gerhardt. *Benjamin. Adorno. Zwei Studien.* Frankfurt am Main: Athenäum/ Fischer, 1974.

Kambas, Chryssoula. *Walter Benjamin im Exil. Zum Verhältnis von Literaturpolitik und Ästhetik.* Tübingen: Niemeyer, 1983.

Kany, Roland: *Mnemosyne als Programm. Geschichte, Erinnerung und die Andacht zum Unbedeutenden im Werk von Usener, Warburg und Benjamin.* Tübingen: Niemeyer, 1987.

Kaufmann, David. "Beyond Use, within Reason: Adorno, Benjamin and the Question of Theology." *New German Critique* 83 (2001): 151–173.

Kaulen, Heinrich. *Rettung und Destruktion. Untersuchung zur Hermeneutik Walter Ben-jamins.* Tübingen: Niemeyer, 1987.

———. "Walter Benjamin und Asja Lacis: Eine biographische Konstellation und ihre Fol-gen." *Deutsche Vierteljahrsschrift für Literaturwissenschaft und Geistesgeschichte* 69, no. 1 (March 1995): 92–122.

Knoche, Stefan. *Benjamin—Heidegger. Über Gewalt. Die Politisierung der Kunst.* Vi-enna: Turia und Kant, 2000.

Köhn, Eckhardt. *Straßenrausch—Flanerie und kleine Form. Versuch zur Literaturge-schichte des Flaneurs bis 1933.* Berlin: Arsenal, 1989.

Koepnick, Lutz. *Walter Benjamin and the Aesthetics of Power.* Lincoln: University of Nebraska Press, 1999.

Konersmann, Ralf. *Erstarrte Unruhe. Walter Benjamins Begriff der Geschichte.* Frankfurt am Main: Fischer, 1991.

Kracauer, Siegfried. "On the Writings of Walter Benjamin" (1928). In Siegfried Kracauer, *The Mass Ornament,* ed. and trans. Thomas Y. Levin, 259–264. Cambridge: Harvard University Press, 1995.

Kurz, Gerhard. "Benjamin. Kritischer gelesen." *Philosophische Rundschau* 23 (1976): 161–190.

Lesley, Esther. *Walter Benjamin. Overpowering Conformism.* London: Pluto, 2000.

Lienkamp, Christoph. "Griechisch-deutsche Sendung oder messianische Historie. Zur geschichtsphilosophischen Auseinandersetzung mit Nietzsche bei Walter Benjamin und Martin Heidegger." In *Allgemeine Zeitschrift für Philosophie* 21 (1996): 63–78.

Lindner, Burkhardt, ed. *"Links hatte noch alles sich zu enträtseln . . .": Walter Benjamin im Kontext.* Frankfurt am Main: Syndikat, 1978. 2nd ed., Frankfurt am Main: Fischer, 1985.

Lindner, Burkhardt. *Benjamin-Handbuch. Leben, Werk, Wirkung.* With the coop. of Thomas Küpper and Timo Skandries. Stuttgart: Metzler, 2006.

———. "Derrida. Benjamin. Holocaust. Zur politischen Problematik der 'Kritik der Gewalt.'" *Zeitschrift für Kritische Theorie* 3 (1997): 65–100.

Long, Christopher P. "Art's Fateful Hour: Benjamin, Heidegger, Art and Politics." *New German Critique* 83 (2001): 89–115.

Makropoulos, Michael. *Modernität als ontologischer Ausnahmezustand? Walter Benjamins Theorie der Moderne.* Munich: Fink, 1989.

Markus, Gyorgy. "Walter Benjamin, or the Commodity as Phantasmagoria." In *New German Critique* 83 (2001): 3–42.

McCole, John. *Walter Benjamin and the Antinomies of Tradition.* Ithaca: Cornell University Press, 1993.

Mehlman, Jeffrey. *Walter Benjamin for Childen: An Essay on His Radio Years.* Chicago: University of Chicago Press, 1993.

Menke, Bettine. *Sprachfiguren: Name, Allegorie, Bild nach Benjamin.* Munich: Fink, 1991.

Menninghaus, Winfried. *Walter Benjamins Theorie der Sprachmagie.* Frankfurt am Main: Suhrkamp, 1980.

———. *Schwellenkunde. Walter Benjamins Passage des Mythos.* Frankfurt am Main: Suhrkamp, 1986.

———. *Unendliche Verdopplung. Die frühromantische Grundlegung der Kunsttheorie im Begriff absoluter Selbstreflexion.* Frankfurt am Main: Suhrkamp, 1987.

Missac, Pierre. *Walter Benjamins Passage.* Frankfurt am Main: Suhrkamp, 1991.

Mosès, Stéphane. *Der Engel der Geschichte: Franz Rosenzweig, Walter Benjamin, Gershom Scholem.* Frankfurt am Main: Suhrkamp, 1994.

Müller, Bernd. *"Denn es ist noch nichts geschehen." Walter Benjamins Kafka-Deutung.* Cologne, Weimar, and Vienna: Böhlau, 1996.

Nägele, Rainer, ed. *Benjamin's Ground. New Readings of Walter Benjamin.* Detroit: Wayne State University Press, 1988.

———. *Theater, Theory, Speculation. Walter Benjamin and the Scenes of Modernity.* Baltimore: Johns Hopkins University Press, 1991.

Opitz, Michael and Erdmut Wizisla, eds. *Aber ein Sturm weht vom Paradies her. Texte zu Walter Benjamin.* Leipzig: Reclam, 1992.

———. *Benjamins Begriffe.* 2 vols. Frankfurt am Main: Suhrkamp, 2000.

Pensky, Max. *Melancholy Dialectics. Walter Benjamin and the Play of Mourning.* Amherst: University of Massachusetts Press, 2001.

Primavesi, Patrick. *Kommentar, Übersetzung, Theater in Walter Benjamins frühen Schriften.* Frankfurt am Main: Stroemfeld/Nexus, 1998.

Rabinbach, Anson. *In the Shadow of Catastrophe. German Intellectuals between Apocalypse and Enlightenment,* 27–65. Berkeley: University of California Press, 1997.

Raulet, Gérard. *Le caractère destructeur. Esthétique, théologie et politique chez Walter Benjamin.* Paris: Aubier, 1997.

Raulet, Gérard, and Uwe Steiner, eds. *Walter Benjamin. Ästhetik und Geschichtsphilosophie/Esthétique et philosophie de l'histoire.* Bern: Lang, 1998.

Regehly, Thomas, ed. *Namen, Texte, Stimmen. Walter Benjamins Sprachphilosophie.* Stuttgart: Akademie der Diözese Rottenburg, 1993.

Reijen, Willem van. *Der Schwarzwald und Paris. Heidegger und Benjamin.* Munich: Fink, 1998.

Reisch, Heiko. *Das Archiv und die Erfahrung: Walter Benjamins Essays im medientheoretischen Kontext.* Würzburg: Königshausen & Neumann, 1992.

Richter, Gerhard. *Walter Benjamin and the Corpus of Autobiography.* Detroit: Wayne State University Press, 2002.

Richter, Gerhard, ed. *Benjamin's Ghosts: Interventions in Contemporary Literary and Cultural Theory.* Stanford: Stanford University Press, 2002.

Rumpf, Michael. "Walter Benjamin und Erich Unger." *Deutsche Vierteljahrsschrift für Literaturwissenschaft und Geistesgeschichte* 71 (1997): 647–667.

Schiller-Lerg, Sabine. *Walter Benjamin und der Rundfunk. Programmarbeit zwischen Theorie und Praxis.* Munich: Saur, 1984.

Schings, Hans-Jürgen. "Walter Benjamin, das barocke Trauerspiel und die Barockforschung." In *Daß eine Nation die andere verstehen möge. Festschrift für Marian Szyrocki,* ed. Hans-Gert Roloff, 663–676. Amsterdam: Rodopi, 1988.

Schneider, Manfred. "Walter Benjamins 'Berliner Kindheit um Neunzehnhundert.'" In Manfred Schneider, *Die erkaltete Herzensschrift. Der autobiographische Text im 20. Jahrhundert,* 105–149. Munich and Vienna: Hanser 1986.

Schöttker, Detlev. *Konstruktiver Fragmentarismus. Form und Rezeption der Schriften Walter Benjamins.* Frankfurt am Main: Suhrkamp, 1999.

Schöttker, Detlev, ed. *Schrift, Bilder, Denken—Walter Benjamin und die Kunst der Gegenwart.* Frankfurt am Main: Suhrkamp, 2004.

Scholem, Gershom. *Walter Benjamin und sein Engel. Vierzehn Aufsätze und kleine Beiträge.* Ed. Rolf Tiedemann. Frankfurt am Main: Suhrkamp, 1983.

Smith, Gary. "'Das Jüdische versteht sich von selbst.' Walter Benjamins frühe Auseinandersetzung mit dem Judentum." *Deutsche Vierteljahrsschrift für Literaturwissenschaft und Geistesgeschichte* 65 (1991): 318–334.

Sontag, Susan. "Under the Sign of Saturn." In Susan Sontag. *Under the Sign of Saturn,* 107–134. New York: Farrar, Straus & Giroux, 1980.

Steiner, Uwe. *"Die Geburt der Kritik aus dem Geiste der Kunst" Untersuchungen zum Begriff der Kritik in den frühen Schriften Walter Benjamins.* Würzburg: Königshausen & Neumann, 1989.

———. "Traurige Spiele—Spiel vor Traurigen. Zu Walter Benjamins Theorie des barocken Trauerspiels." In *Allegorie und Melancholie,* ed. Willem van Reijen, 32–63. Frankfurt am Main: Suhrkamp, 1992.

———. "Elective Affinity. Notes on Benjamin and Heine." *New Comparison. A Journal of Comparative and General Literary Studies* 18 (1994): 57–75.

———. "'Kapitalismus als Religion.' Anmerkungen zu einem Fragment Walter Benjamins." *Deutsche Vierteljahrsschrift für Literaturwissenschaft und Geistesgeschichte* 72 (1998): 147–171.

———. "'The True Politician.' Walter Benjamin's Concept of the Political." *New German Critique* 83 (2001): 43–88.

———. "Von Bern nach Muri. Vier unveröffentlichte Briefe Walter Benjamins an Paul Häberlin im Kontext." *Deutsche Vierteljahrsschrift für Literaturwissenschaft und Geistesgeschichte* 75 (2001): 463–490.

————, ed. *Walter Benjamin 1892–1940. Zum 100. Geburtstag.* Bern: Lang, 1992.

Szondi, Peter. "Hoffnung im Vergangenen. Über Walter Benjamin." In Peter Szondi, *Schriften*, 2: 275–294. Frankfurt am Main: Suhrkamp, 1978.

————. "Benjamins Städtebilder." In Peter Szondi: *Schriften*, 2: 295–309. Frankfurt am Main: Suhrkamp, 1978.

Tiedemann, Rolf. *Studien zur Philosophie Walter Benjamins.* Mit einer Vorrede von Theodor W. Adorno. Frankfurt am Main: Suhrkamp, 1965.

————. *Dialektik im Stillstand. Versuche zum Spätwerk Walter Benjamins.* Frankfurt am Main: Suhrkamp, 1983.

————. *Die Abrechnung. Walter Benjamin und sein Verleger.* Hamburg: Kellner, 1989.

Unseld, Siegfried, ed. *Zur Aktualität Walter Benjamins. Aus Anlaß des 80. Geburtstages von Walter Benjamin.* Frankfurt am Main: Suhrkamp, 1972.

*Walter Benjamin.* Text + Kritik, 31–32. Munich: Edition Text + Kritik, 1971.

Weidmann, Heiner. *Flanerie, Sammlung, Spiel. Die Erinnerung des 19. Jahrhunderts bei Walter Benjamin.* Munich: Fink, 1992.

Weigel, Sigrid. *Body- and Image-Space: Rereading Walter Benjamin.* New York: Routledge, 1996.

————. *Entstellte Ähnlichkeit. Walter Benjamins theoretische Schreibweise.* Frankfurt am Main: Fischer, 1997.

————. *Walter Benjamin. Das Heilige, die Kreatur und die Bilder.* Frankfurt am Main: Fischer, 2008.

Werckmeister, Otto Karl. *Icons of the Left: Benjamin and Eisenstein, Picasso and Kafka after the Fall of Communism.* Chicago: University of Chicago Press, 1999.

Wissmann, Heinz, ed. *Walter Benjamin et Paris. Colloque internationale, 27–29 juin 1983.* Paris: Cerf, 1986.

Witte, Bernd. *Walter Benjamin—Der Intellektuelle als Kritiker. Untersuchungen zu seinem Frühwerk.* Stuttgart: Metzler, 1976.

Wizisla, Erdmut. *Benjamin und Brecht. Die Geschichte einer Freundschaft.* Frankfurt am Main: Suhrkamp, 2004.

Wohlfarth, Irving. "No Man's Land. On Walter Benjamin's 'Destructive Character.'" *Diacritics* (1978): 47–65.

————. "Et cetera? Der Historiker als Lumpensammler." In *Passagen. Walter Benjamins Urgeschichte des XIX. Jahrhunderts,* ed. Norbert Bolz and Bernd Witte, 70–95. Munich: Fink, 1984.

Wolin, Richard. *Walter Benjamin. An Aesthetic of Redemption.* Berkeley: University of California Press, 1994.

## Other Studies

Abbott, Berenice. *Eugène Atget.* Santa Fe: Arena, 2002.

Alewyn, Richard. "Vorwort." In *Deutsche Barockforschung. Dokumentation einer Epoche,* ed. Richard Alewyn. 2nd ed. Cologne and Berlin: Kiepenheuer & Witsch, 1966.

Binder, Hartmut, ed. *Kafka-Handbuch in zwei Bänden.* Vol. 2. Stuttgart: Kröner, 1979.

Böhme, Hartmut, Peter Matussek, and Lothar Müller. *Orientierung Kulturwissenschaft. Was sie kann, was sie will.* Reinbek: Rowohlt, 2000.

Born, Jürgen, ed. *Franz Kafka. Kritik und Rezeption, 1924–1928*. Frankfurt am Main: Fischer, 1983.

Gay, Peter. *Weimar Culture. The Outsider as Insider*. New York: Harper & Row, 1970.

Hitzer, Hans. *Die Straße. Vom Trampelpfad zur Autobahn. Lebensadern von der Urzeit bis heute*. Munich: Callwey, 1971.

Jäger, Lorenz. "Neue Quellen zur Münchner Rede und zu Hofmannsthals Freundschaft mit Florens Christian Rang." *Hofmannsthal-Blätter* (1984): 3–29.

———. *Messianische Kritik. Studien zu Leben und Werk von Florens Christian Rang*. Cologne: Böhlau, 1998.

Jaumann, Herbert. *Die deutsche Barockliteratur. Wertung—Umwertung. Eine wertungsgeschichtliche Studie in systematischer Absicht*. Bonn: Bouvier, 1975.

Jay, Martin. *The Dialectical Imagination: A History of the Frankfurt School and the Institute for Social Research, 1923–1950*. Berkeley: University of California Press, 1996.

Kaulen, Heinrich. "Der unbestechliche Philologe. Zum Gedächtnis Norbert von Hellingraths (1888–1916)." *Hölderlin-Jahrbuch* 27 (1990–91): 182–209.

———. "Rationale Exegese und nationale Mythologie. Die Hölderlin-Rezeption zwischen 1870 und 1945." *Zeitschrift für deutsche Philologie* 113 (1994): 554–577.

Köhnke, Klaus Christian. *Entstehung und Aufstieg des Neukantianismus. Die deutsche Universitätsphilosophie zwischen Idealismus und Positivismus*. Frankfurt am Main: Suhrkamp, 1986.

Lethen, Helmut: *Verhaltenslehre der Kälte. Lebensversuche zwischen den Kriegen*. Frankfurt am Main: Suhrkamp, 1994.

Niethammer, Lutz. *Posthistoire. Ist die Geschichte zu Ende?* Reinbek: Rowohlt, 1989.

Parini, Jay. *Benjamin's Crossing. A Novel*. New York: Henry Holt, 1997.

Peter, Klaus. *Romantikforschung seit 1945*. Königstein, Ts: Athenäum, 1980.

Schnädelbach, Herbert. *Philosophie in Deutschland, 1831–1933*. Frankfurt am Main: Suhrkamp, 1994.

Scholem, Gershom. *Major Trends in Jewish Mysticism*. London: Thames & Hudson, 1955; and New York, NY: Schocken, 1995.

———. *Von Berlin nach Jerusalem. Jugenderinnerungen*. Frankfurt am Main: Suhrkamp, 1978.

Standage, Tom. *The Turk: The Life and Times of the Famous Eighteenth-Century Chess-Playing Machine*. New York: Walker, 2002.

Susman, Margarete. *Ich habe viele Leben gelebt. Erinnerungen*. Stuttgart: Deutsche Verlagsanstalt, 1964.

Taubes, Jakob. *Vom Kult zur Kultur. Bausteine zu einer Kritik der historischen Vernunft. Gesammelte Aufsätze zur Religions- und Geistesgeschichte*. Ed. Aleida and Jan Assmann, Wolf Daniel Hartwich, and Winfried Menninghaus. Munich: Fink, 1996.

Voigts, Manfred. *Oskar Goldberg: der mythische Experimentalwissenschaftler; ein verdrängtes Kapitel jüdischer Geschichte*. Berlin: Agora, 1992.

Von der Leyen, Friedrich. "Norbert von Hellingrath." *Hölderlin-Jahrbuch* 11 (1958–1960): 1–16.

Weitz, Ulrich. *Salonkultur und Proletariat. Eduard Fuchs—Sammler, Sittengeschichtler, Sozialist.* Stuttgart: Stöffler und Schütz, 1991.

Wiggershaus, Rolf. *Die Frankfurter Schule. Geschichte, theoretische Entwicklung, politische Bedeutung.* Munich and Vienna: Hanser, 1986.

Wizisla, Erdmut, and Michael Opitz, eds. *Glückloser Engel. Dichtungen zu Walter Benjamin.* Frankfurt am Main: Insel, 1992.